1,000,000 Books
are available to read at

Forgotten Books

www.ForgottenBooks.com

Read online
Download PDF
Purchase in print

ISBN 978-1-331-18117-0
PIBN 10154981

This book is a reproduction of an important historical work. Forgotten Books uses state-of-the-art technology to digitally reconstruct the work, preserving the original format whilst repairing imperfections present in the aged copy. In rare cases, an imperfection in the original, such as a blemish or missing page, may be replicated in our edition. We do, however, repair the vast majority of imperfections successfully; any imperfections that remain are intentionally left to preserve the state of such historical works.

Forgotten Books is a registered trademark of FB &c Ltd.
Copyright © 2018 FB &c Ltd.
FB &c Ltd, Dalton House, 60 Windsor Avenue, London, SW19 2RR.
Company number 08720141. Registered in England and Wales.

For support please visit www.forgottenbooks.com

1 MONTH OF FREE READING

at
www.ForgottenBooks.com

By purchasing this book you are eligible for one month membership to ForgottenBooks.com, giving you unlimited access to our entire collection of over 1,000,000 titles via our web site and mobile apps.

To claim your free month visit:
www.forgottenbooks.com/free154981

* Offer is valid for 45 days from date of purchase. Terms and conditions apply.

English
Français
Deutsche
Italiano
Español
Português

www.forgottenbooks.com

Mythology Photography **Fiction**
Fishing Christianity **Art** Cooking
Essays Buddhism Freemasonry
Medicine **Biology** Music **Ancient Egypt** Evolution Carpentry Physics
Dance Geology **Mathematics** Fitness
Shakespeare **Folklore** Yoga Marketing
Confidence Immortality Biographies
Poetry **Psychology** Witchcraft
Electronics Chemistry History **Law**
Accounting **Philosophy** Anthropology
Alchemy Drama Quantum Mechanics
Atheism Sexual Health **Ancient History**
Entrepreneurship Languages Sport
Paleontology Needlework Islam
Metaphysics Investment Archaeology
Parenting Statistics Criminology
Motivational

TOWARDS DEMOCRACY

by Edward Carpenter

Complete Edition in Four Parts

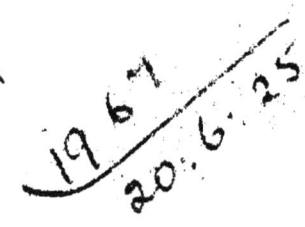

Published by
GEORGE ALLEN AND UNWIN LIMITED
AT RUSKIN HOUSE, 40 MUSEUM STREET,
LONDON, W.C.

TOWARDS DEMOCRACY

by Edward Carpenter

Complete Edition in Four Parts

Published by
GEORGE ALLEN AND UNWIN LIMITED
AT RUSKIN HOUSE, 40 MUSEUM STREET,
LONDON, W.C.

1918.

COPYRIGHT
BY EDWARD CARPENTER
All rights reserved

First Published 1883; Second Edition 1885;
Third Edition 1892; Fourth Part 1902;
Complete Edition 1905; Reprinted 1908, 1909, 1912, 1913.

CONTENTS

PART I
	PAGE
TOWARDS DEMOCRACY (1881-2) ...	3

PART II

O Freedom, beautiful beyond compare ...	111
York Minster ...	112
Sunday Morning after Church	115
High in My Chamber ...	119
Deep Below Deep ...	122
Except the Lord	124
I Come Forth from the Darkness	130
Sunday Morning near a Manufacturing Town	137
In the Drawing Rooms	139
In a Manufacturing Town	144
What Have I to do with Thee	146
As to You, O Moon ...	149
Squinancy Wort	152
Not of Myself ...	154
Lo! I Open a Door	154
By this Heart ...	154
As one who from a high Cliff ...	156
To One in Trouble	156
These Waves of Your Great Heart	156
Thus as I Yearned for Love	158
Eternal Hunger	159
Child of the Lonely Heart	160
To One who is where the Eternal are ...	162
Through the Long Night	165
To a Stranger ...	166
To a Friend ...	166
Of the Love that you poured forth	167
As a Woman of a Man ...	167

	PAGE
O Love, to whom the Poets	169
Who You are I Know Not	171
Have Faith (1884)	172
I Heard a Voice	179
I Know that You are Self-conscious	179
Who are You	180
Among the Ferns	181
I Heard the Voice of the Woods	184
The Wind Chants Well	187
I am a Voice	188
O Sea with White Lines	188
Home...	190
Off Gaspé	190
By the Shore	192
A Military Band	195
Wings	201
On an Atlantic Steamship	203
By Lake Wachusett	213
O Mighty Mother	215
AFTER LONG AGES (1883-4)	218

PART III

We are a menace to you, O civilisation	259
After Civilisation	260
The word Democracy	263
The Meaning of it All	266
These Populations	266
Andromeda	268
The Triumph of Civilisation	269
The Dead Christ	270
Christmas Eve	271
Little Heart within thy Cage	272
When I am near to you	273
Cradled in Flame	273
All Night Long	274
Of the Past	274
Love's Vision	275

Contents

	PAGE
Nearer than ever Now	276
O Thou whose Form	276
The Elder Soldier to the Younger	277
Into the Regions of the Sun (1886)	278
As it Happened	280
Parted Lips	283
Summer-heat	284
A rivederci	284
Who will Learn Freedom	285
After all Suffering	286
When a Thousand Years have Passed	287
A Message Committed to the Waves	288
Rest at Last	290
The Wind of May	291
O Earth, scene of what toil	292
A Voice over the Earth	293
In the Chamber of Birth	301
A Cottage among the Hills	302
Alice	303
Baby Song	304
Early Morning	305
The Golden Wedding	306
The Mother to her Daughter	307
A Sprig of Aristocracy	308
A Scene in London	308
S. James' Park	309
The Twin Statues of Amenophis	311
Artemidorus, Farewell	313
From Turin to Paris	315
To the End of Time	321
On the Eve of Departure	322
Arenzano	323
O Tender Heart	324
The Carter	326
The Stone-cutter	327
The Voice of One Blind	327
A Song in Old Age	329
In Extreme Age	331

Contents

	PAGE
After the Day's Work	332
I saw a Vision	332
Ah ! Blessed is he that hath Escaped	333
The Great Leader	333
I Accept You	333
Sol...	333
A Glimpse	334
The Long Day in the Open	334
The Idler	335
In the Deep Cave of the Heart	335
Fly Messenger! through the Streets of the Cities	336
The Coming of the Lord	337
The Curse of Property	340
Over the Great City	342
Underneath and After All	343
A Hard Saying	344
Not for a Few Months or Years	345
Disentanglement	345
The Mortal Lover	347
The End of Love	349
A New Life	350
The Law of Equality	351
To Thine Own Self be True	352
Abandon Hope all Ye that Enter Here...	353
To One Dead	353
Of all the Suffering	354
A Long Journey	356
The Secret of Time and Satan (1888)	358
Brief is Pain	364
The Body and the Book	366

PART IV

Because the Starry Lightnings	368
Who shall Command the Heart	369
From Caverns Dark	370
The Lake of Beauty	372
The wandering Psyche	373
I hear thy call, Mysterious Being	374

Contents

	PAGE
So thin a Veil divides	376
The open Secret	376
The Songs of the Birds, who hears	377
A Child at a Window	380
Night	381
April	381
Lucifer	382
The Ocean of Sex	383
As the Greeks Dreamed	385
In a Scotch-Fir Wood	386
The Dream goes by	387
Surely the Time will come	388
The one Foundation	390
A Mightier than Mammon	394
O little Sister Heart	407
Forms Eternal as the Mountains	408
Spending the Night alone	408
O Joy divine of Friends	409
O Child of Uranus	410
One at a Time	411
The dead Comrade	412
Philoläus to Diocles	413
Hafiz to the Cup-bearer	416
In the stone-floored Workshop	417
The Trysting	419
The Lover far on the Hills	422
The Babe	423
O Gracious Mother	425
I saw a fair House	426
A Dream of Human Life	428
The Coast of Liguria	429
Easter Day on Mt. Mounier	431
At Mentone	433
Monte Carlo	435
India, the Wisdom-land (1890)	440
Tanzbödeli	442
A Village Church	445

Contents

	PAGE
Sheffield...	450
A Lancashire Mill-hand ...	452
A Trade ...	454
The Ploughboy	455
The Jackdaw	456
By the Mersey ...	457
In the British Museum Library	459
Empire	462
The British, A. D. 1901	467
Portland	468
China, A. D. 1900	471
Standing beyond Time	476
Who but the Lover should know	477
The Everlasting Now	479
Now is the accepted Time	479
A Summer Day	480
The central Calm	481
Widening Circles	482
When I Look upon your Faces	483
Life behind Life	483
The stupid old Body	484
The wandering lunatic Mind	485
As a Mould for some fair Form	487
Nothing less than All	487
Believe yourself a Whole	490
The Body within the Body	491
In an old Quarry	494
The Soul to the Body	494
To become a Creator	497
After Fifty Years	499
Out of the House of Childhood	500
Little Brook without a Name (1902)	502
Lo! what a World I Create	506
A NOTE ON "TOWARDS DEMOCRACY"	509

Part I
TOWARDS DEMOCRACY

TOWARDS DEMOCRACY

The sun, the moon and the stars, the grass, the water that flows round the earth, and the light air of heaven:

To You greeting. I too stand behind these and send you word across them.

I

FREEDOM at last!
Long sought, long prayed for—ages and ages long:

The burden to which I continually return, seated here thick-booted and obvious yet dead and buried and passed into heaven, unsearchable;

[How know you indeed but what I have passed into you?]

And Joy, beginning but without ending—the journey of journeys—Thought laid quietly aside:

These things I, writing, translate for you—I wipe a mirror and place it in your hands.

II

The sun shines, as of old; the stars look down from heaven; the moon, crescent, sails in the twilight; on bushy tops in the warm nights, naked, with mad dance and song, the earth-children address themselves to love;

Civilisation sinks and swims, but the old facts remain—the sun smiles, knowing well its strength.

The little red stars appear once more on the hazel boughs, shining among the catkins; over waste lands the pewit tumbles and cries as at the first day; men with horses go out on the land—they shout and chide and strive—and return again glad at evening; the old earth breathes deep and rhythmically, night and day, summer and winter, giving and concealing herself.

I arise out of the dewy night and shake my wings.

Tears and lamentations are no more. Life and death lie stretched below me. I breathe the sweet æther blowing of the breath of God.

Deep as the universe is my life—and I know it; nothing can dislodge the knowledge of it; nothing can destroy, nothing can harm me.

Joy, joy arises—I arise. The sun darts overpowering piercing rays of joy through me, the night radiates it from me.

I take wings through the night and pass through all the wildernesses of the worlds, and the old dark holds of tears and death—and return with laughter, laughter, laughter:

Sailing through the starlit spaces on outspread wings, we two—O laughter! laughter! laughter!

III

Freedom! the deep breath! the word heard centuries and centuries beforehand; the soul singing low and passionate to itself: Joy! Joy!

Not as in a dream. The earth remains and daily life remains, and the scrubbing of doorsteps, and the house and the care of the house remains; but Joy fills it, fills the house full and swells to the sky and reaches the stars: all Joy!

O freed soul! soul that has completed its relation to the body! O soaring, happy beyond words, into other realms passing, salutations to you, freed, redeemed soul!

What is certain, and not this? What is solid?—the rocks? the mountains? destiny?

The gates are thrown wide open all through the universe. I go to and fro—through the heights and depths I go and I return: All is well.

I conceive the purport of all suffering. The blear-eyed boy, famished in brain, famished in body, shivering there in his rags by the angle of the house, is become divine before me; I hold him long and silently by the hand and pray to him.

I conceive a millennium on earth—a millennium not of riches, nor of mechanical facilities, nor of intellectual facilities, nor absolutely of immunity from disease, nor absolutely of immunity from pain; but a time when men and women all over the earth shall ascend and enter into relation with their bodies—shall attain freedom and joy;

And the men and women of that time looking back with something like envy to the life of to-day, that they too might have borne a part in its travail and throes of birth.

All is well: to-day and a million years hence, equally. To you the whole universe is given for a garden of delight, and to the soul that loves, in the great coherent Whole, the hardest and most despised lot is even with the best; and there is nothing more certain or more solid than this.

IV

Freedom! the deep breath!

The old Earth breathes deep and rhythmically, night and day, summer and winter; the cuckoo calls across the woodland, and the willow-wren warbles among the great chestnut buds; the laborer eases himself under a hedge, and the frog flops into the pond as the cows approach;

In the theatre Juliet from her balcony still bends in the moonlight, and Romeo leans up from the bushes below; in the pale dawn, still, faint with love he tears himself away; the great outlines of the fields and hills where you were born and grew up remain apparently unchanged.

If I am not level with the lowest I am nothing; and if I did not know for a certainty that the craziest sot in the village is my equal, and were not proud to have him walk with me as my friend, I would not write another word—for in this is my strength.

My thoughts are nothing, but I myself will reach my arms through time, constraining you.

These are the days which nourished and fed me so kindly and well; this is the place where I was born, the walls and roofs which are familiar to me, the windows out of which I have looked. This is the overshadowing love and care of parents; these are the faces and deeds, indelible, of brothers and sisters—closing round me like a wall —the early world in which I lay so long.

This is to-day: the little ship lies ready, the fresh air blowing, the sunlight pouring over the world. These are the gates of all cities and habitations standing open; this is the love of men and women accompanying me wherever I go; these are the sacred memories of that early world, time may never change.

And this is the word which swells the bosom of the hills and feeds the sacred laughter of the streams, for man: the purpose which endures for you in those old fields and hills and the sphinx-glance of the stars.

V

I, Nature, stand, and call to you though you heed not: Have courage, come forth, O child of mine, that you may see me.

As a nymph of the invisible air before her mortal beloved, so I glance before you—I dart and stand in your path—and turn away from your heedless eyes like one in pain.

I am the ground; I listen the sound of your feet. They come nearer. I shut my eyes and feel their tread over my face.

I am the trees; I reach downward my long arms and touch you, though you heed not, with enamored fingers; my leaves and zigzag branches write wonderful words against the evening sky—for you, for you—say, can you not even spell them?

O shame! shame! I fling you away from me (you shall not know that I love you). Unworthy! I strike you across the face; does the blood mount to your cheek now? my glove rings at your feet: I dare you to personal combat.

Will you come forth? will you do the daring deed?

will you strip yourself naked as you came into the world, and come before me, and regard unafraid the flashing of my sword? will you lose your life, to Me?

O child of mine!
See! you are in prison, and I can give you space;
You are choked down below there, by the dust of your own raising, and I can give you the pure intoxicating air of the mountains to breathe;
I can make you a king, and show you all the lands of the earth;
And from yourself to yourself I can deliver you, and can come, your enemy, and gaze long and long with yells of laughter into your eyes!

VI

The caddis worm leaves the water, and takes on wings and flies in the upper air; the walking mud becomes amorous of the winged sunlight, and behaves itself in an abandoned manner.

The Earth (during its infancy) flies round the Sun from which it sprang, and the mud flies round the pond from which it sprang.

The earth swims in space, the fish swim in the sea, the bird swims in the air, and the soul of man in the ocean of Equality—towards which all the other streams run.

Here, into this ocean, everything debouches; all interest in life begins anew. The plantain in the croft looks different from what it did before.

Do you understand? To realise Freedom or Equality (for it comes to the same thing)—for this hitherto, for you, the universe has rolled; for this, your life, possibly yet many lives; for this, death, many deaths; for this, desires, fears, complications, bewilderments, sufferings, hope, regret —all falling away at last duly before the Soul, before You (O laughter!) arising the full grown lover—possessor of the password.

The path of Indifference—action, inaction, good, evil, pleasure, pain, the sky, the sea, cities and wilds—all equally used (never shunned), adopted, put aside, as materials only; you continuing, love continuing—the use and freedom of materials dawning at last upon you.

O laughter! the Soul invading, looking proudly upon its new kingdom, possessing the offerings of all pleasures, forbidden and unforbidden, from all created things—if perchance it will stoop to accept them; the everlasting life.

From that day forward objects turn round upon themselves with an exceedingly innocent air, but are visibly not the same;

Fate is leveled, and the mountains and pyramids look foolish before the glance of a little child; love becomes possessed of itself, and of the certainty of its own fruition (which it never could have before).

Here the essence of all expression, and the final surrender of Art—for this the divine Artists have struggled and still struggle;

For this the heroes and lovers of all ages have laid down their lives; and nations like tigers have fought, knowing well that this life was a mere empty blob without Freedom.

Where this makes itself known in a people or even in the soul of a single man or woman, there Democracy begins to exist.

Of that which exists in the Soul, political freedom and institutions of equality, and so forth, are but the shadows (necessarily thrown); and Democracy in States or Constitutions but the shadow of that which first expresses itself in the glance of the eye or the appearance of the skin.

Without that first the others are of no account, and need not be further mentioned.

VII

Inevitable in time for man and all creation is the realisation: the husks one behind another keep shelling and peeling off.

Rama crosses to Ceylon by the giant stepping-stones; and the Ganges floats with the flowers and sacred lamps of pilgrims; Diotima teaches Socrates divine lore; Benedict plunges his midnight lust in nettles and briars; and Bruno stands prevaricating yet obstinate before his judges.

The midnight jackals scream round the village; and the feigned cry of the doe is heard as she crosses the track of the hunter pursuing her young; the chaffinch sits close in her perfect nest, and the shining leaping waters of the streams run on and on.

The great stream of history runs on.

Over the curve of the misty horizon, out of the dim past (do you not see it?) over the plains of China and the burning plains of India, by the tombs of Egypt and through the gardens beneath the white tower of Belus and under the shadow of the rock of Athens, the great stream descends:

Soft slow broad-bosomed mother-stream—where the Ark floats, and Isis in her moon-shaped boat sails on with the corpse of Osiris, and the child-god out of the water rises seated on a lotus flower, and Brahma two-sexed dwells amid the groves, and the maidens weep for Adonis.

Mighty long-delaying vagrant stream! Of innumerable growing rustling life! Out of some cavern mouth long ago where the cave-dwellers sat gnawing burnt bones, down to to-day—with ever growing tumult, and glints of light upon thee in the distance as of half-open eyes, and the sound of countless voices out of thee, nearer, nearer, past promontory after promontory winding, widening, hastening!

Now to-day, turbid wild and unaccountable in sudden Niagara-plunge toward thy nearer oceanic levels descending—

How wonderful art thou!

VIII

Lo! to-day the falling waters—the ribbed white perpendicular seas—shaking the ground with their eternal thunder! Lo! above all rising like a sign into the immense height of the sky, the columned vapor and calm exhalation of their agony—

The Arisen and mighty soul of Man!

[The word runs like fire along the ground; who shall contain it? the word that is nothing—as fire is nothing and yet it devours the land in a moment.]

Lo! to-day the eagle soul that stretches its neck into the height, looking before and after; the living banner calling with audible inaudible voice through all times; the spirit whose eyes are heavy with gazing out over the immense world of MAN!

[O spirit! spirit! spirit! spirit! stretching thy arms out over the world,

Calling to thy children—spirit of the brow of love and feet of war and thunder—

Thou art let loose within me!

No delicate fiction art thou to me now—the sound of thy steps appals me with joy as thou stridest—fills me with joy and power.

Go, go, my soul, stream out on the wind with this one—I laugh as the ancient cities shake like leaves in the din and tumult;

Go shout on the winds that the world is alive, that the Arisen one controls it—

I laugh as the ground rocks under my feet, I laugh as I walk through the forest, and the trees reel to and fro, and their great dead branches chatter——

Shout on the winds, though the foaming hell grows hoarse with gusty thunder, shout that the crashing distracted hurrying eddying world is taken

Prisoner in the highest!]

Ah! the live Earth trembles beneath thy footsteps;

the passionate deep shuddering words run along the ground: who shall contain, who shall understand them?

Surely, surely, age after age out of the ground itself arising, from the chinks of the lips of the clods and from between the blades of grass, up with the tall-growing wheat surely ascending——

Deep-muttered, vast, inaudible—they come—the strange new words, through the frame of the great Mother and through the frames of her children trembling:

Freedom!
And among the far nations there is a stir like the stir of the leaves of a forest.

Joy, Joy arising on Earth!
And lo! the banners lifted from point to point, and the spirits of the ancient races looking abroad—the divinely beautiful daughters of God calling to their children.

The nations of the old and of the new worlds!
See, what hastening of feet, what throngs, what rustling movement!

Lo! the divine East from ages and ages back intact her priceless jewel of thought—the germ of Democracy—bringing down! [Gentle and venerable India well pleased now at last to hear fulfilled the words of her ancient sages.]

Lo, Arabia! peerless in dignity, eternal in manhood of love and war—pivoting like a centre the races of mankind; Siberia, the aged mother, breaking forth uncontrollable into exultant shouting, from Kokan to farthest Kamschatka and the moss-morasses of the Arctic Sea!

See how they arise and call to each other! Norway

with wild hair streaming, dancing frantic on her mountain tops? Italy from dreams, from languid passionate memories amid her marble ruins, to deeds again arising; Greece; Belgium; Denmark; Ireland—liberty's deathless flame leaping on her Atlantic Shore!

O the wild races of Africa, beautiful children of the sun, hardy and superb, givers of gifts to the common stock without which all the other gifts were useless! The native tribes still roaming in the freedom of the earth and the waters: the Greenlander and his little boy together in their canoe towing the dead seal, the tawny bronzed Malay, and Papuan, and Australian through the interminable silent bush tracking infallibly for water or the kangaroo!

Lo! the great users and accumulators of materials, the proud and melancholy Titans struggling with civilisation! England, ringed with iron and with the glitter of her waves upon her; Germany; France; Russia—and the flow of East and West, and the throes of womanhood and the future; lo! Spain—dark, proud, voiceless, biting her lips, with high white arm beckoning beckoning! And you, too, ye manifold Stars and Stripes—unto what great destiny!

The peoples of the Earth; the intertwining many-colored streams!

China, gliding seemingly unobservant among the crowd, self-restrained, of her own soul calmly possessed; the resplendent-limbed Negro and half-caste (do you not see that old woman there with brow and nose and jaw dating conclusively back from far away Egypt?); the glitter-eyed caressing-handed Hindu, suave thoughtful Persian, and faithful Turk; Mexico and the Red Indian (O unconscious pleading eyes of the dying races!); Japan and the Isles of the Pacific, and the caravan wanderers and dwellers in the oases of Sahara.

O glancing eyes! O leaping shining waters! Do I not know that thou Democracy dost control and inspire, that thou, too, hast relations to these—and a certainty—

As surely as Niagara has relations to Erie and Ontario?

IX

Lo! the spirit floats in the air.

On his lips it kisses the young man from China, and the patient old man, and the spiritual-faced boy;

And on his lips the long-eyed Japanee; and on his thick lips the Negro:

Come!

And to the forlorn emigrant, to the old Irish woman with shriveled brown anxious face, and to her barefoot beautiful daughter, and to the young fair-haired woman from Sweden:

Come!

And to the Portuguese lad with shining teeth and smiling mouth, and to the long-haired Italian, and to the ruddy Scot;

And to the young Tamil boy holding up flowers and pouring his morning libation of water to the Sun, and to his grandmother superintending the household with quiet loving care; and to the rows of Hindu villagers squatted by the water tanks at early morning, bathing and chatting, and to the women their wives cleaning their brass-glancing waterpots; and to the noble Mahratta women, and to the beautiful almond-eyed women of Egypt, and to the shifty clever Eurasian, and to the stunted dweller by the sacred unfrozen lake of Thibet:

Come!—and to the wanderers lighting their camp-fires at the feet of the world-old statues at Thebes; and to the sacred exiles on the march to Irkutsk; to the wild riders across the plains of Wallachia;

And to the sweet healthy-bodied English girl, and to the drink-marked prostitute, and to the convicted criminals, the diseased decrepit and destitute of all the Earth:

Lo! my children I give myself to you; I stretch my arms; on the lips each one in the name of all I kiss you:

Come! And out of your clinging kisses, see! I create a new world.

X

Who understands?

Who draws close as a little child?

Ah! who is he who stands closest? And has heard the word, himself, uttered out of the ground from between the clods?

Who is the wise statesman who walks hand in hand with his people, guiding and guided?

Who is the child of the people, moving joyous, liquid, free, among his equals, touching nearest the serene untampered facts of earth and sky?

Who is the poet whom love has made strong strong strong with all strength?

Ah! who is he who says to the great good Mother: *Cling fast, O Mother, and hold me; clasp thy fingers over my face and draw me to thee for ever?*

XI

THE scene changes; the sun and the stars are veiled, the solid earth alone is left. I am buried (I too that I may rise again) deep underfoot among the clods.

Each one a transparent miracle, competent with man and his vast-aspiring religions and civilisations—but for me they are only dirt.

Level wastes of sand and scrub; mudflats by the mouths of rivers; old disheveled rocks and oozy snow; trickling slime-places and ponds and bogs and mangrove marshes and chattering shale-slopes and howling deserted ridges and heaps of broken glass and old bones and shoes and pots and pans in blind alleys and fogs along flat shores and crimes betrayals murders thefts respectability, bad smells by house doors, filthy-smelling interiors of factories and drawing-rooms, stale scents, gas, dirt, evil faces, drunkenness, cruelty to animals, and the cruelty of animals to each other——

This is the solid earth in the midst of which I am buried.

O I am mad! the lightning flashes on evil raw places. I stretch uneasily in my grave and tumble the towers of great cities with my feet; the volcanos lurch and spill their molten liquor.

I hate those nearest me, and am closed, captious and intolerant. I sweep a great space round me and sulk in the middle of it.

Now underneath the earth on which you walk I sport in the fire of Hell;

Satan is my friend and vicious blood-spilling lusts and clenched teeth push the way for me to destruction. I dance in the flames and will claw every one in: take care how you cross me!

Your talk of goodness I despise. To every conceivable sin I hold out my hand. My touch blackens you. I crawl forth out of slime and worms and blink at the sun. I press my way madly through the gallows-crowd to him who bears my reprieve held up on high.

This is the Cross; these are the eyes of Christ—and of the crossing-sweeper;

This is the Divine love which encloses and redeems all evil. Ah! here is peace!

Flat curtains hang round me in every direction (as they hang round you), and behind them the live people go dancing and laughing: but we are not going to be baffled.

Sex still goes first, and hands eyes mouth brain follow; from the midst of belly and thighs radiate the knowledge of self, religion, and immortality.

XII

The clods press suffocating closer and closer—grit and filth accumulate in the eyes and mouth, I can neither see nor speak—the devil and the worms dance around.

The immortal worms make their obeisance to you, and the religious devil grins at you—they compliment you on your superiority.

The Earth is for you, and all that is therein—save what anyone else can grab; and universal love is for you—and to sleek yourself smoother than others in the glass; and to fly on from world to world, leaving sweet odors behind you, and to get cleverer and cleverer and better and better as you go, and to be generally superior!

How very nice! the devil and the worms thank you for your kind invitation to accompany them; but regret that they are engaged.

XIII

This is poison! do not touch it—the black brew of the cauldron out of which Democracy firks its horned and shameless head.

O disrespectable Democracy! I love you. No white angelic spirit are you now, but a black and horned Ethiopian—your great grinning lips and teeth and powerful brow and huge limbs please me well.

Where you go about the garden there are great footmarks and an uncanny smell; the borders are trampled and I see where you have lain and rolled in a great bed of lilies, bruising the sweetness from them.

I follow you far afield and into the untrodden woods, and there remote from man you disclose yourself to me, goat-footed and sitting on a rock—as to the Athenian runner of old.

You fill me with visions, and when the night comes I see the forests upon your flanks and your horns among the stars. I climb upon you and fulfil my desire.

XIV

The heights heighten and the depths deepen; from beneath the eyelids of man look forth new heavens and a new earth. The glitter of sunlight upon the waves is there.

Here underneath, the great lubricous roots grasp downward in darkness at the rocks; there the tall shaft shoots into air, and the leaves float poised in the sunshine —but the word conceals itself.

Of the goat-legged God peering over the tops of the clouds; of the wild creature running in the woods of whom the rabbits are not afraid; of him who peeps his horns in at the windows of the churches, and the congregation cross themselves and the parson saws his loudest; of the shameless lusty unpresentable pal; of the despised one hobbling on hoofs—I dream.

Of the despised and rejected, arising with healing in his wings, of the sane sweet companion in the morning, of the Lover who neither adorns nor disguises himself—I dream.

XV

O Democracy, I shout for you!

Back! Make me a space round me, you kid-gloved rotten-breathed paralytic world, with miserable antics mimicking the appearance of life.

England! for good or evil it is useless to attempt to conceal yourself—I know you too well.

I am the very devil. I will tear your veils off, your false shows and pride I will trail in the dust,—you shall be utterly naked before me, in your beauty and in your shame.

For who better than I should know your rottenness, your self-deceit, your delusion, your hideous grinning corpse-chattering death-in-life business at top? (and who better than I the wonderful hidden sources of your strength beneath?)

Deceive yourself no longer.

Do you think your smooth-faced Respectability will save you? or that Cowardice carries a master-key of the universe in its pocket—scrambling miserably out of the ditch on the heads of those beneath it?

Do you think that it is a fine thing to grind cheap goods out of the hard labor of ill-paid boys? and do you imagine that all your Commerce Shows and Manufactures are anything at all compared with the bodies and souls of these?

Do you suppose I have not heard your talk about Morality and Religion and set it face to face in my soul to the instinct of one clean naked unashamed Man? or that I have not seen your coteries of elegant and learned people put to rout by the innocent speech of a child, and the apparition of a mother suckling her own babe!

Do you think that there ever was or could be Infidelity greater than this?

Do you grab interest on Money and lose all interest

in Life? Do you found a huge system of national Credit on absolute personal Distrust? Do you batten like a ghoul on the dead corpses of animals, and then expect to be of a cheerful disposition? Do you put the loving beasts to torture as a means of promoting your own health and happiness? Do you, O foolishest one, fancy to bind men together by Laws (of all ideas the most laughable), and set whole tribes of unbelievers at work year after year patching that rotten net? Do you live continually farther and farther from Nature, till you actually doubt if there be any natural life, or any avenging instinct in the dumb elements?—And then do you wonder that your own Life is slowly ebbing —that you have lost all gladness and faith?

I do not a bit. I am disgusted with you, and will not cease till I have absolutely floored you. I do not care; you may struggle; but I am the stronger.

Ah, England! Have I not seen, do I not see now, plain as day, through thy midst the genius of thy true life wandering—he who can indeed, who can alone, save thee—

Seeking thy soul, thy real life, out of so much rubbish to disentangle?

Plaintive the Divine Child haply a moment by some cottage door, or by the side of some mechanic at his bench, lingering, passes on;

Through the great magnificent land, through its parks and country palaces and bewildering splendors of the resorts of wealth and learning, shy and plaintive, passes:

Is there no hand held out?

Do not the learned people know him? Have the wealthy nothing to give? Will not the philanthropic reach a hand to this one?

The guides are all talking. They are settling the affairs of the universe. [They never cease.]

They have not settled yet which way to go themselves: how shall they give help to an ignorant child?

They are busy moreover distributing money and pamphlets: and surely nothing more can be needed.

They are very busy. They are worn out and rest not. Their faces are without sleep.

Nevertheless they go on. Was it said that any man could be contented? It is a lie;—or happy? It is mere foolishness. These things are the dreams of youthful ignorance.

The affairs of the universe and the continual fluctuations of the Stock Exchange are too great an anxiety.

Meanwhile the old woman was staggering homeward under a load of sticks—but none offered to relieve her of her burden. But indeed when you think of it, how could they? for it would have spoiled their clothes.

The poor boy was taken with a fit upon the doorstep, but it was best not to take him all dirty and slavering into the nicely-carpeted house!

The criminal had suffered shipwreck in life and was deserted; but of course it would not have done to be seen consorting with him.

O happy happy guides! to whom such mighty issues are confided!

Happy happy Child! who need not stay to hear the end of their talk! whom I saw, in vision, silent and musing within itself, pass away from among those people.

XVI

Will you continually deny yourself, you? Will you for ever turn aside? These are not the times, remember, of canary birds—when the thunder growls along the horizon.

O England, do I not know thee—as in a nightmare strangled tied and bound?

Thy poverty—when through thy filthy courts from tangles of matted hair gaunt women with venomous faces look upon me?

When I see the thin joyless faces of their children, and the brick walls scarcely recognisable as brick for dirt, and the broken windows; when I breathe the thick polluted air in which not even plants will live; when oaths and curses are yelled in my ears, and the gibbering face of drink starts upon me at every corner;

When I turn from this and consider throughout the length and breadth of the land, not less but more hateful, the insane greed of riches—of which poverty and its evils are but the necessary obverse and counterpart;

When I see deadly Respectability sitting at its dinner table, quaffing its wine, and discussing the rise and fall of stocks; when I see the struggle, the fear, the envy, the profound infidelity (so profound that it is almost unconscious of itself) in which the moneyed classes live;

When the faces of their children come to me pleading, pleading—every bit as much as the children of the city poor—pleading for one touch of nature: Of children who have been stuffed with lies all their lives, who have been told that they cannot do without this and that and a thousand things—all of which are wholly unnecessary, and a nuisance, (as who should tell one that it were not safe to walk on the naked Earth, but only on ground embarrassed with straw and all manner of rubbish up to one's knees;)

Of children who have been taught to mix the nonsense manners and diarrhœa of drawing-rooms with their ideals of right and wrong; to despise manual labor and to reverence ridicule; to eat and drink and dress and sleep in unbelief and against all their natural instincts; and in all things to mingle the disgust of repletion with the very thought of pleasure—till their young judgments are confused and their instincts actually cease to be a guide to them;

Of strong healthy boys who positively believe they will starve unless they enter the hated professions held out to them;

When I see avenues of young girls and women, with sideway flopping heads, debarred from Work, debarred from natural Sexuality, weary to death with nothing to do, (and this thy triumph, O deadly respectability discussing stocks!)

When I see, flickering around, miserable spectrums and nostrums of reform—mere wisps devoid of all body—philanthropic chatterboxes, [Nay, I do not hold with you! For if you kill me to death talking to me in a drawing-room, what in the name of heaven are you going to do to the unfortunate in hospital?]

When I hear and see the droning and see-sawing of pulpits; when the vision of perfect vulgarity and commonplaceness arises upon me—of society—and of that which arrogates to itself the sacred name of England;

The puppet dance of gentility—condescension, white hands, unsoiled dress, charitable proprietorship—in the street, the barracks, the church, the shop, the house, the school, the assembly,

In eating drinking and saying Good morning and Good night—of the theory of what it is to be a lady or a gentleman;

Of exclusiveness, and of being in the swim; of the drivel of aristocratic connections; of drawing-rooms and levees and the theory of animated clothespegs generally; of belonging to clubs and of giving pence to crossing-sweepers without apparently seeing them; of helplessly living in houses with people who feed you, dress you, clean you, and despise you; of driving in carriages; of being intellectual; of prancing about and talking glibly on all subjects on the theory of setting things right—and leaving others to do the dirty work of the world; of having read books by the score, and being yet unable to read a single page; of writing, and yet ignorant how to sign your name; of talking about political economy and politics and never having done a single day's labor in your life; of being a magistrate or a judge and never having committed a common crime, or been in the position to commit one; of being a parson and afraid to be seen toping with Christ in a public; a barrister and to travel in a third class carriage; an officer and to walk with one of your own men;

When I see the sea, spreading, of infidelity, of belief in externals—in money, big guns, laws, views, accomplishments, cheap goods—towncouncilors, cabinet ministers, M.P.'s, generals, judges, bishops—all alike;

When I look for help from the guides and see only a dead waste of aimless abject closeshaven shabby simpering flat pompous peaked punctilious faces:

O England, whither—strangled tied and bound—whither whither art thou come?

XVII

I choke!

[Or should choke—did I not know very well I could tear all these bonds to pieces like withes of dry grass: did I not know too that these are after all in place as they are, nor could be better than they are:

The natural sheath protecting the young bud—fitting close, stranglingly close, till the young thing gains a little more power, and then falling dry, useless, their work finished, to the ground.]

Strangled, O God? Nay—the circle of gibbering faces draws closer, the droning noises become louder, the weight gets heavier, unbearable—One instant struggle! and lo!

It is Over!—daylight! the sweet rain is falling and I hear the songs of the birds.

Blessings and thanks for ever for the sweet rain; blessings for the fresh fresh air blowing, and the meadows illimitable and the grass and the clouds;

Blessings and thanks for you, you wild waters eternally flowing: O come flowing, encroaching, over me, in my ears: I salute you who are pure and sweet (ah! what designs, what love, are hid within you!)—

I praise you for your faithfulness for ever.

XVIII

To descend, first;

To feel downwards and downwards through this wretched maze of shams for the solid ground—to come close to the Earth itself and those that live in direct contact with it;

To identify, to saturate yourself with these, their laws of being, their modes of life, their needs (the Earth's also), thoughts, temptations and aspirations;

This—is it not the eternal precept?—is the first thing: to dig downwards. Afterwards the young shoot will ascend—and ascending easily part aside the overlying rubbish.

These are not the times of canary birds—nor of trifling with art and philosophy and impertinent philanthropic schemes; this is the time of grown Men and Women:

Of or among the people; always living close to the earth and the people, and creating what they create, out of them.

Young Men and Women, I—though not of myself alone—call you: the time is come. (Is not the sweet rain falling?)

You—for whom the bitter cup and the sweet are so strangely mixed—how strangely none but you can tell;

You—in whom divine strength is one with the uttermost weakness;

In soberness of spirit, as to some long and patient task in death alone ending, I call.

Strong in peace, strong in turmoil and conflict, strong in yourselves, undaunted, with large hearts, with large strong hands,

Spreaders of health (better than any doctor) to individuals, to the diseased prostrate nation, sustainers of ridicule, clearers of the ground laden with the accumulated wreck and rubbish of centuries,

Lovers of all handicrafts and of labor in the open air, confessed passionate lovers of your own sex,

Arise!

Heroes of the enfranchisement of the body (latest and best gift long concealed from men), Arise!

As the North wind in summer runs over the world, making a clear light down to the very horizon—so is the world prepared for you.

Come! I too call you. I too have looked in your eyes, O you of great faith and few words; you cannot escape, now.

Under your eyelids I have seen, shy, hidden away, pure without taint, one with the fresh air to sweeten all the world —lo! the greatest faith of all.

You sacred ones, first interpreters, you holders up of new ideals, you greatest and least,

You who are and by your mere presence create Democracy—Arise!

Thou Woman, gentleborn and sensitive, yet incapable of being shocked or disgusted—Arise!

Thou one strong Man in love sufficient, out of the heart of the people—Arise!

XIX

HEROES, lovers, judges; despised, outcast, ridiculed; princes and kings and destitute; drudges and slaves; mothers, free women and feminine neuters; actors, parsons, squires, capitalists, rich dinners, fine houses (it is all the same: I go back upon my own words), the parks and the opera; unobtrusive, unguessed, day by day, and year by year; talking loud, talking soft, in the fashion, and out; dreaming of duty, love, release, nature, organisation, hatred, death; ascetic, lusty, genial, maimed, incoherent, proud; by tradition military, money-broking, official, commercial, idle, literary, church, chapel and club; in all forms and in all places; weary yet unwearied; before dawn rising and through the window peering at the untroubled sky; weak yet indomitable; suffering yet filled with exceeding joy—

Age after age, under the Earth, hidden, the womb of the dead generations arising to life again, myriads of seeds, chrysalids, pupæ, cysts, rootlets, transparent white bulbs of souls in Hades, by faith working many miracles; thrills of magnetism through the whole vast frame, summer heat and winter cold and the kiss of the living air; death and decay and weakness and prostration and poisonous inbreaths, and nearer nearer nearer nearer life and joy everlasting.

Through the city crowd pushing wrestling shouldering, against the tide, face after face, breath of liquor, money-grubbing eye, infidel skin, shouts, threats, greetings, smiles, eyes and breasts of love, breathless, clutches of lust, limbs, bodies, torrents, bursts, savage onslaughts, tears, entreaties, tremblings, stranglings, suicidal, the sky, the houses, surges and crests of waves, white faces from afar bearing down nearer nearer, almost touching, and glances unforgotten and meant to be unforgotten.

XX

I do not forget you: I see you quite plainly.

Tangles of social claims, convenances, toy-duties, fine soft-carpeted house, array of servants, failing and failing health, growing and settled sadness, ennui, wearisome pleasures, hyper-sensitiveness.

Golden hand-cuffs, the prison life of Custom without one touch of nature, desperate beating of wings and breast against the bars, trailing slime and winding web of lies impossible to escape from.

Careful obediences; sleek hat and well-brushed coat; blameless deference to public opinion; the desk, the counter, the Exchange, the walk home, the favorable comments of passers-by;

And within, blinding burning hatred, bottomless yawning pits opening in the midst of life—of love, of jealousy, of desire—vast gales and whirlwinds carrying away the superstructure and the plans of years.

Waves and storms of the ocean within; shipwreck and disaster of life; fortune, health, honor, love, gone down seeming irretrievably in the great signless waste; and still the stars shining calm on the flying spray, and the immense placid heaven unmoved going back to innumerable other worlds and radiant birth-places and pilgrimages and possessions of the Soul without end.

XXI

I do not forget you. I see you quite plainly.

But why should one god leave his throne to scrape favors at the feet of other gods?

Surely it is enough to be here—and always to be Here.

I weave these words about myself to form a seamless web without beginning or ending. I do not spin a yarn for you to reel off at your leisure; nor do I pour out water into pots.

This is one of my bodies—of the female—which if you penetrate with true sexual power, clinging it shall conceive, and you shall know me in part—by the answer of the eyes of children, yours and mine, looking up from the grass and down from the sky upon you as you walk.

And if you understand me I will draw you away from all sorrow—so that no evil can happen to you. Not at first will it be so, but afterwards, after a time.

XXII

You cannot escape me (and this place of my Presence I will never leave till I have saturated myself, till the waves of my love have traveled over the whole vast ocean of existence from where I stand):

The horse galloping over the plains cannot escape the plains it gallops over.

Leagues and leagues out in the sunlight I lie, the winds of heaven blow over me—I desire nothing more, I am perfectly content.

Yes, you cannot escape me.

At night I creep down and lie close in the great city—there I am at home—hours and hours I lie stretched there; the feet go to and fro, to and fro, beside and over me.

Oaths and curses and obscene jokes; the group of laughing men and girls tumbling out of the doors of the beershop, the haggard old woman under the flaring gas-jet by the butcher's stall (the butcher sometimes gives her a bit of waste meat in charity), the butcher himself with his smooth grisled hair and florid face—you cannot escape me.

You, soaring yearning face of youth threading the noisy crowd, though you soar to the stars you cannot escape me.

I remain where I am. I make no effort. Wherever you go it is the same to me: I am there already.

The murmuring of many voices is in my ears. As I lie on my side hour after hour the drowse of myriads of feet is upon me:

Hour after hour, hour after hour,—and I sleep, well content.

XXIII

Closer and closer will I come, till I lay hold of you—myself and none other.

As one grasps a drowning man with a grasp that will not be relaxed, so will I grasp you—you shall not escape me.

Ah! Death, and Hell with thy gaping jaws, into thee at length I am curious to descend; curious am I to go where the old empty masks of Fear and Disaster are kept, and to see where they hang—hereafter useless for ever.

XXIV

Are you laughed at, are you scorned? Do they gaze at you and giggle to each other as you pass by? Do they despise you because you are mis-shapen, because you are awkward, because you are peculiar, because you fail in everything you do—and you know it is true?

Do you go to your chamber and hide yourself and think that no one thinks of you, or when they do only with contempt?

My child, there is One that not only thinks of you, but who cannot get on at all without you.

Are you alone in the world?

Have you sinned? have you a terrible secret within you which must out, yet you dare not reveal it?

Have you a face so disfigured that no one will look straight in your eyes?

Have you a mortal disease? do you feel the beating pulse of it in the dead of the night? At midday when the passers by go to and fro in the bright sunshine, do you feel the shadowy call of it to another world?

Are you tormented with inordinate clutching lusts which you dare not speak? are you nearly mad with the sting of them, and nearly mad with terror lest they should betray you?

My child, there is One who understands perfectly. There is nothing betrayed, and there is nothing to betray.

It is all straightforward.

There is no fraction of your days, your body, your thoughts, your passions, which has not deliberately and calmly been prepared—and which shall not deliberately and calmly be removed again when it has played its part.

There is no prejudice here, or weakness or self-righteousness, nor any apartness at all;

You are included, and all that is done and felt by you is done and felt at the same instant by not you;

Whatever you are and whatever you do, there is One who will and does look you candidly in the face, and understands you.

You may recoil from that gaze; but if you learn to encounter and return it (whether in one or many lifetimes) you will see that from it at length all secret terrors, shams, disfigurements, death itself, vanish away;

And you will not only not be alone in the world, but you will be a sovereign lord over the world.

XXV

Apart from all evil—from all that seems to you evil—your Soul, my friend, that towards which you aspire, which will become you one day—your true Self—rides,

Above your phantasmal self continually.

Do not fear: it is there.

Through all the baffling and confusion, through all the seeming haphazard and labyrinth darkness of life, it is there —overseeing; quietly selecting, directing, ordaining. It is lord of all.

If there were chance, it were evil: but there is not. The soul surrounds chance and takes it captive;

And all experience—what you call good and what you call evil, alike—it takes and greedily absorbs, nor ever can have enough.

Are you not sometimes aware of your own body how it goes about, moving hither and thither? are you not aware of it in the street among others, exchanging greetings (and those who exchange the greetings absolutely equal before you)?

Are you not aware of it at night, lying awake, perhaps in pain? Are you not aware of it wandering over the hills at sunrise, or out at sea—in the agonised white faces of the people on board—and the ship is foundering?

Are you not aware of it North and South, East and West, by day and night, in winter and summer, in childhood and in age, gathering, culling, assimilating, without end, and with unerring instinct?

And You, all the time—YOU ?

What ?—Like some great Egyptian King-God, seated, marble, with wide eyes looking out over the procession, chariots and horsemen, which creeps past in his honour—over them to the plains and the winding river.

Do not fear ; do not be discouraged by the tiny insolences of people. For yourself be only careful that you are true.

The dreams of the dark-faced yearning swift-souled Egyptians, conceiving into stone eternal types of calm passion, the dreams of Pheidias, the dreams of the dreamers of all the earth falling passionate before the visionary beauty of womanhood and manhood—Are true.

The dust, the wretched blur and distortion are but for a moment. They are no more than they are. When you shall behold yourself in the clean mirror of God you shall be wholly satisfied.

The body is a root of the soul. As the body in air, so the soul sustains itself in love.

The medium in which the Knowledge of Yourself subsists is Equality. When you have penetrated into that medium (as the young shoot penetrates into the sunlight) you shall know that it is so—you shall realise Yourself—but not till then.

Hereafter the face of Nature, the faces of the sea and the fields, the faces of the animals—hereafter the faces of them that pass in the street—are changed.

Nothing escapes, the line is cast over them all, they

cannot choose but yield themselves—to you, my friend—delivering the essence of their life to you.

Hereafter certain things, all-important before, become indifferent; certain thoughts with which you had tormented yourself torment you no longer; the chains fall off. On the other hand the ways which were forbidden and inaccessible become accessible—on all hands the doors stand open to your touch.

XXVI

Wonderful! The doors that were closed stand open. Yet how slight a thing it is.

The upturning of a palm? the curve of a lip, an eyelid? Nothing.

Nothing that can be seen with the mortal eye or heard by the ear, nothing that can be definitely thought, spoken, or written in a book—

Yet the doors that were trebled-bolted and barred, and the doors weed-overgrown and with rusty old hinges,

Fly open of themselves.

XXVII

Did you once desire to shine among your peers—or did you shrink from the knowledge of your own defect in the midst of them?

Did you, friend, covet so to be more beautiful, witty, virtuous—to be able to tell a story or sustain an argument well, or to be able to discourse on any subject, or to be a skilful rider or a good shot?

Or shrank from the ridicule which the reverse of these excited—which was certain and is still certain to come upon you?

Was it really your own anxious face you used to keep catching in the glass? was it really you who had so many things, one way or another, you wanted to conceal from others—so many opinions too to disguise?

All that is changed now.

But what if your prayers had been granted? What if you had become exceptional and had secured for yourself a place with the strong and the gifted and the beautiful?

What if when you arrived the eyes of all had been turned upon you; and when you had passed by—one by one, sad, thoughtful, depressed, the weak more conscious of his or her weakness, the stupid more conscious of stupidity, the deformed more painfully conscious of his or her deformity, to their solitary chambers they had gone apart and prayed they had never been born?

What if you had taken advantage of the weak and defenceless and oppressed of the whole Earth—and had bartered away belief in the Soul standing omnipotent in the most despised things?

What if you had gladly disguised and covered your own defect, allowing thus the ignorant ridicule of the world to fall more heavily on those who could not or would not act a lie?

What if you had been a rank deserter, a cowardly slave, taking refuge always with the stronger side?

Ah! what if to one weary traveler in the world, in the

steep path painfully mounting, you making it steeper still had added the final stone of stumbling and despair?

Better to be effaced, crazy, criminal, deformed, degraded.

Better instead of the steep to be the most dull flat and commonplace road.

Better to go clean underfoot of all weak and despised persons—so that they shall not even notice that you are there;

None so rude and uneducated but you shall go underfoot of them, none so criminal but you shall when the occasion serves go underfoot of them, none so outcast but they shall pass along you and not even notice that you are there.

XXVIII

The undistinguished old Earth! the dusty clods!

The mere brown handfuls crumbled through the fingers, out of which proceed the trees and the grasses and the animals roaming through them, and man with his vast-aspiring religions and civilisations.

The common and universal;

The servant girl tying up her hair before the broken mirror hung from a nail in the wall; the daisy child-face looking at you from the side of the path as you pass; the slow humor of old gaffers on the village seat in the sun:

These contain you. With all your ambitions you cannot escape and go beyond these. It is impossible.

The bride attiring herself in her white veil, the brilliant and admired wit of the salons, the mathematician in his study, cannot go beyond these,

Any more than the earth can go beyond and fly out of space. It is impossible; it is unthinkable.

Far around and beyond whatever is exceptional and illustrious in human life stretches that which is average and unperceived;

All distinctions, all attainments, all signal beauty, skill, wit, and whatever a man can exhibit in himself, swim and are lost in that great ocean.

The subtle learning of the learned, the beauty of the exceptionally beautiful, the wit of the witty, the fine manners and customs of the courtly—all these things proceed immediately out of the common and undistinguished people and those who stand in direct contact with Nature, and return into them again.

The course of all is the same; they are tossed up thinner and thinner, into mere spray at last—like a wave from the breast of the Ocean—and fall back again.

You try to set yourself apart from the vulgar. It is in vain. In that instant vulgarity attaches itself to you.

If it did not, you would cease to exist.

XXIX

Gold is not finer than lead, nor lead than gold (every atom of each has its own life movement intelligence, and ridicules epithets);

The stars are not more human to the soul than is the deep background of Night behind them. And what would the shoal of merry leaping children playing there in the sun be without the mother-love in which they swim all the while as in an ocean?

To be Yourself, to have measureless Trust; to enjoy all, to possess nothing.

That which you have, your skill, your strength, your knack of pleasant thoughts—they belong to all. It is a fact, and the others looking on you know it.

That which you have not, your scornful defects, your dumbnesses, your aches and pains and silent hours of suffering, to understand that you can give of them too, inexhaustible store—as the old brown earth gives out of her heart, to men; and she knows it, but they do not know it.

To walk along the path which has an equal good on either hand; to give the sign of equality;

To entertain no possible fear or doubt about the upshot of things—to be Yourself, to have measureless Trust:

Perhaps that is best of all.

XXX

Curious how much—and the disentangling of self—depends upon Ideals!

Who is this, for instance, easy with open shirt, and brown neck and face—the whites of his eyes just seen in the sultry twilight—through the city garden swinging?

The fountain plashes cool in its basin, and mixes its murmur with the sound of feet going to and fro upon graveled walks;

The massed foliage above catches the evening light,

catches the rising wind, and sways like the sea on a calm day; the voices of children are heard—but who is this?

[Who anyhow is he that is simple and free and without afterthought? who passes among his fellows without constraint and without encroachment, without embarrassment and without grimaces, and does not act from motives?

Who is ignorant or careless of what is termed politeness, who makes life wherever he goes desirable, and removes stumbling-blocks instead of creating them?]

Grave and strong and untamed,
This is the clear-browed unconstrained tender face, with full lips and bearded chin, this is the regardless defiant face I love and trust;
Which I came out to see, and having seen do not forget.

And not I alone.
See! on the little public round the fountain scattered—on the seats lounging, or walking to and fro—the strange effect!
The dressed-up man of the world eyes him curiously—and does not forget;
The pale student eyes him: he envies his healthy face and unembarrassed manner;
The delicate lady sees him well, though she does not seem to; secretly now she loathes her bejeweled lord and desires piteously the touch of this man's muscular lithe sun-embrowned body;
The common people salute him as their equal and call him by his name; the children know him: they run after him and catch him by the hand.

Curious! how all the poetry, the formative life, of the scene—the rushing scent of the lime trees, the evening light, the swaying of the foliage, the rustle of feet below,

The yearning threads of the fine lady's life—how the sympathy of the little public by the fountain—all gathers round this figure.

There was a time when the sympathy and the ideals of men gathered round other figures;

When the crowned king, or the priest in procession, or the knight errant, or the man of letters in his study, were the imaginative forms to which men clung;

But now before the easy homely garb and appearance of this man as he swings past in the evening, all these others fade and grow dim. They come back after all and cling to him.

And this is one of the slowly unfolded meanings of Democracy.

XXXI

The world travels on—and shall travel on.

A few centuries shall not exhaust the meanings of it. In you and me too, inevitably, its meanings wait their unfolding.

No old laws, precedents, combinations of men or weapons, can retard it; no new laws, schemes, combinations, discoveries, can hasten it; but only the new births within the Soul, you and me.

Sacred for this is the Day and sacred is the Night, sacred are Life and Death because, O wonderful, of this!

When Yes has once been pronounced in that region

then the No of millions is nothing at all; then fire, the stake, death, ridicule, and bitter extermination, are of no avail whatever;

When the Ideal has once alighted, when it has looked forth from the windows with ever so passing a glance upon the Earth, then we may go in to supper, you and I, and take our ease—the rest will be seen to;

When a new desire has declared itself within the human heart, when a fresh plexus is forming among the nerves—then the revolutions of nations are already decided, and histories unwritten are written.

XXXII

I charge you, O traveler, that you disbelieve not—a voice comes in the cool of the evening:

I charge you that in the secret unspoken word you disbelieve not, sacred, and the first almighty Thing,

Moving among cities and over the open sea—advancing to deliverance in us;

Night and day, youth and old age, willing and unwilling—advancing to deliverance in us.

Dumb and of no account, her beauty now and then only (or at night when no one is near) before the glass disrobing, trembling, lonely, unresponded—yet mightier than all the array and splendor of the Earth—I charge you that you do not disbelieve!

Outwards all proceeds: Brahma from himself sheds and shreds the universes; I from myself, you from yourself.

To-day the slave goes first, in his chains, and the voiceless, and those that are without arguments and always in the wrong;

And the prisoner with slouched head, and the suspected and insulted in rags, and those whose hearts bleed silently because of what they see;

And the old forsaken mother, and the cast-aside woman, and the child, and the favorless and the drunkard shall go first;

The mechanic to-day shall go before his master, the bricklayer shall be saluted in the street before the architect, the navvy shall be accounted more than the politician, and I will give the illiterate the advantage of those that read and write.

The scouted and the exiled and the unheard-of, laborers in the fields and in mines, quarrymen and limekilners and brickburners and makers and cleaners of drains and household drudges, shall be nearest in honor: the burdened of every day, and the sufferers, the over-worked and hope-forlorn, and the concealers of sin and sorrow and despair, shall head the procession.

And with them One (of whom I have spoken) moving unseen hither and thither—side by side first with one and then with another—shall resume and make all plain, shall be himself the beginning and ending of it all.

XXXIII

When He descends, when He comes to take dominion—

Do you think that anything else will do? do you think that he will perhaps be put off by offers sufficiently liberal, and arguments?

Do you think that he will be deeply impressed by your grave How, how? and It cannot be?—or that he will ascend into your high houses and take his ease with you, and lounge smoking and looking wearily at the sky till he forgets what he has come for?

Do you think he will pay great attention to your hat and boots, or to what they write before or after your name, or to what they say of you next door—or will ask what church you go to, or what conventicle or schism-shop, or enquire into the soundness of your investments?

Do you think he will drive about with you in your carriages dispensing charities like an Oriental prince—and occasionally even say a few words to the coachman—or that it will be pretence or mere kindly patronage if he prefers the coachman's company to yours?

Do you think that perhaps he will be very bland and gentle, and never be rude or coarsely dressed, and that he will be highly interested in what you tell him, and that he won't at a single look know all that ever you did?

Do you suppose that he will not know which is the top and which is the bottom of things, or that he will be impressed by your cleverness and smart repartees, or that he will reckon you up by the number of books you have read?

Do not deceive yourself—for it is yourself that you are trying to deceive—not Him.

XXXIV

The magistrate sits on the bench, but he does not exercise judgment; the doctor dispenses medicine but has heard no tidings of what health is; the parson opens his mouth, but no intelligible sound comes forth; the merchant distributes evils just the same as goods.

Do you suppose it is all for nothing that disbelief has gone out over the world; that weariness has taken possession of the souls of the rich, and that fatal darkness enfolds the head of wealth and education;

That men disbelieve in the human heart and think that the source of power is set otherwhere than in its burning glowing depths: that the powers which they worship are but so many withered emblems of power—dead scoriæ nodding and jostling over the living lava-stream?

Do you suppose it is all for nothing that the eyes of brothers avoid in the street, and none sees what is before him; that the heel is upon the head, and Earth alone regards the faces of them that are oppressed—that the stones in the wintry fields are become confidants, and the ground is sown with compressed thought, like seeds?

[When yet there is peace over the world, as of the Sea swooning away into its hollows; and differences are sullen like rocks at ebb-tide, and brackish dismal mudflats lie between, and the sun stands motionless overhead, and Contempt trickles malarious, and Avoidance and Negation and Fear loom up against the sky, and men cling like rotting weeds about their bases, and the soul stifles for the swingeing life of the waves and the breath of the wind that blows from one end of the world to the other.]

Do you suppose it means nothing that that which satisfied once satisfies now no more (not till the whole round has been made), but unrest and hunger are eating through men's souls?

That a new need gone up is more than all precedent, and History shrivels before the will, even if it be only of one man; that the pilgrimage has begun, and men are leaving their long-loved homes by thousands—and the tenderest-hearted are the first to sever the old ties?

That centuries of suffering have compressed thought and purpose into one—till they are harder than rock; so that you shall remove mountains, but you shall not remove the word which has gone forth?

That expediency and logic expostulate in vain, and man has become wholly unreasonable, and is calm to drop utility into the bottomless pit; and the wise cover their lights, but the fools flash theirs and are whirled away—like fireflies in a thunderstorm?

Do you suppose it means nothing when the godlike Hand comes forth—the awful hand, sacred with the kisses of the generations of men?

When the hand of Necessity comes forth from the cloud and covers dark the faces of them who have never known it, turning them back from their ruin—but stands in the clear sky, beckoning bright, like a pillar of fire for weary fugitives?

When the awful vision moves across the sky, and the earth is electric under it—and the grass stands stiffly, and the blue thistle in the hedge is erect with meaning,

And men are amorous for the naked stinging touch of the world, and to wrestle limb to limb with the wind and the waves;

When poverty and hardship smile for their espousal, and fierce endurance is fused in one passion with love, and the glitter of concealment is torn away, and the loins are compressed and the eyes aflame with lust,

Towards that which shall surely be born?

When Wealth is slowly and visibly putrefying and putrefying the old order of things;

When the surface test is final—the rainbow-colored scum—and society rotting down beneath it; a trick of clothing or speech, metallic chink in the pocket, white skin, soft hands, fawning and lying looks—everywhere the thrust of rejection, the bond of redemption nowhere; the sacred gifts all violated stale and profaned—men and women falling off from them listless, like satiated leeches;

When Labor is not loyal and true, nor the Laborers loyal and true to each other; when a man has no pride in the creation of his hands, nor rejoices to make it perfect; when machinery is perfectly organised and human souls are hopelessly disorganised;

Do you think all these things mean nothing?

XXXV

Ah, England! Ah, beating beating heart!

No wonder you are weary! weary of talk!

Weary seeking amid the scramble, amid the scramble of words and the scramble of wealth,

Amid the fashionable, the scientific, the artistic, the commercial, the political, the learned and literary scramble—weary,

Seeking, seeking, seeking for a God!

As it ever was and will be—
As a thief in the night, silently and where you least expect,
Unlearned perhaps, without words, without arguments, without influential friends or money—leaning on himself alone—
Without accomplishments and graces, without any liniments for your old doubts, or recipes for constructing new theological or philosophical systems—
With just the whole look of himself in his eyes—
The Son of Man shall—yes, shall—appear in your midst. O beating heart, your lover and your judge shall appear.

He will not bring a new revelation; he will not at first make any reply to the eager questions about death and immortality; he will present no stainless perfection;
But he will do better: he will present something absolute, primal—the living rock—something necessary and at first hand, and men will cling to him therefor;
He will restore the true balance; he will not condemn, but he will be absolute in himself;
He will be the terrible judge to whom every one will run;
He will be the lover and the judge in one.

The Son of Man—
Ponder well these words.
After all I cannot explain them: it is impossible to explain that which is itself initial and elementary.
You will look a thousand times before you see that which you are looking for—it is so simple—

Not science, O beating heart, nor theology, nor rappings, nor philanthropy, nor high acrobatic philosophy,

But the Son—and so equally the Daughter—of Man.

XXXVI

I HEAR the sound of the whetting of scythes.

The beautiful grass stands tall in the meadows, mixed with sorrel and buttercups; the steamships move on across the sea, leaving trails of distant smoke. I see the tall white cliffs of Albion.

I smell the smell of the newmown grass, the waft of the thought of Death; the white fleeces of the clouds move on in the everlasting blue, with the dashing and the spray of waves below.

It comes and recedes again, and comes nearer—out of the waves and the tall white cliffs and the clouds and the grass.

XXXVII

The towers of Westminster stand up by the river, and, within, the supposed rulers contend and argue, but they hear nothing. It comes to them last.

The long lines of princely mansions stretch through Belgravia and Kensington—closelipped, deaf, plaguestricken.

Lines of carriages crowd the Park; tier above tier at the Opera are faces and flowers; there are clubs and literary cliques and entertainments, but of the voice of human joy, native once more in the world, there is scarcely a note.

Over all the towns and villages of the land the fingers of the spires point dumb to the driving clouds.

York Minster stands up like a watchtower in the rising sun, and from the midst of its Roman walls looks out over leagues of meadows and cornfields; Salisbury stands up, and Ely lonesome among its old-world fens; but they report nothing seen.

From the Hoe at Plymouth the promenade loafers look down upon the decks of passing vessels; the line of the breakwater stretches, and the wild sea beyond;

The convicts, thousands, motionless-faced, in yellow-dressed gangs dot the thinly-grassed rocks and fortress walls of the Isle of Portland.

Victoria, the Queen, peers from the high windows of Osborne back upon Portsmouth crowded with shipping, and the grass downs of the Island that lies behind it.

The mail-steamers go to and fro, of Dover and Folkestone, the passengers arrive from the Continent, idlers are watching the arrivals, and police officers in disguise—but they report nothing;

Winchelsea and Rye stand forgotten by the water, on rocks beaten now only by the waving meadows; the old martello towers dot the long low shores.

Down the Thames with the tide the great vessels come swinging; St. Paul's looks out upon them, white, in far glimpses over the great city; the sea-gulls dip and hover where the waters meet. The cutters of Yarmouth leave the river and make between the long sands for the open sea and the banks.

XXXVIII

England spreads like a map below me. I see the mud-flats of the Wash striped with water at low tide, the embankments grown with mugwort and sea-asters, and Boston Stump and King's Lynn, and the squaresail brigs in the offing.

Beachy Head stands up beautiful, with white walls and pinnacles, from its slopes of yellow poppy and bugloss; the sea below creeps with a grey fog, the vessels pass and are folded out of sight within it. I hear their foghorns sounding.

Flamborough Head stands up, dividing the waves. Up its steep gullies the fishermen haul their boats; in its caves the waters make perpetual music.

I see the rockbound coast of Anglesey with projecting ribs of wrecks; the hills of Wicklow are faintly outlined across the water. I ascend the mountains of Wales; the tarns and streams lie silver below me, the valleys are dark. Moel Siabod stands up beautiful, and Trifan and Cader Idris in the morning air.

I descend the Wye, and pass through the ancient streets of Monmouth and of Bristol. I thread the feathery birch-haunted coombs of Somerset.

I ascend the high points of the Cotswolds, and look out over the rich vale of Gloucester to the Malvern hills, and see the old city clustering round its Church, and the broad waters of the Severn, and the distant towers of Berkeley Castle.

The river-streams run on below me. The broad deep-bosomed Trent through rich meadows full of cattle, under tall shady trees runs on. I trace it to its birthplace in the hills. I see the Derbyshire Derwent darting in trout-haunted shallows over its stones. I taste and bathe in the clear brown moor-fed water.

I see the sweet-breathed cottage homes and homesteads dotted for miles and miles and miles. It comes near to them. I enter the wheelwright's cottage by the angle of the river. The door stands open against the water, and catches its changing syllables all day long; roses twine, and the smell of the woodyard comes in wafts.

The Castle rock of Nottingham stands up bold over the Trent valley, the tall flagstaff waves its flag, the old market-place is full of town and country folk. The river goes on broadening seaward. I see where it runs beneath the great iron swing-bridges of railroads, there are canals connecting with it, and the sails of the canal-boats gliding on a level with the meadows.

The great sad colorless flood of the Humber stretches before me, the low-lying banks, the fog, the solitary vessels, the brackish marshes and the water-birds; Hull stretches with its docks, vessels are unlading—bags of shell-fish, cargoes of oranges, timber, fish; I see the flat lands beyond Hull, and the enormous flights of pewits.

The Thames runs down—with the sound of many voices. I hear the sound of the saw-mills and flour-mills of the Cotswolds, I can see racing boats and hear the shouts of partisans, villages bask in the sun below me; Sonning and Maidenhead; anglers and artists are hid in nooks among tall willow-herbs; I glide with tub and outrigger past flower-gardens, meadows, parks; parties of laughing girls handle the oars and tiller ropes; Teddington, Twickenham, Richmond, Brentford glide past; I hear the songs, I hear Elizabethan echoes; I come within sound of the roar of London.

I see the woodland and rocky banks of the Tavy and the Tamar, and of the arrowy Dart. The Yorkshire Ouse winds sluggish below me; afar off I catch the Sussex Ouse and the Arun, breaking seaward through their gaps in the Downs; I look down from the Cheshire moors upon the Dee.

In their pride the beautiful cities of England stand up before me; from the midst of her antique elms and lilac and laburnum haunted gardens the grey gateways and towers of Cambridge stand up; ivy-grown Warwick peeps out of thick foliage; I see Canterbury and Winchester and Chester, and Worcester proud by her river-side, and the ancient castles —York and Lancaster looking out seaward, and Carlisle; I see the glistening of carriage wheels and the sumptuous shine of miles of sea frontage at Brighton and Hastings and Scarborough; Clifton climbs to her heights over the Avon; the ruins of Whitby Abbey are crusted with spray.

I hear the ring of hammers in the ship-yards of Chatham and Portsmouth and Keyham, and look down upon wildernesses of masts and dock-basins. I see the observatory at Greenwich and catch the pulses of star-taken time spreading in waves over the land. I see the delicate spider-web of the telegraphs, and the rush of the traffic of the great main lines, North, West, and South. I see the solid flow of business men northward across London Bridge in the morning, and the ebb at evening. I see the eternal systole and diastole of exports and imports through the United Kingdom, and the armies of those who assist in the processes of secretion and assimilation—and the great markets.

I explore the palaces of dukes—the parks and picture galleries—Chatsworth, Hardwicke, Arundel; and the numberless old Abbeys. I walk through the tall-windowed hospitals and asylums of the great cities and hear chants caught up and wandering from ward to ward.

I see all over the land the beautiful centuries-grown villages and farmhouses nestling down among their trees; the dear old lanes and footpaths and the great clean highways connecting; the fields, every one to the people known by its own name, and hedgerows and little straggling copses, and village greens; I see the great sweeps of country, the rich wealds of Sussex and Kent, the orchards and deep lanes of Devon, the willow-haunted flats of Huntingdon, Cambridge and South Lincolnshire; Sherwood Forest and the New Forest, and the light pastures of the North and South Downs; the South and Midland and Eastern agricultural districts, the wild moorlands of the North and West, and the intermediate districts of coal and iron.

The oval-shaped manufacturing heart of England lies below me; at night the clouds flicker in the lurid glare; I hear the sob and gasp of pumps and the solid beat of steam and tilt-hammers; I see streams of pale lilac and saffron-tinted fire. I see the swarthy Vulcan-reeking towns, the belching chimneys, the slums, the liquor-shops, chapels, dancing saloons, running grounds, and blameless remote villa residences.

I see the huge warehouses of Manchester, the many-storied mills, the machinery, the great bale-laden drays, the magnificent horses; I walk through the Liverpool Exchange; the brokers stand in knots; the greetings, the frock-coats, the rosebuds; the handling and comparing of cotton samples.

Leeds lies below me; I hear the great bell; I see the rush along Boar Lane and Briggate. I enter the hot machine shops, smelling of oil and wooldust. I see Sheffield among her hills, and the white dashing of her many water-wheels, and the sulphurous black cloud going up to heaven in her midst.

Newcastle I recognise, and her lofty bridge; and I look out over the river gates of the Mersey.

XXXIX

I see a great land poised as in a dream—waiting for the word by which it may live again.

I see the stretched sleeping figure—waiting for the kiss and the re-awakening.

I hear the bells pealing, and the crash of hammers, and see beautiful parks spread—as in toy show.

I see a great land waiting for its own people to come and take possession of it.

XL

The clouds fly overhead still, and the waves curdle in the blue beneath; the smell of the newmown grass comes, and the tall white cliffs stand up.

All depends upon a Word spoken.

Do you think perhaps that there is no answer? do you think that the high lighthouses looking out over the water, the sea itself careering beyond them, that the ploughed lands, and the rocks that are hewn into great cities, are indifferent to who own, to who trespass upon them? that they are dumb, dead, and of no account?

Do you think that they have nothing to say to all this, that they will not deliver themselves upon whom they choose, that they have it not in their power to bless and to curse, ah! that they cannot repay love a hundredfold?

Do you not know that the streets, houses, public buildings of the city where you live, have tongues, arms, eyes? that they are on the watch? that the trees and streams around you are alive with answers, and that the common clay knows the tread of its true owner?

Do you think that England or any land will rise into life, will display her surpassing beauty, will pour out her love, to the touch of false owners—to people who finger banknotes, who make traffic, buying and selling her, who own by force of titledeeds, laws, police—who yet deny her, turning their backs upon her winds and her waves, and ashamed to touch her soil with their hands?

Do you think that she will arise to the call of these? O do you not know how she yearns for the mastery of her true owners, how she leans herself backward, displaying her charms, inviting—breathing courage even into faint souls to know their manhood—to come upon her boldly, to let none stand between?

O know well that it shall be. That the land they dwell on, that the Earth, for whatsoever people is worthy, shall become impossible to be separated from them—even in thought.

Of those who are truly the People, they are jealous of their land; the woods and the fields and the open sea are covered with their love—inseparable from life.

Every hedgerow, every old lumb and coppice, the nature of the soils in every field and part of a field, the suffs, the bedrock, pastures, ploughlands and fallows; the quarries and places of the best stone for roadmending, building, walling, roofing, draining; the best stuff for mending footpaths; the best water for miles round, and the taste and quality of the various wells and springs; the clays for puddling and for brickburning, the basseting out and dips of the beds; the cattle and livestock up and down, their various breeds, treatment and condition; the moors, forests, streams, rivers, seacoasts, familiar by sunlight, moonlight, starlight, and on dark nights—every nook and corner of them; the old trees and their histories, the waterside trees, and where pheasants frequently roost, and the places for netting rabbits and hares, or for spearing trout by lantern-light; or where the crab-apple and cluster-berry and mountain-flax and agrimony grow;

The haunts of the wild duck and snipe, the decoy of the corncrake, the nests of the storm-cock and the water-hen and the pewit; the legends told of old hollows and caves and crags; the bold and beautiful headlands, the taste of the air upon them; the old streets in the towns, and their histories, and the histories of the houses in them, and of those who lived in the houses; the old villages and their traditions, customs, specialties, notorious characters, feasts and frolics;

The knowledge of the arts of sea and river fishing, oyster and scallop dredging, the trawl, the seine and the drift-net, farming, fruit-growing, timbergrowing pilling and dressing, canal-making, sea-walling, ship-building, irrigation; the great crafts in stone, wood, iron—of the mason's, the smith's, the joiner's, the tool-maker's work; of the clean use of tools, of all faithful and perfect work, and the joy and majesty that comes of it—

Everything that the land has—calls an answer in the breasts of the people, and quickly grows love for the use of those that live on it.

Without this love no People can exist; this is the creation nourishment and defence of Nations. It is this that shall save England (as it has saved Ireland); which ultimately —of the very Earth—shall become the nurse of Humanity.

Between a great people and the earth springs a passionate attachment, lifelong—and the earth loves indeed her children, broad-breasted, broad-browed, and talks with them night and day, storm and sunshine, summer and winter alike.

[Here indeed is the key to the whole secret of education.]

Owners and occupiers then fall into their places; the trees wave proud and free upon the headlands; the little brooks run with a wonderful new music under the brambles and the grass.

[Determined—is the word henceforth—to worship nothing, no ownership, which is unreal; no title-deeds, money-smells, respectabilities, authorities;

To be arrogant, unpersuadable, faithful, free—not unworthy of the trees waving upon the high tops and of the earth rolling through the starlit night.]

Government and laws and police then fall into their places—the earth gives her own laws; Democracy just begins to open her eyes and peep! and the rabble of unfaithful bishops, priests, generals, landlords, capitalists, lawyers, kings, queens, patronisers and polite idlers goes scuttling down into general oblivion.

Faithfulness emerges, self-reliance, self-help, passionate comradeship.

Freedom emerges, the love of the land—the broad waters, the air, the undulating fields, the flow of cities and the people therein, their faces and the looks of them no less than the rush of the tides and the slow hardy growth of the oak and the tender herbage of spring and stiff clay and storms and transparent air.

All depends upon a word spoken or unspoken.

The clouds fly overhead still, and the smell of the new-mown grass is wafted by. It comes and recedes again.

I hear the awful syllable Change, and see all things, qualities, impersonations, gliding from the embraces of their own names; but I hear beyond;

I hear beyond the sound of the hone and strickle, and look in the eyes of the Mower, under the shade of his broad straw hat.

It comes and recedes again, and comes nearer.

The little waves lip up against the great black ship as she glides down river—

O sailor sitting on a plank over the side, beware!

The ship itself, the rigging, the tidal river, the docks, the wharves, and long busy streets, and country beyond— the shows of life and death—

Who makes and who unmakes them?

I touch you lightly. I am the spray.

I touch you that you remember, and forget not who you are.

XLI

I look upon him who makes all things.

I sit at his feet in silence as he lights his pipe, and feel the careless resting of his fingers upon my neck.

I see the fire leaping in the grate; I see the nodding of grasses and blackberry sprays in the hedges; I hear the long surge and hush of the wind;

I hear his voice speaking to me.

O rivers and hills of Albion, O clouds that sail from the Atlantic to the North Sea, and wrinkled old Abbeys and modern towers and streets of heavily laden drays,

Behind your masks I am aware of an imperceptible change: surely it must be the appearance of a Face.

XLII

The word travels on.

I have been on tramp, and my boots are dusty and hobnailed, and my clothes are torn: do not ask me into your house; (God knows; I might spoon my food with a knife!)

Give me a penny on the doorstep and let me pass on. I have sat with you long, and loved you well, unknown to you, but now I go otherwhere.

XLIII

The word travels on.

Out of the mists of time, out of innumerable births, of endless journeys, transfigurements, lives, deaths, sorrows, emerging, my voice sounds to myself, to you, nearer than all thought: tentatively trying the first notes, wonderingly at its beauty, of the Song—strange word!—of Joy.

To spread abroad over the earth, to be realised in time: Freedom to be realised in time, for which the whole of History has been a struggle and a preparation:

The dream of the soul's slow disentanglement.

[O Blessed is he that has passed away!

Blessed, alive or dead, whom the bitter taunts of existence reach not—nor betrayals protruded from dear faces, nor weariness nor cold nor pain—dwelling in heaven, and looking forth in peace upon the world.

Blessed, thrice blessed, by day, by night! Blessed who sleeps with him, blessed who eats walks talks, blessed who labors in the field beside him; blessed whoever, though he be dead, shall know him to be eternally near.]

I am the poet of hitherto unuttered joy.

A little bird told me the secret in the night, and henceforth I go about seeking to whom to whisper it.

I see the heavens laughing, I discern the half-hidden faces of the gods wherever I go, I see the transparent-opaque veil in which they hide themselves; yet I dare not say what I see—lest I should be locked up!

Children go with me, and rude people are my companions. I trust them and they me. Day and night we are together and are content.

To them what I would say is near; yet is it in nothing that can be named, or in the giving or taking of any one thing; but rather in all things.

Laughter, O laughter! O endless journey! O soul exhaled through suffering, arising free! Little bird petrel through the stormy seas diving darting—thy boundless home—O clouds and sunshine shattering! Elf in thine own dark eyes gazing! O beckoner of companions, hastening onward—winged spirit divine, girt round with laughter, laughter, laughter.

XLIV

I AM come to be the interpreter of yourself to yourself;
  [Do I not stand behind the sun and moon, do I not wait behind the air that you breathe, for this!]
  Born beyond Maya I now descend into materials.

  The dandelion by the path, and the pink buds of the sycamore, and the face of the sweep who comes to sweep your chimney, shall henceforth have a new meaning to you, (how do you know that I am not the chimney-sweep?)
  The nettles growing against the gate post, and the dry log on the grass where you stop and sit, the faithful tool that is in your hand and the sweat on your forehead, the sound of the dear old village band across far fields—
  These shall be for memorials between us, and I in them will surely draw towards you.

  And to you, when I am dead, they shall deliver the words which still I had not sense and courage to speak. Hear them.
  Where I was not faithful these shall be faithful to you; where I was vain and silly these shall look you clear of all vanity and silliness; where I was afraid to utter my thoughts dumb things shall utter for you words impossible to be misunderstood.
  The sun shall shine, the clouds draw across the sky, the fire leap in the grate, the kettle boil—to purposes which you cannot fathom; the simplest shall look you in the

face to meanings ever profounder and profounder than all Thought.

Behind them, behind the woven veil—accepting, not rejecting, my own vanities, cowardices, giving them also their due place—I too wait in silence, till the full-armed shall come to give me birth again.

XLV

In silence I wait and accept all—the glare of misapprehension I accept—I sit at the fashionable dinner-table and accept what is brought to me.

I am a painter on the house-side, the sight of the distant landscape pleases me, and the scraps of conversation caught from the street below. My back aches singling turnips through the long hot day; my fingers freeze getting potatoes.

I help the farmer drive his scared cattle home at midnight by the fitful flicker of lightning. I go mowing at early morning while the twilight creeps in the North East—I sleep in the hot hours—and mow again on into the night.

I am a seeing unseen atom traveling with others through space or remaining centuries in one place; again I resume a body and disclose myself.

I am one of the people who spend their lives sitting on their haunches in drawing-rooms and studies; I grow gradually feebler and fretfuler. I am a boy once more in tall hat and gloves walking wearily among crowds of well-dressed (hopelessly well-dressed) people, up and down a certain promenade.

I enter the young prostitute's chamber, where he is

arranging the photographs of fashionable beauties and favorite companions, and stay with him; we are at ease and understand each other.

I dance at the village feast in the upper room of a public; my partner shows me the steps and figures. The elderly harper, so noble and dignified, accompanies his son's fiddle—or goes round to collect the pence—but all the while his thoughts are with his only daughter in Australia.

The wheel turns, but whatever it brings uppermost is well.

XLVI

I lie abed in illness, and experience strange extensions of spirit. I am close to those afar off, and the present and near at hand are discounted. I spend nights of pain and loneliness.

I dream of the beautiful life. I go down to the sea with fisher folk, and spend chill nights on the great deep under the stars; the sun rises on faces round me of freedom and experience. I see everywhere the old simple occupations—the making and mending of nets, the growing of flax and hemp, the tending of gardens, cattle—the old sweet excuses for existence, their meaning now partly understood—the faith that grows in the open air and out of all honest work till it surrounds and redeems the soul.

The blacksmith blows up his fire; he listens for the sound of the great heat. He taps the glowing iron in advance of the blows of the striker, and turns it deftly with the tongs.

The budder of roses bends among the low bushes;

with a quick motion he flirts out the wood and binds the bud on the wild stock. The wire-weaver stands at his loom, working the treadles with his foot and throwing the shuttle with alternate hand.

The old coach-body maker stands at his bench, grey-haired, worn, thoughtful—the young apprentice comes down whistling from the trimming shop to ask him a question.

The sunlight streams in broad shafts through the chinks of the blinds into the carpenter's shop; with grizzled beard and hair, and something of a stoop in his shoulders, the governor stands penciling out a fresh job; a tall young fellow sits astride of a door-style, cutting a mortise, and a dab of light on the floor sends a reflection up in his arch-humored face.

The bathers in the late twilight, almost dark, advance naked under the trees by the waterside, five or six together, superb, unashamed, scarcely touching the ground.

The budding pens of love scorch all over me—my skin is too tight, I am ready to burst through it—a flaming girdle is round my middle. Eyes, hair, lips, hands, waist, thighs—O naked mad tremors; in the dark feeding pasturing flames!

O soul, spreading, spreading—impalpable sunlight behind the sunlight!

The tall thin grey-bearded man I meet daily in the street—with lined brow, silent, full of experience;

The stout matron in the greengrocer's shop, loquacious, clear-eyed, with clear indubitable voice;

The thick-thighed hot coarse-fleshed young bricklayer with the strap round his waist;

The young printer (but he has a wife and family at home) with large dreamy projecting eyes, going absent, miles away, over his work—thinking of Swedenborg and the dance of atoms and angels;

The young woman at the refreshment bar, her thick light-colored hair, her well-formed features, and the bored look in her eyes as she returns the chaff of the carefully-dressed young man across the counter;

The military-looking official at the door of the hotel—the despondency of drink which he conceals beneath his loud-voiced smart exterior;

The ragged boy with rare intense eyes not to be misunderstood—in the midst of much dirt and ignorance the soul through suffering enfranchised, exhaled—here too shining like the sunlight, redeeming justifying all it lights on;

The slut of a girl who has become a mother, the ready doubt among her neighbors who was the father; the stupid loving way in which she crams the child to her breast—sitting on a stone by the fire-side utterly oblivious of opinion;

The good-natured fair-haired Titan at work in the fields; the little woman with large dark eyes who is so clever and managing among the poor, and with their children;

The thin close-lipped friz-haired commercial traveler, unwearied, walking long distances to save railway or coach fare, well posted in all local information for fifty miles round;

His wife, so comfortable and fore-thoughtful at home, so evil-tongued abroad, and the bevy of red-haired red-cheeked girls, well drilled in scrubbing and cooking, and not without a veneer of accomplishments;

The railway lamp-foreman, tall, strong, fleet of foot, with gentle voice—lover of the fields and flowers, going long walks Sundays or late evenings by moonlight—sending the balance of his earnings to support his aged father and mother;

The bright sunny girl-child with long beautiful hair (envied of the other children) and poignant blossoming lips and eyes;

The girl in the tobacconist's shop, her drooping lashes, her taper fingers, and provocative inimitable composure—and all the time her mother is incurably dying;

The hunch-backed cobbler, young, thwarted, thinking incessantly of Jesus—praying night and day for the gift of preaching;

The drunken father reeling home in the rain across country—he has more than a mile to go—singing, cursing, tumbling hands and knees in the mire; his son following unbeknown at a little distance (he had been watching a long time for his father outside the beershop); the late moon rising on the strange scene, the hiccuped oaths of the old man through the silence of the night.

XLVII

Lo! I touch you.

Softly yearningly I touch you, and pass on—dreaming the dream of the soul's slow disentanglement.

Sharp-cut, thin-lipped, sad, scholastic; plain-featured,

unembarrassed, affectionate; and you, beautiful careless boy! and you, strange eternal anxious mother-face!

How shall I say what I have to say? How shall I speak the word which sums up all words that are spoken? How shall I speak that for which the moon and the stars and running waters and the universe itself subsist, to speak it?—which if it could be uttered in a word there were no need of all these things.

O Death, take me away.
Take me away, kindly Death; lead me forth, lead me through the entire universe.
Let me pass; hold me back, I say, no longer; for I am tired, I am sick, of talking—and I forebode other ways.

For I would be the dust;
And I would be the silver rays of the moon and the stars, and the washing sound of the midnight sea;
And nourishing sweet air and running water, for the lips of them that I choose;
To pass, to put on the invisible cap, to run round about the world, unseen.
And I will be the plain ungarnished facts of life, with continual nearnesses;
The train arriving at the station shall not be nearer or more solid; nor the lifting and transporting of boxes and goods, nor the grasp of the handles to them that open and shut the doors.

I will be the ground underfoot and the common clay;

The ploughman shall turn me up with his ploughshare among the roots of the twitch in the sweet-smelling furrow;

The potter shall mould me, running his finger along my whirling edge (we will be faithful to one another, he and I);

The bricklayer shall lay me: he shall tap me into place with the handle of his trowel;

And to him I will utter the word which with my lips I have not spoken.

XLVIII

I arise and pass.

I am a spirit passing by, a light air on the hills saying unto you: In death there is peace.

Out of all mortal suffering, out of the bruised and broken heart, out of tears, tears—falling seen, falling inward and unseen—out of the withering flame of desire, and out of all illusion,

My spirit exhaled—floats free—my brother and sister—for you—over the world eternally.

[Joy, O joy!]

For you, too, beyond this visible—through the gates of mortal passion and suffering—for the exhaled spirit,

For you, too, beyond this broken dream, this bitter waking in tears,

Something—how can I tell it?—which I have seen,

which I might perhaps give you: and yet which I cannot give you, but in me waits also for you—O how long?

Something that I have promised. I give you the token. Faithfully when you recognise and return it shall you have that you desire.

I am the light air on the hills—deny me not; my desire which was not satisfied is satisfied, and yet can never be satisfied.

I pass and pass and pass.

From the hills I creep down into the great city—fresh and pervading through all the streets I pass;

Him I touch, and her I touch, and you I touch—I can never be satisfied.

I who desired one give myself to all. I who would be the companion of one become the companion of all companions.

The lowest and who knows me not, him I know best and love best;

The child of the suffering heart I take; my arms pass under his shoulders and under the hollow of his thighs; his arm lies around my neck, my lips yearn close to his—on my breast at length he slumbers peacefully and long.

The blind and aged woman descends the steps leading to the basement of the tall London house; the east wind blows bitter with dust along the street; she feels along the wall, and for the door, and timidly knocks. I cannot see who opens the door, but it is slammed immediately in her face. I take her by the hand and speak words to her, and her sightless eyes are as though they saw once more.

Once I walked the world of rocks and grass, of space

and time, of ambition and action, and could imagine no other—for I was in that one; now I roam through other fields and have the freedom of worlds innumerable, and am familiar where before was darkness and silence.

XLIX

I arise and pass.

In her tall-windowed sitting room—alone—
[The setting sun casts long shafts of light across the path and beneath the trees where knee-deep in grass a milkwhite calf is browsing,]
In her tall-windowed sitting room, with its antique pier-glasses and profuse handsome ornaments—alone—
The old dowager sits.

Her silver-grey hair lies smooth under a lace cap; lace and silk are her dress, her thin fingers are well stocked with rings.

Lonely is the great house; her old life and the voices of children have long passed away. She goes to the window to pass the time and through the glass looks out upon the still landscape; after a while she turns and rings a bell—a tall young footman appears.

Her voice is quiet and gentle as she gives her order, and flexible still with intelligence; very taking with their old-fashioned refinement are her manners;

But in a moment what she requires is there, and she is alone again—everything is done for her.

Into her chair once more she resigns herself, to knit an antimacassar.

Without, how peaceful the scene!

The crisp sound of browsing, the liquid blue-violet eyes of the white calf, her budding horns, her sweet breath, her muscular tongue encircling the tufts of grass, the impatient sideway thrust of the head with which she tears them,

The fearlessness with which she gives her head to be caressed and hugged by the little girl just come down from the farm.

The sun withdraws his rays; the many shadows are merged in one;

The sweet odor of the white campion comes floating, and of the wild roses in neighboring hedgerows, and of the distant bean-fields;

Twilight comes, and dusk comes, and the height of the sky lifts and lifts;

The last of the long daylight fades:

Over the fields and by the hedgerows and along the sprawling suburban streets of London the last of the long daylight fades:

Over the roof of the high opera-house—late grey and ghostly in contrast with the myriad twinkling lamps below—by those within unthought of, it fades:

Where—amid a blaze of light and color, elate, to her full height drawn, tier upon tier of faces, thousands of eyes confronting, and saturated with the excitement of the moment, every vein in her beautiful body bounding—

The prima donna lifts clear and unfaltering in the finale her splendid voice,

And retires amid a storm of flowers.

The sower goes out to sow, alone in the morning, the early October morning so beautiful and calm.
The flanks of the clods are creeping with thin vapor, and the little copse alongside the field is full of white trailing veils of it;
While now like a flood the rising yellow sunlight pours in, among the brambles and under the square oak-boughs, and splashes through in great streaks of light over the ploughed land.

Beautiful is the morning. Alone over the field, to and fro, to and fro, with ample alternate hand-sweep he goes. At every step, right and left, the grain broadcast flies in a glittering shower.
With the Sun and the Earth for companions, with browned arms and face and dazzle-lidded eyes, thick-booted, untiring, all day the sower goes sowing—
What in due time shall become daily bread in the mouths of thousands.

The caravan has halted: it is the hour of prayer, the tents are already pitched;
On his carpet the old Sheikh kneels upright—his arms and eyes uplifted; above, the living blue breathless miracle bends—the sky!
The others are round him with their faces buried in the sand; the camels are tethered a few paces off.
His voice ascends. By the doors of the tents from the

scanty fires just lighted three columns of smoke, perfectly straight, also ascend.

That is all. The smoke creeps upward and is lost continually in the blue; his voice who prays creeps upward and is lost.

Around spreads, silent, with loose stones and a few weeds, the desert; above, the sky.

The Sky!

L

I arise and pass.

After eighty years, having been once like the rest a little vacant-eyed child in his mother's arms; having thence lived and toiled and enjoyed much hither and thither over the earth; Now being very weary, and day after day and week after week growing more and more weary; all all old interests refusing, for death longing—the old lawyer lies down to sleep.

It is but for an hour or two. Death comes not yet. The leaves still tremble in the evening wind, the clouds in solemn transformation float on, voices of children call in the garden below.

The last few miles, the old familiar country—the well-known roads and garden-lands—yet no glance thereon.

The strange immortal instinct pressing—the veiled figure always in front, beckoning.

Now at this time the creatures of the forest to their lairs retiring await the approach of night; the great mountains stand in awe amid the hush of their own waters; twilight fades and the stars once more appear.

Deep under dead leaves in the wood or buried in the earth, the baby fly, white and unformed—the two dark specks which will be its eyes just appearing—in its oak-spangle cradle sleeps. With their mother plaited in a ball of dry grass, warm and soft, the young fieldmice lie quiet, or chirrup nosing for their food. The pools of water are full of creatures that cannot rest; to the starlit surface rising they spread wings and fly forth into the fields of air. In heaven whirled by resistless tradition and necessity descending from God knows when, Jupiter the great planet swims—and swathes itself wondrous in clouds—prophetic.

Heaven bends above, the Earth opens disclosing innumerable births beneath. He lies weary, slumbering for a moment. The pen, the desk, the half-finished letter, are there; the gas makes a slight singing noise overhead.

Solid walls and stones grow transparent and penetrable: the earth and all that is in it fade and recede to make way for the Traveler.

LI

I arise and pass.

An unfinished house standing at the edge of a field is burning—and the roof has caught first.

One vast sheet of flame ascends spiral in the night, and casts its glare upon thousands of faces in the street and fields below.

Lo! the wonderful colors of the flame! The pitchy night

above; the dazzling white and red mixed with the greens and blue-greens of the burning metals; and the great twisted column of tawny smoke, with red sparkles flying on the wind.

Lo! the strange light cast upon the wall of full-foliaged elms; and far more wonderful than all, at their feet, the crowd of living faces—

The mad pushing sweating crowd, the flushed eager faces—dominated all, controlled and riveted by that flaming sign.

Holy! holy! holy!
Night and flame, night and flame, entering in! entering (O arched wonder of many eyes!) through the visible into the invisible—

Holy! holy! holy!
Night and flame entering in (and one with you, treading softly through the myriad marvelous chambers)—

To dwell; to dwell for months, years; to transfuse, enlarge, to touch with wonder, ardor, exultation; to be remembered afterwards, years and years perhaps, upon his bed, by that child there: the jets of flame through the roof, the strange wreathing smoke, the solemn dark of the sky, the bravery of the firemen, the thrill of the falling timbers; to mix with the yearnings of the growing lonely boy, to be a strange symbol burning in his heart; to fire the slumbering train (in some compressed girl-soul) of adventurous resolve; to mingle with the fears of motherhood;

At last to merge and become indistinguishable—in each one of these to merge, night and flame!—leaving out not one.

Holy! holy! holy!
And lo! the crowd still standing.

And now out of all two alone.
By the curbstone, in the forefront of the crowd, a man —a navvy—with his hands clasped in front of him on the breast of his little son!
The boy, timid, standing between his father's feet, pressing back against his legs, with his own little hands the great hands clasping;
The two, equal childlike, with parallel upward eyes by the flame riveted,
Their rapt unconscious demeanor, the strong likeness between them,
And the meanings, apart, which the wonderful roaring gesticulating flame in the night signifies secretly to each.

LII

I arise and pass.

With struggles and strange exhausting birth-leapings, with long intervals of sleep,
[When it is all over, with long long sweet sleep;]
With the unwashed wet of birth, of love, still upon me;
With the clinging of the love of men and women, with

the sweat of night-long companions, with the bruised sweetness of love;

With sleep, sleep, with the wine of life and death, with kisses given and received, with the reaching of arms round neck and shoulder, and the answer of quiet eyes;

With nakedness unashamed, with divine comradeship, and laughter; with the enclosing shadow of Death, far lost in daring outposts on the verge of the Unknown; with soldiership and armor unremitted, exultant;

With childhood and the least trifle content; with eternal Nowness; with perfected Carelessness; with night, day, rain, sun, winter, summer, morning, evening, solitude, pain, pleasure, and the looking forth of innumerable faces;

With Chastity and Ascendancy; with invulnerability and superhuman power; with Unchastity and Effusion; with live clinging threads of love reaching down to the remotest time;

With the endless journey begun; with trades by sea and land; simple food, coarse clothing, common features; with the breath of the common air, and the freemasonry of the old crafts all over the world;

Shaggy coat-shakings, revolts, rejections of accepted things, travels, disappearances, re-appearances, swoonings away, oblivions; arising again on earth, irresistible, to supreme mastery,

To Savagery and the wild woods, with unfettered step; to rocks and hanging branches; to the dens of the animals, to wind and sun, blowing shining through, and I through them, to evade and arise;

With joy over the world, Democracy, born again, into heaven, over the mountain-peaks and the seas in the unfathomable air, screaming, with shouts of joy, whirling the nations with her breath, into heaven arising and passing,

I arise and pass—dreaming the dream of the soul's slow disentanglement.

LIII

Where you are:

Where the firelight flickers about your room, and the wind moans in the window, and the railway whistle over suburban roofs sounds hollow through the night;

Where you sit alone, and your thoughts spread making a great space about you;

Where you go forth at early morning with your bass of trusty tools, and your shadow shoots long before you down the frosty sparkling road—where you return at evening weary and out of humor with your life,

I dream the dream.

Where you open your eyes upon the world, and the beauty of it is upon you like the touch of beloved fingers;

Where the still flame burns in your soul, hidden away from the lightest breath of curious man; where the fire of consecration burns;

Yet the world closes in at last, and the lamp grows dim, and you lie like one half dead—of the bitter wounds of the faces of men and the taunts of existence;

I dream the dream: I dream the dream of the soul's slow disentanglement.

Where you bend ankle-deep in mud all day in the rice plantations for a few half-pence; and the sun sails on—slow, slow—over the steamy land;

Where you walk following the old employ, shepherding sheep in the sweet crisp air of the high lands;

Where you stand pale and worn-eyed in the gloomy North amid the hot smell of machinery and the wicked scream of wheels; where you stand adjusting the threads, making the same answering movement of the hand for the millionth time;

Where you lie wedged in under a coal seam, working by the light of a tallow dip stuck in clay; or grind scythes all day, bending over, or race your wheel with the racing steel;

Where you sit high up on the fragrant mountains of Ceylon, with a great flood of moonlight at your feet, leaning your soul out from the verandah to the slow lifting and floating of palm-fronds in the exquisite breeze; and memories come trooping back upon you like the clouds of small yellow butterflies that along your coasts—between the sand and the sea—beat annually up against the wind;

Where you recline by your camp-fire in the African wild, watching the moonlight dances of the natives—the fantastic leaps of the dancer, the rhythmical hand-clapping of the spectators;

Where you drop down the river in the sun, past the dreaded mud-banks and wildernesses of mangroves;

I dream the dream.

LIV

Where you sit in your armchair by the hearth, sleeping long and long; where you wake to look back upon your life lying hushed below you—like one who looks back from the summit of a mountain;

And the children that came to you in the morning have gone from you at evening dusk,

And the lesson of unfulfilled longing is yours, and of the inflow of immortality;

Where they go out over the earth, where the children of the universal mother go; and the wind carries them over the sea, blowing them into all lands; where they flow through the straits and narrows and over the great oceans of the earth, dwelling for nights together among the white leaping crests under the stars;

Where strange faces meet, under other-slanting suns, amid new scenes and colors;

Where light encounters dark, and in their meeting glance lie new social ideals and civilisations slumbering;

Where the mother of them all sits dreaming;

Where the young poet peers in by moonlight through the bars of the tomb of Dante, and turns away with a silent prayer;

Where the artist with easel and palette sits swathed in coats upon a hillside watching the untroubled dawn;

Where the old Hindu feeling the approach of death leaves his family and retires to a hut in the jungle, there to spend his last days in prayer and solitude;

Where royalty dwells lonely in spacious chambers, or moves along corridors past scarlet-coated footmen;

Where young and old at eventide in the dreamy flicker of firelight sit silent, or go away wandering in thought after the brother, the son, and lover of their dreams, following quickly softly with each and kissing the sacred footsteps through the dark;

Where the young mother prays for hours bending over the face of her sleeping child; where the young man dreams all night of the face of his new-found friend and the kisses of his lips;

Where the river glides down by night past the great city broadening to the sea;

I dream the dream.

The wind blows up fresh and cold where the waves are slapping against the jetty; red and green lights skim rapidly over the water;

The cold light of the half moon stands overhead, breaking its way through combed fleece clouds, the horizon stretches misty white like the edge of an ice-bound sea;

The moon pushes her way for a moment through the clouds, to look down upon the stilled scene of human toil and suffering; the wind blows up keen against those who still linger on the jetty;

Keenly it blows away over the waste sea, and wraps itself round a thousand solitary watchers of the deep.

On the wind I ride,

And dream the dream of the soul's slow disentanglement;

LV

I have passed away and entered the gate of heaven. I am absolved from all torment. All is well to me.

A tiny infant am I once more, leaning out from my mother's arms as one leans from a balcony. But the world hangs flat before me like a painted curtain: the sun and the moon and men's faces are all alike. This is my dream. The sound of music comes calling to me, calling, calling. Listening I lean forward with open mouth and far-distant gaze, and am profoundly still. [Let who looks upon me see with his own eyes my dark soul's myriad re-awakening.]

I am a wild cat crouching at night in the angle of a bough. I am Arjuna reasoning on the battle-field with Krishna—learning the lessons of divine knowledge. I am a teacher scanning the faces of those who sit opposite to me. All is well.

I labor all day in the drizzle with pick and shovel; the smell of fire I strike from the rock pleases me; I return home tired and wet in the early dusk to my tea.

I am one of a rustic party of actors; in the old farm-parlor we rehearse our parts, with shouts of laughter. I go into the cowshed last thing at night with my lantern to see that all is well.

I am a shepherd on the breezy hills; the wholesome aromatic odors of the grass transfuse me; my sheep graze on and on through the noonday; I lie in the sun and think and speak of little beside ewes and tups.

I stand in the chamber of Death and gaze upon the swathed larval form—the solid world recedes around it;

through the just open window come the cries of hawkers and the creak of cart-wheels.

I laugh and chat with the other girls and women in the edge-tool warehouse; I run home in the evening to my old mother and to prepare the dinners for next day.

The din of the riveting shop goes on round me; I hate the bully red-faced master coming on his rounds—with his insulting voice—and answer him not: murderous thoughts haunt my mind.

I plot with others to murder the captain on board ship. I am satisfied with the deed and experience no remorse. It is off the coast of China. I go ashore afterwards and spend the night at a sing-song shop.

All is well. The least action as well as the greatest. The beautiful and the deformed are alike beautiful. I am happy now and not to-morrow, and am absolved from motives.

On the northern-most point of Australia, decent in my single cowry-shell, I stand. The white man comes ashore in his boat from the great ship, and gives me some old hoop-iron, and I give him a few wooden lances in return.

I am a long-eyed Japanee. In the shadow of the sacred thicket I lie—where the great seated image of Buddha (hollow within for a shrine) breaks above me against the blue sky. The sharp shadows lie under his sleepy lids and soft mouth smiling inwardly. I see on his forehead the sacred spot, and from between his feet the emblematic lotus springing.

[All is well.]

In the shadow of the thicket I lie spreading my fevered limbs to the cool breeze, bruising their unslaked passion against the stony earth—in the cool shadow I lie and gaze at his face I know so well, and through the immortal calm of it the spirit of the Holy One steals upon me; the fever of life departs.

I stand near the door of my cottage, busy with the week's washing, thinking of my husband; in the doorway to and fro my baby swings in the little seat he has made; petulant soft wafts of spring air steal in, this warm February morning. I am very happy.

I am very happy. By the door of my own little house at last I stand entranced. I look out upon the world and know not which way to go.

O world you have been very gentle to me! Strangely as to the dead your beauty comes to me now. Little house where I have lived so long, I thank you too: I know well that you are different from what you appear.

· Disembodied I cry, I cry, over the earth—I shake the sleepers in their tombs with unutterable joy:

O arise! O air and elements break forth into singing! Great sea washing the shores of earth! O earth of countless tombs! the hour of your disclosure is at hand; the bounds of mortality at length are past!

I arise and pass once more: I travel forth into all lands: nothing detains me any longer. By the ever beautiful coast-line of human life, in all climates and countries, wandering on, a stranger, unwearied, I meet the old faces: I come never away from home.

I lift the latch of the cottage door, and the place I love is laid for me for supper; I depart, yet never to depart again.

Laws and limitations fade, time and distance are no more, no bars can hold me, no chamber shut me in: on those that bear me to the grave I descend in peace.

The arched doors of the eyebrows of innumerable multitudes open around me: new heavens I see, and the earth made new because of them.

I will stop here then. I will not leave the earth after all. I am content and need go no farther.

And was this, O love, the cause of your so long aching? That you might have the adit, that you might enter in at last and be at rest?

LVI

SLOWLY on You, too, the meanings: the light-sparkles on water, tufts of weed in winter—the least things—dandelion and groundsel.

Have you seen the wild bees' nest in the field, the cells, the grubs, the transparent white baby-bees, turning brown, hairy, the young bees beginning to fly, raking the moss down over the disturbed cells? the parasites?

Have you seen the face of your brother or sister? have you seen the little robin hopping and peering under the bushes? have you seen the sun rise, or set? I do not know—I do not think that I have.

When your unquiet brain has ceased to spin its cobwebs over the calm and miraculous beauty of the world;

When the Air and the Sunlight shall have penetrated your body through and through; and the Earth and Sea have become part of it;

When at last, like a sheath long concealing the swelling green shoot, the love of learning and the regard for elaborate art, wit, manners, dress, or anything rare or costly whatever, shall drop clean off from you;

When your Body—for to this it must inevitably return—is become shining and transparent before you in every part (however deformed);

Then (O blessed One!) these things also transparent possibly shall surrender themselves—the least thing shall speak to you words of deliverance.

The stones are anywhere and everywhere: the temple roof is the sky.

The materials are the kettle boiling on the fire, the bread in the oven, the washing dolly, the axe, the gavelock—the product is God;

And the little kitchen where you live, the shelves, the pewter, the nightly lamp, the fingers and faces of your children—a finished and beautiful Transparency of your own Body.

LVII

I saw the cow give birth to her first-born calf; I saw the beautiful helpless creature laid under her nose; I saw the calm woman who sprinkled the young thing with meal and tended the exhausted mother.

I see the many women who manage cattle well, and gardens, and understand the breeding of sheep;

I see the noble and natural women of all the Earth; I see their well-formed feet and fearless ample stride, their supple strong frames, and attitudes well-braced and beautiful;

On those that are with them long Love and Wisdom descend; everything that is near them seems to be in its place; they do not pass by little things nor are afraid of big things; but they love the open air and the sight of the sky in the early morning.

Blessed of such women are the children : and blessed are they in childbirth. The open air and the sun and the moon and the running streams they love all the more passionately for the sake of that which lies sleeping within them.

LVIII

Recurved and close lie the little feet and hands, close as in the attitude of sleep folds the head, the little lips are hardly parted;

The living mother-flesh folds round in darkness, the mother's life is an unspoken prayer, her body a temple of the Holy One.

I am amazed and troubled, my child, she whispers— at the thought of you; I hardly dare to speak of it, you are so sacred;

When I feel you leap I do not know myself any more—

I am filled with wonder and joy—Ah! if any injury should happen to you!

I will keep my body pure, very pure; the sweet air will I breathe and pure water drink; I will stay out in the open, hours together, that my flesh may become pure and fragrant for your sake;

Holy thoughts will I think; I will brood in the thought of mother-love. I will fill myself with beauty: trees and running brooks shall be my companions;

And I will pray that I may become transparent—that the sun may shine and the moon, my beloved, upon you,

Even before you are born.

LIX

Out of Night and Nothingness a Body appears.

The threads of a thousand past ages run together in it; out of its loins and the look of its eyes a thousand ages part their way into the future.

Eyes out of which I see, Ears through which I hear—formed in my mother's womb in silence;

Mother of mine, walking the earth no more (to me closer than ever), out of all tears, suffusing light over the world, equal with God—for whose sake Night and Day evermore are sacred;

Body, by which I ascend and know Myself—Mysteries of life and death slowly parting and transforming around me:

O glad, not for one year or two but for how many thousands, I out of deep and infinite Peace salute you.

The doctor does not give Health, but the winds of heaven;

Happiness does not proceed by chance, nor is got by supplication, but is inevitable wherever the Master is.

Doubt parts aside. I hear grown and bearded men shouting in the woods for joy, shouting singing with the birds; I hear the immense chorus over all the world, of the Return to Joy.

Come, my friend, in the still autumn morning, while the sun is yet low upon the hills, among the dead leaves come walk with me.

Those and the like of those that have been my companions are with You also, and shall be to all time. I give you but a hint and a word of commendation. I open a door outwards.

The gentle and stormy winds, the clouds sailing in heaven; the plough-stilts, the boat-tiller; sitting at dinner with the winter sun looking in at the open door, natural men and women (common as unquarried rock) around you; love, granted or not granted; the companionship of the dead;

The savage eternal peaks, the solitary signals—Walt Whitman, Jesus of Nazareth, your own Self distantly deriding you—

These are always with you.

Have you doubted?—It is well. But now you shall forget your doubts.

Have you suffered?—It is good to suffer; but soon you shall suffer no longer.

Have you looked at the sky and the earth and the long busy streets and thought them dead of all poetry and beauty?—It is you have been ill, nigh to death; but be at peace: life shall surely return to you.

I have seen your struggles, your long wakeful nights; I have sat by you. I have heard the voice which calls you. Come with me. Here is Rest, here is Peace I give you. A little while by the edge of this wood sitting, I with You; then to depart; yet never to depart again.

Words unspoken, yet wafted over all lands, through all times, eternal; no more mine than yours—I give them again to the wide embracing Air.

Haply a little breath for you to breathe—to enter, scarcely perceived, into your body—a little time to dwell, transforming, within you.

Haply mementos, indications, broken halves of ancient changeless Symbols, eternal possessions, treasures incorruptible,

Of Love which changes not—to be duly presented again —the broken halves to be joined.

I a child sitting at your feet, content—the odor of dead leaves all around; or walking with you, your comrade, through the night (often we lean and touch each other's lips as we go); or very old, and near and dear to Death:

Are you sure you know me when you look upon me?

Behold a mystery!—these eyes, these lips, this hair, these loins—see you me in them, you shall see me where they are not.

Long looking, the face of the world shall change—surely by the edge of the little wood I will come and sit with you.

All riches promised, and far more, I give to you.
Have you used the Summer well, then the Winter shall be beautiful to you. Have you made good use of Life, then Death shall be exceeding glorious.

All this day we will go together; the sun shall circle overhead; our shadows swing round us on the road; the winter sunshine shall float wonderful promises to us from the hills; the evening see us in another land;
The night ever insatiate of love we will sleep together, and rise early and go forward again in the morning;
Wherever the road shall lead us, in solitary places or among the crowd, it shall be well; we shall not desire to come to the end of the journey, nor consider what the end may be: the end of all things shall be with Us.

LX

This is my trade; teach me yours and I will teach you mine.
Are you a carpenter, a mason, a grower of herbs and flowers, a breaker of horses? a wheel-wright, boat-builder, engine-tenter, dockyard-laborer? do you take in washing or sewing, do you rock the youngest in the cradle with your foot while you knit stockings for the elder ones? It is well—Weaning yourself from external results learn the true purposes of things.

Wherever the sea and the land are, is my trade, and it has been known since the eldest Time: the ancient Mysteries and Oracles hinted at it, the venerable sages of India knew it, and men and women who walked this earth before all history; in the remotest stars it is exactly the same as here, and in all the circles of intelligences whether they dwell in fire or water or in the midst of what is solid, or in the thinnest vacuum.

Many an old woman sitting by her cottage door is far more profoundly versed in it than I am. Many a fisherman pouncing on crabs along the shores of the Mediterranean has in it long ago served his apprenticeship. If you think or desire by coming with me to know more or be better than these, you mistake me and what I have to tell you.

Learning and superiority are of no use in the face of all this: they depart much as they came. But to come near to understanding the use of materials is divine, and he that has never despised a weaker or more ignorant than himself is nearest to this.

Many are the roads, but there is one end to which they all lead; there are many profitable trades, but there is one whose profits are past all reckoning.

LXI

Hand in hand for an hour I sit with you in the Great Garden of Time

Equals We, possessors and enjoyers, ask no more than simply to be. This hour, equal of all others that were or shall be, itself perfect: the other hours as they come or go, perfect.

Meeting once, to meet often and often again (is not the whole garden ours?), we shall not forget, we will not hasten or delay.

. From this day it is not so much we that change, as the hours that glide past us; each bends low as it passes with a gift.

Earth-kings on their thrones faintly fore-shadowed this; the old myths and legends of heaven were the indistinct dreams of the everlasting peace of the soul.

LXII

And you too, ye hours of suffering and warfare, grim unrest, we confront, each perfect; we contain you; storms and darkness surging around, we have seen round you.

Hours of pain and darkness within, evil conscience and heavy burdens of concealment! hours of black and obstinate desire, eyes turning aswerve, trembling guilty tongue—hungry mortal hours! caught in the cleave of your jaws, I deny you not.

Far from it: I welcome you. You are my friends as good as any, I give you equal places with the rest, if not better—for what indeed should I understand if you had not taught me?

Each beautiful, countless myriads to be known,
Over the hills and green plains of Eternity pasturing, for ever widening—mortal, immortal, swift-footed, slow-footed—O ye Hours and Desires, you are all mine!

My herd, my beauties! my glossy, supple, with arched

necks, my gentle and caressing, my wild, fierce, passionate—divine, satanic—there is room, and plenty, for you all!

O beautiful creatures! not because sometimes you show your teeth at each other will I disown you; not if you should all turn upon one to rend him, will I cast that one out—never so black or ungainly be he.

Avaunt! Over the hills with lightning speed fly, tossing your nostrils: but know that I easily outspeed you all—you cannot delude or escape Me.

Wild herd! begetting and begetting innumerable progeny (all mine),

See if to my chariot at length harnessed I will not drive you, irresistible and triumphant, through all the kingdoms of Space.

LXIII

Beautiful is the winter by the sea; the gray waves come rolling with locks tossed back by the North wind.

In his hut on the beach the fisherman cooks his dinner; the clock that belongs in the herring-boat ticks against the wall; the drift-nets are mended; the boat is overhauled and repaired, the boat-lanterns and the pump are painted.

Out on the great deep the balance and plunge goes on; the sail steadies in the wind; the land and well-known points fade; the circle of water completes itself.

Beautiful is the winter inland; the wind and wild clouds with rain rush over the world; the valleys are full of the sound of streams.

The farmer cleans out his ditches and drains, and mends the foot-paths across his fields; the turnip-pit is completed; and the apples and potatos are picked over in the store-room.

The snow descends upon the young blade of corn; the soft-fingered flakes wrap all the world in white; frost seals the earth in silence.

He stands by the door of the house-place at night; the moon leans out, and the stars and the great planets from heaven; Orion hunts with his dogs. In the morning the field-fares and starlings go by in flights.

Do I ask of you perfections? do you think that Winter is perhaps less perfect than Summer? or that there is not perfection everywhere, where the soul casts its light?

Be not careful about perfections: I declare to you the day shall come when everything shall be perfect to you.

To be ungainly or deformed shall after all be no hindrance, your ignorance and rags shall not avail for a disguise;

Past your own futility and vanity you shall walk unfettered, and just gaze upon them as you go by; if learning and skill admit you to wonders, ignorance and awkwardness shall give you entrances equally or more desirable.

Take care (I have warned you before) how you touch these words: with curious intellect come not near, lest I utterly destroy you; but come with bold heart and true and careless, and they shall bless you beyond imagination.

I do not turn you back from self-seeking; on the contrary I know that you shall never rest till you have found your Self;

If you seek it in money, fame, and the idle gratification of inordinate organs and bumps—that is all very well for a time; but you will have to do better than that.

If you seek it in Duty, Goodness, Renunciation, they also are very well for a time; but you will do better.

LXIV

Beautiful is the figure of the lusty full-grown groom on his superb horse: the skin of the animal is saturated with love.

Radiant health!

O kisses of sun and wind, tall fir-trees and moss-covered rocks! O boundless joy of Nature on the mountain tops—coming back at last to you!

Wild songs in sight of the sea, wild dances along the sands, glances of the risen moon, echoes of old old refrains coming down from unimagined times!

O rolling through the air superb prophetic spirit of Man, pulse of divine health equalising the universe, vast over all the world expanding spirit!

O joy of the liberated soul (finished purpose and acquittal of civilisation), daring all things—light step, life held in the palm of the hand! O swift and eager delight of battle, fierce passion of love destroying and destroying the body!

Eternal and glorious War! Liberation! the soul like an eagle—from gaping wounds and death—rushing forth screaming into its vast and eternal heaven.

See! the divine mother goes forth with her babe (all creation circles round)—God dwells once more in a woman's womb; friend goes with friend, flesh cleaves to flesh, the path that rounds the universe.

O every day sweet and delicious food! Kisses to the lips of sweet-smelling fruit and bread, milk and green herbs. Strong well-knit muscles, quick-healing glossy skin, body for kisses all over!

Radiant health! to breathe, O joy! to sleep, ah! never enough to be expressed!

For the taste of fruit ripening warm in the sun, for the distant sight of the deep liquid sea!

For the sight of the naked bodies of the bathers, bathing by the hot sea-banks, the pleasant consciousness of those who are unashamed, the glance of their eyes, the beautiful proud step of the human animal on the sand;

For the touch of the air on my face or creeping over my unclothed body, for the rustling sound of it in the trees, and the appearance of their tall stems springing so lightly from the earth!

Joy, joy and thanks for ever.

LXV

For the face of the farm-lad who came and sat beside me, the handfuls of pease that he offered me—for the taste of their juicy sweet pods;

The pressure of the Earth against me as I lay on it, the light sense riding on it of tremendous forces charioting me onward; for the like sense in my will and actions, of being borne along!

O the splendid wind careering over earth and ocean, the sun darting between the great white clouds! O the lifting of arms to Nature—heaven wrapped around one's body!

The unflagging pleasure of food, the crisp and toothsome growths of the soil! draughts of running water in summer;

The evenings by the fire in winter, the ease after labor, the steady sleepy heat, the sleepy flicker on the wall, the presence of others in the room; for the voices of children;

For the beautiful faces—and ever more beautiful appearing—of those I meet in the doorway or at meals, the mortal father mother sister brother faces;

For the glorified face of him I love: the long days out alone together in the woods, the nights superb of comradeship and love.

O joy returning morn noon and night! day-long as in a dream walking over earth enchanted, waking deep midnight out of sleep in the ocean of joy! [Lo! the beautiful surface, the rippling of waves, the moon shining down.]

Deep deep draughts of all that life can give, drawn in to feed the flame—

Joy, joy and thanks for ever.

[O burning behind all worlds, immortal Essences, Flames

of this ever-consuming universe, never-consumed—to laugh and laugh with you, and of our laughter

Shake forth creation!]

Wonderful! wave after wave; clouds, rain, wind, day and night;

The sea by night in storms, and the morning over the hills, for grief and joy, for solitude and companionship; for the birth of babes and the putting away of the husks of the feeble and aged in the ground;

For the great processions of the seasons over the Earth, and the dead lying below; and the dead rising again in the pure translucent air to begin a new existence, with unutterable joy bursting outwards from them beyond all mortal bounds—

With shouts and pæans into the blue æther of God—

Joy, joy and thanks for ever.

And for the strange individual decree of each one,

The daily hunger and thirst after sympathy, ever-new, for the pleasant putting-forth of affection, and for the excess —for prostrate unspeakable love!

For the pleasant moods of the soul, for the finite masterly enjoyment of the world; and for the painful moods, for the vicious agony and the vast dark after-death of desire— for the transcendent pouring and pouring of the soul out into other worlds!

For the tragic moments of life, and for the long same stretches of the commonplace;

For the wonderful looming rise upon one of the great

Arch of Death as one approaches it, for the dim perception of the infinite stretches beyond!

For the final deep abiding sense of rest—in Thee;

For the touch of Thyself growing continually out of everything more actual, starlike, perfect;

And for all experience;

Joy, joy and thanks for ever.

LXVI

O the sound of trumpets, the wild clangor of wings! forging aloft into the air! O Freedom for men!

Sounds of innumerable voices singing! Starry lamps twinkling to each other across the huge concave of Time!

Dread Creators of the flying earth through space! Travelers yourselves upon it! Fliers through all forms! Enduers of all disguises!

In your hut by the sea shore looking back upon the myriad constellations whence you descended! In the eyes of her you love, in the faithful face of your enemy in battle, aware at last of the drift of Creation!

O joy! joy! inextinguishable joy and laughter!

Lo! the Conscience, the tender green shoot in each one, growing, arising, Ygdrasil casting its leaves, elements and nations, over the universe!

Lo! the Moral laws so long swathing the soul, loosing, parting at last for the liberation of that which they prepared.

Lo! Death in majesty appearing, tender and beautiful, walking on earth the floor of heaven, through the night, through the long transparent night singing singing—

In her arms the children of all creation, all creatures of the field and the children of men, nursing,

In their ears singing low, singing soft, the song—the interpreting song—that the darting sun sings, and the maiden by her window, the song of the leaping waters and of love—

And of joy, of inconceivable joy, O ecstasy! thrilling every object of thought.

LXVII

I hear the electric thunderbolt strike the earth. It shivers and it staggers in its orbit.

Leap, children of men, arise! Set your faces dead as flint. For great is the prize before you.

The hour has struck! the Masters appear! Back, O elements and destiny!

From this hour, War! ever more splendid and glorious War! the long tradition of the Earth!

The flame of the Soul, burning through all materials!

Long the battle, clouds of dust hiding heaven. Earth trembles like a startled horse.

They that fight descend, radiant with eternal lightnings. The gods blaze forth upon each other.

The flags fly of all nations up and down. The long result of history, and penetrating and preceding all history, completes itself.

Lo, Freedom! haughty, magnificent, moving like a dream before the half-awakened eyes of men—never faithless to her, never at last one faithless.

LXVIII

And so I heard a voice say What is Freedom?

I have heard (it said) the lions roaring in their dens; I have seen the polyp stretching its arms upward from the floor of the deep;

I have heard the cries of slaves and the rattling of their chains, and the hoarse shout of victims rising against their oppressors; I have seen the deliverers dying calmly on the scaffold.

I have heard of the centuries-long struggle of nations for constitutional liberty—the step-by-step slowly-won approaches as to some inner and impregnable fastness;

I know the wars that have been waged, the flags flying to and fro over the earth; I know that one tyranny has been substituted for another, and that the forms of oppression have changed:

But what is Freedom?

Villeins and thralls become piece-men and day-tal men, and the bondsmen of the land become the bondsmen of Machinery and Capital; the escaped convicts of Labor fit admiringly the bracelets of Wealth round their own wrists.

I have seen the slaves of Opinion and Fashion, of Ignorance and of Learning, of Drink and Lust, of Chastity and Unchastity:

One skin cast leaves another behind, and that another, and that yet another;

I have seen over the world the daily fear of Death and Hell, of Pain and momentary overhanging Chance;

I have seen recluses craning their lives up into impossible heavens, thinkers hopelessly meditating after philosophic Truth, incurables lying covered with bed-sores, household drudges running from the hearth to the slopstone and from the slopstone to the hearth all their lives;

Something of all these slaveries I know—they are very well in their way—

But what is Freedom?

And I heard (in the height) another voice say:
I AM.

In the recluse, the thinker, the incurable and the drudge, I AM. I am the giver of Life, I am Happiness.

I am in the good and evil, in the fortunate and the unfortunate, in the gifted and the incapable, alike; I am not one more than the other.

The lion roaring in its den, and the polyp on the floor of the deep, the great deep itself, know ME.

The long advances of history, the lives of men and women—the men that scratched the reindeer and mammoth on bits of bone, the Bushmen painting their rude rock-paintings, the mud-hovels clustering round mediæval castles, the wise and kindly Arab with his loving boy-attendants, the Swiss mountain-herdsman, the Russian patriot, the English mechanic,

Know ME. I am Happiness in them, in all—underlying. I am the Master, showing myself from time to time as occasion serves.

I am not nearer to one than the other; they do not seek me so much as I advance through them.

Out of all would YOU emerge?
Would you at last, O child of mine, after many toils and endless warfare (for without such all is in vain) emerge and become MY EQUAL?
[Wonderful, wonderful is this that I tell you! Would you too become a Master—when you have seen and known all slaveries, and have ceased to put one before the other?]
Would you, whom I have often silently been with, to whom in the early morning I have come kissing you on the lips to leave Happiness for your waking, whom I have taught long and long my own ways, even for this—become my Equal? would you look me at last in the face?

It shall be then. The way is long but the centuries are long. Faint not. Does my voice sound distant? Faint not.
Even now for a moment round your neck, advancing, I stretch my arms; to my lips I draw you, I press upon your lips the seal of a covenant that cannot be forgotten.

LXIX

I—WHO write—translate for you these thoughts: I wipe a mirror and place it in your hands [look long, O friend, look long, satiate yourself]—

I bring you to your own, to take, or leave for a while, as pleases you best. I have perfect faith in you.

And can wait: the whole of Time is before me.

LXX

The little red stars appear once more shining among the hazel catkins; the pewit tumbles and cries as at the first day, the year begins again,

The wind blows east, the wind blows west, the old circle of days and nights completes itself;

But henceforth the least thing shall speak to you words of deliverance; the commonest shall please you best;

And the fall of a leaf through the air and the greeting of one that passes on the road shall be more to you than the wisdom of all the books ever written—and of this book.

Part II

CHILDREN OF FREEDOM

O Freedom, beautiful beyond compare, thy kingdom is established!

Thou with thy feet on earth, thy brow among the stars, for ages us thy children

I, thy child, singing daylong nightlong, sing of joy in thee.

York Minster

SOLID and ghostly in the pale winter morning—
    Thy vast floor worn, worn by the tiny foot-falls of centuries,
The great grey Alps, thy columns, cutting sharply their strong lines against the delicate tracery of roof and window—
Solid and ghostly, in visionary beauty thou stretchest O nave,
All desolate—vast and desolate.

The murmurs of the outer world tremble faintly along the roof like the murmur of the sea in some vast sea-shell;
Below, nothing visible moves save one ancient verger, pacing to and fro or drowsing in his armchair by the stove.

But hark now; from behind the screen the droning mumble of morning prayers!
It ceases, and the thin boy-voices of the scanty choir take up the chant.
Strangely from its invisible source, like some river once running strong but now losing itself in runlets in the sand,
As from out the old mediæval world, faint and far comes sounding that refrain—

The quaint barbaric tentative uncertain-toned Gregoric refrain, soaring,
Soaring, soaring, through the great desolate nave wandering, in the ears of the one drowsy verger dying.

And all around over the world spreads winter,
Heavy and silent;
There is no music heard in the streets, nor sound of hope or of pleasuring—but pinched faces are there,
And in wretched homes reign cold and starvation.

The Church is dead. Snow covers the ground. Silence and heavy misery spread their wings dull against the faces of the people. The Church is dead.

All the long years of Christianity have come to this;
All the preaching and the prayers and the psalm-singing of centuries have come to this;
All the rapt outpourings of the soul to God, and hidden yearnings of ages, to this?
The Church is dead. Snow covers the ground. Snug in their firelit homes, with closed shutters and surrounded by every luxury, the Wealthy the Pious and the Respectable sit—
And without, the People are dying of cold and starvation.

A nation is dying—
Dying slowly and surely of Unbelief—and there can be no deadlier disease: no plague of the middle ages, no cholera epidemic, deadlier.

A nation is dying—

Rotting down piece-meal, lethargic even in its misery, weary and careworn even in its luxury, to the grave.

And I sit and sing.

All the dark winter night, and though the night were ten times pitchier than it is,

I sit and sing.

Though the gloom spread all around me, though the wan pinched faces plead terribly upon me, in the midst still I sit and sing: J$_{oy}$! Joy!—for I have seen;

Deep in the wide wan eyes I have seen:

And what I have seen—is sufficient.

O what lies deeper far than the life and death of nations—

As the calm Ocean lies deep below the storms which vex its surface;

What all the ages and ages of human life on earth has never never failed;

What is to humanity as the sun rising in the morning is to nature—

Ever fresh and young and potent, creating new worlds for itself as it were by merely looking forth upon them;

What rises winged out of all graves—with laughter—leaving the long vistas of corpses behind; and out of the graves of nations;

What for each man rises out of his own grave, and is never vanquished;

Deep deep—below all words—in the eyes of these wan children,
I have seen—and that is sufficient.

O the fresh fresh air blowing!
Here on the summit of this leafless poplar, under the immense night, while the tender growing light just outlines the distant hills,
To sit and sing—for pure joy simply to sit and sing!

Sunday Morning after Church

SUNDAY morning just after church—and a light warm wind from the North flutters laden with the scent of hay out to sea;
The sea lies crisp and calm, slate-green, stretching itself miles and miles to the wind—wonderful, ecstatic, pushing back with liquid-velvet paws upon the shore.

On the sea-side esplanade there is a good-sized crowd —perhaps a thousand grown men and women walking up and down on one exclusive and fashionable stretch of grass.
It is quite a sight. Scarlet parasols and blue and white lined with pink, tall hats shining speckless, kid-gloves reaching to the elbow—with glitter of gold and silver bangles, and soft sheen and rustle of dresses. All subdued and polite, colors carefully chosen, voices low, movements measured:

Let us take a seat here. How pleasant the air is! and the shade of the great clouds! and the dazzling effect of so many going to and fro!

Here comes one—her face not very easy to be seen for her parasol—but her chin is softly rounded, and the tinge and tissue of her skin most delicate. She wears a very light salmon-pink silk slashed with blue. She is with her mother and an elder sister, and seems to be doing her best, gentle child, to be the correct thing.

Here another of bolder sort—dark handsome eyes, just flashing often enough to keep him amused on the man who is walking beside her; lips a trifle too red, but contrasting well with the great yellow rose on her shoulder and the violet velveteen tunic; figure admirable, but her face somewhat wan beneath its petulance and inquisitiveness.

There goes an old beau, carefully brushed grizzled hair, faultless boots—knows everybody, a good-natured and amusing crony; here a grey-haired baronet and his wife, both demure and short-sighted (no question but they have been to church); there again, a few steps to the left, three young men arm in arm, carefully got up, exchanging whispered comments.

Hist! this elderly matron and her daughter are coming to sit beside us!

Heavy and heated, in rich silks deeply flounced and embroidered, and tight spindle-heeled boots—they seem glad of a rest.

The dress of the elder one especially is a study—the

flounces, the innumerable quantity of beads, the formless mass of plaits and gathers, the wonderful arrangement of whalebones in the body, the strict lacing down the back, the frills and lace round neck and shoulders, the several rings seen on the for a moment ungloved hand, the lump of trinkets suspended from her waist, and the usual headgear [—one cannot help thinking of the chaotic mass of human work this idle red easy-tempered woman carries about on her body].

I close my eyes for a moment. How pleasant still and soft the air is!

A vision goes past of dark and unspoken things—of criminals in prison, of rags and disease and destitution.

Naked and outcast forms hurry by;

The mother snatches some half-pence from her boy match-seller, and makes for the nearest gin-shop; squalid streets and courts are in the background, and filthy workshops;

Forms of humanity pass before me, unclothed; voices hover round, wordless;

Strange clinging voices call; through the long high arches floating, through the night strange voices call.

O freedom! O shadow and night! and forms half-shapen in the womb of night—to the outlet of deliverance!

These naked and outcast—I contemplate them long, undisguised; what they are is not hidden from me, I go back of them and beyond.

I pass as one among them, and feel the touch of their bodies, and of their arms twining—and turn down tired and sleep beside those who sleep;

Half-human, crazy, hungry, condemned, bitter-lipped, forsaken,

The young man with divine face so pale and misshapen I see—I see the poor thin body of the dying mother.

[She is ignorant and unlettered, but when she talks to me in perfect child-like trust of the future of her orphaned children I think I have heard the words of the profoundest Wisdom that ever were uttered.]

The rags fall off, the prison doors fly wide.

In vast phalanx, as out of night and oblivion,

Unclothed, majestic, with wounds and disfigurements, as of him who hung upon the Cross—

With stretched arms, shadow-gigantic and shining, as just alighted on the earth—they stand. I hear their voices call—

Strange wild and inarticulate—

Through the long high arches floating, through the night their voices call.

I open my eyes again. The gay crowd still glides past, exchanging greetings, the flounces and lace are still on the chair beside me. I catch the fluffy smell.

I rise and pass down towards the sea. It lies there, unnoticed as before, slate-green and solemn, stretching miles and miles away; but the wind has risen and is rising, and in the distance here and there it is fretful with sharp white teeth.

HIGH IN MY CHAMBER

HIGH in my chamber I hear the deep bells chime
—Midnight.
The great city sleeps with arms outstretched supine under the stars—deep-breathing, hushed;
Into the kennels of sleep are gone the loud-baying cares of day, and hunted man rests for a moment.

The spangled stream has gone.
The long procession of carriages through fashionable quarters, the stream of faces past gay shop-windows,
And high above them the weary face of the needle-woman straining the last hour of daylight—
All are gone.
Into the hidden chamber of the dark the stream of life has poured itself,
For the conception of a new day.

The note of sorrow sleeps;
The weary throbbing brain and heart are lulled—assuaged is the tossing sea;
The wretched prisoner—the prisoner of the needle and dingy attic—is released: she dreams her impossible dream;
The prisoners of here and there, and of Necessity gripping close as a vice, are at liberty: they roam out beyond the star-circled walls of time and hear strange secrets whispered.

But the hour swings onward.

To good and evil alike—to the watching and the sleeping heart alike;

To the mother as she lies beside her infant, sleeping, yet wakeful to its slightest movement; to the father as he sleeps beside the mother;

To the young man as he lies beside his new-made bride, worshiping sleepless on her bosom;

To the folded bud of childhood, sleeping deep as on a tranquil sea—to the bud just disclosed from Eden; and to the child-like relaxed sleep again of extreme old age;

The hour swings onward.

To the waking fever of remorse;

To the long cadaverous vigil of physical pain;

And to the long vigil of the heart-broken wife praying vainly for respite from thought;

The hour swings onward.

High in heaven over the supine city—over the wilderness of roofs beneath the stars—

The hour swings surely onward.

Again the great bell booms.

Blossoming out of silence the rich music swells—

Then dies away—the second stroke of midnight.

And now as if awoken by that note of warning, over the vast city clash a thousand brazen chattering tongues,

Ding, ding, clack, clack,

High in My Chamber

From far and near, from railway-tower and steeple—blurring the thoughtful night—ding ding, clack clack,
With scrambling stroke they hurry to tell the hour—and so straightway are silent.
But the great bell goes booming slowly on,
High in its tower in heaven among the stars,
Thoughtful, deep-voiced, alone—till it has finished.

So pass the hours, the spacious solemn hours, the shrill chattering hours,
Out into the night they pass, out into the morning,
For the conception of a new day.

2

High in my chamber I hear the deep bells chime,
Deep deep deep, past all mortal hearing, down in the kennels of sleep below the world—
The slow and muffled chime.

The strokes of the changing hours of Man,
The slow spacious thoughts of the changing generations—
Through the night rising I hear.
The thoughts of them who gather the generations into the great fold;
Through whose hearts the trampling millions pass—as surely indeed as through city streets;
The thoughts of them through whose hearts the weary exiles, the prisoners of time, pass, liberating their souls in prayer till the air is charged with lightning—

Through the night rising I hear.

These are they who dream the impossible dream—and it comes true;
Who hear the silent prayers, who accept the trampling millions, as the earth dreaming accepts the interminable feet of her children;
Who dream the dream which all men always declare futile;
Who dream the hour which is not yet on earth—
And lo! it strikes.

3

High in my chamber I hear the deep Bell chime.

Softly softly up through the universe,
Vibrant in every leaf soft-answering, scarce audible ascending,
The great undertone—the deep rich musical solvent, swelling over the world, saturated with love, soft like the winds of spring (O who will give it utterance?)—
Through the night rising I hear.

Deep Below Deep

DEEP below deep,
    Tearless, impenetrably frozen in misery—
Is it a child or an old man?
[His face is the color of ashes: it is like a vacant spot without light.]

Deep Below Deep

A child surely, by his top-heavy knock-kneed gait and perching semi-perceptive ways;

An old man, by the two deep horizontal furrows in his brow.

Come in my child out of the bitter wind, and sit awhile by my fire, and eat.

You need not speak or explain yourself: just sit down, and when you have eaten draw your chair close and get warm.

[Perhaps he will thaw, I think, and tell me the story of his life.]

But he sits silent—his hand in mine—with his head deep on his breast; and hardly moves—except once or twice to pick a bit of rag off the end of his trousers and throw it into the fire.

Now his cap is off I see it is a fine head—a well-formed head and brow with short light curling hair;

But when he lifts it his eyes are bleared and slow, with heavy lids, and they refuse to meet mine.

We sit awhile silent; then with slow fitful answers, only now and then volunteering a word:

It was my own fault:

I went into t' pit when they did not want me to;

They gave me a good education—I can read and write well enew—but I would go into t' pit.

The very first day I was crushed by a wagon and was

laid up a twelve-month : It **was** my legs that was crushed—but I got over it.

Then my father died. My mother behaved very bad to me: I don't live with them now. When I am in work I lodge down by the Brewery, but now I sleep where I can.

I have had twelve year at it. I am now twenty-three.

It was all right at first, but times have been very bad lately. When you work half time you can't save nothing.

I have been out of work three months. They shortened hands, and I was thrown out. They don't care: when times is bad they throw you out to make it worse.

There's hundreds clemming one place or another, and they don't care.

It's all the same to them that's well off themselves, and they have done it to spite us.

Silence.

Again the sunken head, again the impenetrable weary crushed frozen look—

There was no thaw or change whatever.

I knew him for many months, but there was no thaw or change to speak of.

Except the Lord Build the House

SHE lies, whom Money has killed, and the greed of Money,

The thrice-driven slave, whom a man has calmly tortured,

And cast away in the dust—and calls it not murder,
Because he only looked on; while his trusted lieutenants
Supply and Demand pinned the victim down—and her own mother Nature slew her!

The old story of the sewing machine—the treadle machine;

Ten hours a day and five shillings a week, a penny an hour or so—if the numbers were of importance.

Of course she fell ill. Indeed she had long been ailing, and the effort and the torture were slowly disorganising her frame; and already the grim question had been asked: "Might she have rest?" (—the doctor said *must*—and for many a month, too.)

And the answer came promptly as usual. "Have rest? —as much as she wanted! It was a pity, but of course if she could not work she could go. They would make no difficulty, as Supply would fill up her place as soon as vacant."

One more struggle then. And now she *must* go, for work is impossible, and Supply *has* filled her place, and there is no difficulty—or difference—except to her.

For her only the hospital pallet, and the low moaning of the distant world;

For her only the fever and the wasting pain and the nightmare of the loud unceasing treadles;

And the strange contrast in quiet moments of the still chamber and the one kindly face of the house-surgeon, stethoscope in hand, at her bedside;

For her only, hour after hour, the dull throbbing recollection of the injustice of the world,

The bleak unlovely light of averted eyes thrown backwards and forwards over her whole life,

And the unstaunched wound of the soul which is their bitter denial.

And at last the lessening of the pain, and a sense of quietude and space, and through the murky tormented air of the great city a light, a ray of still hope on her eyes peacefully falling;

And then in a moment the passing of the light, and a silence in the long high-windowed ward;

And one with an aster or two and a few chrysanthemums and one with a blown white rain-bewept rose half-timidly coming,

To lay on her couch, with tears.

And so a grave.

In the dank smoke-blackened cemetery, in the dismal rain of the half-awakened winter day,

A grave, for her and her only.

And yet not for her only, but for thousands—
For hundreds of thousands—to lie undone, forsaken,
Tossed impatiently back from the whirling iron—
The broken wheels, or may be merely defective—
Who cares?—
That as they spin roll off and are lost in the darkness,
Run swiftly away (as if they were alive!) into the darkness, and are hidden;

Except the Lord Build the House

Who cares? who cares?
Since for each one that is gone Supply will provide a thousand.

Who cares? who cares?
O tear-laden heart!
O blown white rose heavy with rain!
O sacred heart of the people!
Rose, of innumerable petals, through the long night ever blossoming!
Surely by thy fragrance wafted through the still night-air,
Surely by thy spirit exhaled over the sleeping world, I know,
Out of the bruised heart of thee exhaled, I know—
And the vision lifts itself before my eyes:—

Except the Lord build the house, they labor in vain who build it.

In vain millions of yards of calico and miles of lacework turned out per annum;
In vain a people well clad in machine-made cloth and hosiery;
In vain a flourishing foreign trade and loose cash enough for a small war;
In vain universal-congratulations and lectures on Political Economy;
In vain the steady whirr of wheels all over the land, and men and women serving stunted and pale before them, as natural as possible;

Except Love build the house, they labor in vain who build it.

O rich and powerful of the earth!

Behold, your riches are all in vain—you are poorer than the poorest of these children!

Against one such whom you have wronged your armies your police and all the laws that you can frame shall not prevail.

Your palaces of splendor are reared from the beginning upon a foundation of lies, and the graves that you have dug for others shall be for your own burial.

The word is gone forth!

The wealth the power that you have coveted crumble from your grasp as in a dream.

You have thought to drive armies of starving slaves to win idleness and luxury for you;

But it shall be as a dream: they shall surely elude you.

Behold, your armies shall vanish away—even while the word is on your lips, while your hand of command is lifted,

Your armies shall vanish away like smoke, they shall surely surely elude you.

In Death shall they vanish away,

(O fragrance wafted through the still night-air!)

In Death shall they breathe through your bonds and become as the impalpable winds.

Like deserters at night stealing away in thousands out of a camp,

They shall pass a ghostly army to the other side:
Broken and worn and sick—a ghostly army shall they pass and vanish;
And ye shall dream that they are gone.

But they are not gone.
For with the morning, out of the ground,
Out of their mother Earth—star-thick, and ye cannot bind them more than ye can bind the stars—
Out of the heart of their mother, and out of the hearts of the asters and star-shaped chrysanthemums,
Arising—
Through the hollow air and down the rustling flowing rivers,
Over the meadows with the feet of the wind whitening the grass,
From the mystic chambers of their innumerable homes —out of the mystic doors—
Out of the doors of Death and Birth, in thousands, out of the doors of preparation,
Full-equipped hastening, from all sides swiftly gathering,
A radiant army into your great towns pouring,
Down your long streets striding, they shall return.

Spirits of awful knowledge,
(Clad anew with fleshly hands and feet, through sunlit eyes still glancing,)
And of deep-gathered silent age-long experience;
Spirits of the suffering brotherhood, spirits of awful authority—

Before whom materials shrivel and the accumulations of Custom are blown on the wind like chaff—

A self-appointed army they shall return

Out of whom the word of transformation—
Whispered on many a half-awakened winter day to the silent earth alone—

Shall be spoken aloud as with a trumpet over the world—and the world shall be changed.

I Come Forth from the Darkness

I COME forth from the darkness to smite Thee.—
Who art thou, insolent of all the earth,
With thy faint sneer for him who wins thee bread,
And him who clothes thee, and for him who toils
Daylong and nightlong dark in the earth for thee?
Coward, without a name!
Ignorant curse!—and yet with names as many
Alas! almost as Wealth has. Unclean life
That makest a blight wherever thou alightest!
I smite thee back.
Darest thou yet be seen? (How long, how long,
O patient suffering men will ye endure?)
Darest thou yet be seen?
I smite thee back. Go, return whence thou camest.
The gardens and the beautiful terraces,
The palaces and theatres and halls
Of our fair cities shall not see thee more.

I Come Forth from the Darkness

From this day the word is gone forth which waited long to be spoken.
Who walks the streets shall see the lightning which is not in the clouds but in the eyes of men,
Poising itself to strike.

O shallow-pate, walking for ever in indifferent ignorance!
Thou with the languid averted eyes and impossible patronising airs,
Thou forged bank-note which the great winds will blow crackling into the coping of heaven,
Hast thou yet never opened wide thine eyes?

Thou at thy club or country seat or in thy study, or sitting in the front pew at church—so luxurious, refined, learned,
So pious—yet all out of other men's labor;
Thou eager after elegant recognitions through the street hastening—
Vulgar and infidel—from her path the poor woman with her bundle impatiently pushing;
Thou in the household, in the shop, on the railway, with nameless airs the shameful difference marking;
Thou oily in the pulpit ever preaching: Peace, peace —where there is no peace;
Hast thou yet never opened wide thine eyes—
To see and still to see—to stare with astonishment
Over this wide and troubled Ocean, washing so near-importunate upon thee?

This strange thing that it throws up in thy path!
With wild eyes, bloodshot, haggard!
Hast thou observed it?—hast thou well regarded?
In thy smooth progress, say, hast well regarded?

What? and thou seest nothing?—O look look!
The grey old Ocean shivers in his sleep:
Dreamwalker by the perilous brink, O look!
The grey old Ocean shivers, turns his lids
Whose lashes are the lightning, and arises
Staggering from his hollows (Hear, O hear
The hoarse wolf-howling in the pitchy night).
The thunder of his footsteps shakes the interminable shore:
Dream-walker, look!
This white thing in thy path!
Art mad? O look!—the wild eyes seest thou not?
The warning arm?—no flimsy phantom this,
No pale stray figment of thy brain: but He.

Thus by the shore continually,
Pale spectral close-lipped haggard full in thy path warning He stands,
And thou complacent languid with averted eyes passest by him and onward, continually, to thy doom.

Thou shalt never open thine eyes: (deep flashes to deep:)
But the lightning which thou seest not shall wither thee up,

I Come Forth from the Darkness

And suddenly, in a moment, the flood uprising shall erase thee.

O Deep flashing upward continually,
Wild beautiful Ocean of faces!
Ocean of glittering salt spray of tears!
Of proud perpetual faith glooming through the long night!
Ocean of day and night!
With white waves riding up continually,
White faces nearing through the gloom—eager in endless beauty!
Not lightnings only:
Tenderest phosphorescence over the wide-heaving surface gleaming,
This also is thine.

O pity! pity!
And it might draw the heart of a man in pity from him!
If he had eyes—to see, and still to see—
To and fro through the streets wandering starless,
Faces *not* charged with lightning, but with sorrow, voiceless unsmiting distant-luminous,
(Auroral surely towards some greater day,)
Eyes wistful-ignorant—the bloom of youth so fast going never to return—
From dirt-bespattered countenances pathetically looking,
Trustful reliant eyes—and whom to rely on?

(Whom, these dumb thousands of years?)
Parted lips yearning,
Pale woman lips mute-appealing,
Through the gay street unnoticed passing,
From the haunts of fashion flying, from the blank stare of the houses of wealth and refinement,
To hide their sorrow where none shall understand,
Joyless, unaccusing.
(O lips, your accusation is it not heard in the topmost heaven?)

Faces of the world's deliberate refusal;
Dead-pale faces, shrunken, as of leaves that the frost kills,
Going about to hide themselves from the sun, to lie rotting and rotting in the dark, like the leaves—
In the dark soil which their generations enrich.

Face of the stedfast eyes, growing ever paler—of the weary human shuttle,
Swift between factory and slum to the terrible engine-pulse of necessity alternating.
Sacred pathetic face of the aged slave, out of the world descending,
Of the old woman, mender of carpets—giver of much and receiver of little in this life;
Face of unquestioning submission, kindly consecrating face, out of the world at length with farewell benedictions descending,
Sublimely ignorant of all offence.

Weak face of the drunkard—soon to be labeled suicide;
Pale covert-eyed face of the thief;
Faces ever, faces riding up continually, eager in endless beauty,
O it might draw the heart of a man from him with pity to behold you.

But the world which has deliberately refused you, how shall it dare to pity you?
[O vulgar and infidel and shallow and insolent of all the earth, and ye who have taught yourselves so that ye *can* give no help,
Come ye not here. Is it not sacred ground?
Come ye not here. Defile not with your pity.
Nay, for ye are smitten back and gone whence ye shall never return—
You and your pity—abolished into the void.]
Dumb awful prisoners! who except Death shall dare to pity you?
To kiss you with the close kiss of deliverance?
To take you up unto the mountain tops and show you the country you have conquered for men?

The word which waited so long to be spoken, behold it is gone forth.
Lo! shooting of swift auroral gleams,
Thoughts hither and thither spreading, coherent,
Words; hark! babbling multitudinous,

Waves to and fro in the sunlight flowing, lisping—
Louder and louder lisping—into one consent waking!

O hearts, not in vain!
Joy, joy—so long a stranger upon earth—
Joy is come up! see the great laughing Ocean!
The deep floor paved with flowers!
Joy is come up. Its waves flow over the world!
To and fro, to and fro, tossing, tumultuously dancing,
The sunlight-smitten waves flow over the world!
How is the great deep changed! Joy is come up.
Wealth the great gloom, the last worst tyranny,
Sinks—is gone down for ever. Arise! arise!
The gardens and the beautiful terraces,
The palaces and theatres and halls
Of our fair cities await your smiles, O Man:
Your solemn love which is their dignity,
Your earnest solemn love, their sacrament,
With outstretched arms they wait.
Arise, O Man!
The long inheritance of the ages waits:
Lo! the fair earth is thine—at length is thine.
Joy! Joy!
The light air and the nimble winds, the blue
Cloud-islanded seas of heaven, the great glad fields
Waving with golden grain, green orchards dusk
With pensive shadows—all the round earth is thine.

Child that shalt bless thy mother,
Joy, joy! The earth is thine.

Sunday Morning

Sunday Morning near a Manufacturing Town

SUNDAY, a still autumn morning, and all the roads on the outskirts are throng with people.

Where the streets begin to run wild towards the country, with patch-work of garden-allotments, and occasional hedgerows and overhanging trees, they go—

Pale-faced men and girls hardly escaped for an hour or two from breathing the eternal smoke.

The sun shines softly—it is very pleasant.

Here comes a whole family: the mother holds a baby to her breast, the father carries the little boy on his arm—two other children play around them;

There go two factory girls, with faded shawls thrown over their heads—their arms round each other's necks; both have clear soft eyes, and both have fawn-colored opaque skins, marked with the small-pox;

Here shambling along in the opposite direction a group of ill-made boys, carrying dinner-kerchiefs crammed and purple-stained with blackberries. They have been out early and are returning.

Most of the men stand about in knots on the road or in their gardens, some smoking—some with fox-terriers and coursing-dogs.

Handsomely stand the yellow and the lilac dahlias on their tall stalks; and the marigolds and other flowers look well amid the green. The air is full of the scent of celery.

Some are banking up their celery-beds, some are getting potatos, others lie on their backs enjoying the lazy air, others are gathering flowers.

Here comes one with a nosegay of all sorts, here another with a great armful of dahlias nodding amid their leaves as he walks, here another with quantities of brown and yellow calceolaria—almost every one has a flower of some sort.

There is plenty of chaff as the groups of young mechanics pass the groups of chatting laughing girls—some go apart arm in arm together.

Withal the wan look of many faces there is I know not what sense of naturalness and wholesome feeling abroad to-day (the stuffy people are safe out of the way in church)—

The air is full of voices and laughter; from some of the neighboring cottages come sounds of music.

It is well. I welcome you, O crisp uprising life!

I welcome you, O crisp green shoot which the still bright morning has called forth!

It does not need much to see how deep your roots are fed in the strong soil of necessity;

Not much to see how native and fresh a life you indicate,

And that the limp decaying leaves and dead things of the earth will not overlie you much longer.

IN THE DRAWING ROOMS

IN the drawing-rooms I saw scarce one that seemed at ease;
They were half-averted sad anxious faces, impossible pompous faces, drawling miowling faces, peaked faces well provided with blinkers,
And their owners kept standing first on one leg and then on the other.

I felt very depressed.
Wherever I went it was the same—it was like a nightmare—I could not escape from it.
Ever the same miowls and drawls, the same half-averted sad uneasy looks, the same immensely busy people doing really nothing, the same one-legged weary idling, mutual boredom, and vampire business.
In the street I could not escape it—at the soirée, the lecture room, the concert; I felt stifled; the sky above me was like lead, and the earth—I could have lain on it and cried as a child,
For I felt like one deprived of his natural food, exhausted, and faint with starvation.
[For indeed it is so, that man can not live by bread alone. This is the silent decree of immortality whereby into his body are wrought for its nourishment unseen intangible essences—of the faces of his fellows and of the touch of their bodies and the breath of their lives about him. Which avenues if they be shut—if the faces be like closed

doors, and the hands be withdrawn, and the breath of society about him be corrupt—a man shall shrivel and die, as surely as an infant from its mother's breasts forbidden.]

And at the railway station, and in the train flying over field and river through the dark, I could not escape that vampire horror.

Was this then the sum of life?

A grinning gibbering organisation of negations—a polite trap, and circle of endlessly complaisant faces bowing you back from all reality!

Was it that men should give all their precious time and energy to the plaiting of silken thongs and fetters innumerable—

To bind themselves prisoners—to condemn themselves to pick oakum of the strands of real life for ever?

Was it mere delusion and bottomless nightmare? really at last the much talked-of and speculated-about existence in two dimensions only?

And as I thought of the fields and rivers below me in the dark, returning life thrilled in a faint wave of laughter through me from the beautiful bounding earth;

And as a woman for the touch of a man,

So I cried in my soul even for the violence and outrage of Nature to deliver me from this barrenness.

Well, as it happened just then—and as we stopped at a small way-station—my eyes from their swoon-sleep opening encountered the grimy and oil-besmeared figure of a stoker.

In the Drawing Rooms

Close at my elbow on the foot-plate of his engine he was standing, devouring bread and cheese,

And the firelight fell on him brightly as for a moment his eyes rested on mine.

That was all. But it was enough.

The youthful face, yet so experienced and calm, was enough;

The quiet look, the straight untroubled unseeking eyes, resting upon me—giving me without any ado the thing I needed.

[Indeed because they sought nothing and made no claim for themselves, therefore it was that they gave me all.]

For in a moment I felt the sting and torrent of Reality.

The swift nights out in the rain I felt, and the great black sky overhead, and the flashing of red and green lights in the forward distance,

The anxious straining for a glimpse sideways into the darkness—cap tied tightly on—the dash of cold and wet above, the heat below:

All this I felt, as it had been myself.

The weird look of hedgerows and trees in the wild glare as we pass, the straining and leaping of the engine, and the precious human freight madly borne behind,

The great world reeling by, the rails and the ballast ribbon-like unreeling—out of darkness arriving—phantasmal inexorable flawless!

[Stand firm, bridge of many arches while we pass swiftly over the tops of the trees!

Hold, ties and struts and well-braced girders, hold while our iron feet ring resounding over the river!

Hold firm, phantasmal world, even as thou dost—inexorably firm—whether for good or evil, hold!]

O the mad play!

And the dumb sense of tension when wife or sister or friend is one of the precious freight;

And the long hours of unremitted watchfulness, and the faithful unremitting service of the machinery;

And the faithful responsive wheeling of the stars, fulfilling the hours,

The slow lifting of the Moon through the clouds, the changes of light, west and east,

And the breaking of the morning.

All these in his eyes who stood there, lusty with well-knit loins, devouring bread and cheese—all these and something more:

Nature standing supreme and immensely indifferent in that man, yet condensed and prompt for decisive action:

True eyes, true interpreters, striking as a man wielding a sledge strikes, in whom long practice has ensured the absolute consent of all his muscles!

True eyes, true interpreters—of abounding gifts free givers—

Without wrigglings and contortions, without egotistic embarrassments, grimaces, innuendos,

Without constraint and without stint, free!

In the Drawing Rooms 143

O eyes, O face, how in that moment without any ado you gave me all!

How in a moment the whole vampire brood of flat paralytic faces fled away, and you gave me back the great breasts of Nature, when I was rejected of others and like to die of starvation.

I do not forget.

It is not a little thing—though you passed away so quickly and were wholly unconscious of it.

It is not a little thing, you—wherever you are—following the plough, or clinging with your feet to the wet rigging, or nursing your babe through the long day when your husband is absent, or preparing supper for his return, or you on the foot-plate of your engine—

Who stand mediating there against Necessity, wringing favors and a little respite for your fellows, translating the laws for them, making a channel for the forces;

In whom through faithful use, through long patient and loyal exercise the channels have become clean—

[Clean and free the channels of your soul, though your body be smirched and oily—]

It is not a little thing that by such a life your face should become as a lantern of strength to men;

That wherever you go they should rise up stronger to the battle, and go forth with good courage.

Nay, it is very great.

•

I do not forget.

Indeed I worship none more than I worship you and such as you,
Who are no god sitting upon a jasper throne,
But the same toiling in disguise among the children of men and giving your own life for them.

In a Manufacturing Town

As I walked restless and despondent through the gloomy city,
And saw the eager unresting to and fro—as of ghosts in some sulphurous Hades;
And saw the crowds of tall chimneys going up, and the pall of smoke covering the sun, covering the earth, lying heavy against the very ground;
And saw the huge refuse-heaps writhing with children picking them over,
And the ghastly half-roofless smoke-blackened houses, and the black river flowing below;
As I saw these, and as I saw again far away the Capitalist quarter,
With its villa residences and its high-walled gardens and its well-appointed carriages, and its face turned away from the wriggling poverty which made it rich;
As I saw and remembered its drawing-room airs and affectations, and its wheezy pursy Church-going and its gas-reeking heavy-furnished rooms and its scent-bottles and its other abominations—

I shuddered:

For I felt stifled, like one who lies half-conscious—knowing not clearly the shape of the evil—in the grasp of some heavy nightmare.

Then out of the crowd descending towards me came a little ragged boy:

Came—from the background of dirt disengaging itself—an innocent wistful child-face, begrimed like the rest but strangely pale, and pensive before its time.

And in an instant (it was as if a trumpet had been blown in that place) I saw it all clearly, the lie I saw and the truth, the false dream and the awakening.

For the smoke-blackened walls and the tall chimneys, and the dreary habitations of the poor, and the drearier habitations of the rich, crumbled and conveyed themselves away as if by magic;

And instead, in the backward vista of that face, I saw the joy of free open life under the sun:

The green sun-delighting earth and rolling sea I saw,

The free sufficing life—sweet comradeship, few needs and common pleasures—the needless endless burdens all cast aside,

Not as a sentimental vision, but as a fact and a necessity existing, I saw

In the backward vista of that face.

Stronger than all combinations of Capital, wiser than all the Committees representative of Labor, the simple need and hunger of the human heart.

Nothing more is needed.

All the books of political economy ever written, all the proved impossibilities, are of no account.

The smoke-blackened walls and tall chimneys duly crumble and convey themselves away;

The falsehood of a gorged and satiated society curls and shrivels together like a withered leaf,

Before the forces which lie dormant in the pale and wistful face of a little child.

What Have I to do with Thee

WEARY with the restless burden of this world last night I fell

Dreaming on my couch, in Nature's bosom, and the dream was well;

For with morning I awoke triumphant like a child in glee,

Singing: World, I prithee tell me, What have I to do with thee?

I who am a child, content if but with wonder and with love,

With the quiet Earth beneath me and the splendid Sun above,

To whom laughter comes unbidden in the watches of the night,

· Whom a daisy in the meadow fills with ever new delight—

What Have I to do with Thee

World, unquiet world I dwell in, with thy wearisome grimaces,
(Like an old and odious lover, who importunately paces
Ever up and down before one,) world of fashion, world of cant,
World of philanthropic schemes, committee-meetings, crazes, rant,
World of void affected duties, world quite dumb of love's decree,
O thou solemn prig, pray tell me, What have I to do with thee?

I whom nature made rejoicing in my meed of strength and skill,
Proud with those I love to labor, lingering in the sweet air, till
Twilight brings the firelit home and faces, whom she e free
To all her stores, nor stayed to reckon, whom she taught the mystery
Of the whole Earth inly heaving with desire hid at the core,
Whom she filled with tender grieving, whom she smote with passion sore—
World of brick walls in perspective, world of avenues of dirt,
World of hideous iron railings, stucco and the window-squirt,
World of pigmy men and women, dressed like monkeys, that go by,

World of squalid wealth, of grinning galvanised society,
World of dismal dinner-parties, footmen, intellectual talk,
Heavy-furnished rooms, gas, sofas, armchairs, girls that cannot walk,
Books that are not read, food music novels papers flung aside,
World of everything and nothing—nothing that will fill the void;
World that starts from manual labor, as from that which worse than damns,
Keeps reality at arm's length, and is dying choked with shams,
World, in Art and Church and Science, sick with infidelity,
O thou dull old bore, I prithee, What have I to do with thee?

Who is master? Tell me that. Didst thou make me? or thinkest thou
By the bold array thou donnest, by thy frowns and puckered brow,
To impose that flam upon me? Nay! for far too clearly through
Thy false life and fancy make-up, through the artificial hue
Health paints not upon thy cheek, thy glassy eyes with sunken rims
Staring, and the meaningless spasmodic corpse-dance of thy limbs—
Right through thy whole being looking into what once was thy heart

I behold how hollow lifeless and corrupt a thing thou art.

Strange!—yet so it is—that stronger than a world on granite piled,
More than all Wealth and Tradition is the weak sigh of a child.
We—the future's dreamers—come, and coming look thee in the face:
"World, to *Right-about*" we bid thee; "*March*—and quickly—into space!"

As to You O Moon

As to you O Moon—
I know very well that when the astronomers look at you through their telescopes they see only an aged and wrinkled body;
But though they measure your wrinkles never so carefully they do not see you personal and close—
As you disclosed yourself among the chimney-tops last night to the eyes of a child,
When you thought no one else was looking.

Gustily ran the wind down the bare comfortless street, the clouds flew in long wild streamers across your face, the few still on foot were hurrying homewards—
When, as between the wisps of rain O moon you shone out wonderfully bare and bright,
Lo! far down in the face of a boy I saw you.

Dashed with rain, wet with tears,

Stopping suddenly to lean his head against a wall, caught by your look—

The pale smudged face, the tense glittering eyes, never swerving a moment,

The curls fringing his dirty cap, the rare pale light of wonder and of suffering :

Yes, far down, as in a liquid pool in the woods, centuries down under the surface, as I passed I distinctly saw you.

I should like to know what you were doing there,

You old moon, with your magic down in that boy's soul so powerfully working,

While all the time the appearance of you was journeying up above in the sky!

I should like to know how many thousands and thousands you have looked at like that, so quietly and calm-deceptively :

Why, the reflected light is in their eyes yet—pale sleepless maidens looking out from ivied casements, choral processions winding upwards at dusk to the groves of Ashtoreth, cave-dwellers ages ago sitting at the mouths of their caves—I see the glitter of sparkles as from an immense ocean.

You are an artful old (heavenly) body!

One might almost think that there really was nothing behind those wrinkles,

And that the effluences of gravitation and magnetism which the astronomers think so much of were really the last

As to You O Moon

word to be said about you—as a child might know an elderly dame by the camphor bag which she carried in her pocket, and nothing more.

Yet I fancy that as you jog along round the earth you take very good note in your quiet way of the limpid faces looking up at you, peering deep—centuries down—into each;

I fancy that you are not ill-pleased to pass as you do for a harmless old lady—plucking thus with the less hindrance the flowers that you love;

I fancy that somewhere among the niches and chasms of those rugged craters you surely treasure them up, sacred and faithful, against a day that we little dream of;

Anyhow I see plainly that like all created things you do not yield yourself up as to what you are at the first or the thousandth onset,

And that the scientific people for all their telescopes know as little about you as any one—

Perhaps less than most.

How curious the mystery of creation, the juggle of the open daylight! and all things sworn conspirators to that end!

Lo! the quiet moon in the sky—yet to a child it has told its secret.

SQUINANCY-WORT

WHAT have I done?—
    I am a little flower,
Out of many a one
That twinkles forth after each passing shower.
White, with a blushful glow,
In the sweet meadows I grow,
Or innocent over the hill tops sport and run.—
What have I done?

Many an age agone,
Before man walked on earth,
I was. In the sun I shone;
I shook in the wind with mirth;
And danced on the high tops looking out seaward—
    where I had birth.
Web-footed monsters came
And into the darkness went
In ponderous tournament,
Many an age agone.
But on the high tops I dwelt ever the same,
With sisters many a one,
Guiltless of sin and shame!—
What have I done?

What have I done?—*Man* came,
Evolutional upstart one!

Squinancy-Wort

With the gift of giving a name
To everything under the sun.
What have I done?—Man came
(They say nothing sticks like dirt),
Looked at me with eyes of blame,
And called me "Squinancy-wort."

What have I done? I linger
(I cannot say that I live)
In the happy lands of my birth;
Passers-by point with the finger;
For me the light of the sun
Is darkened. Oh, what would I give
To creep away and hide my shame in the earth!—
What have I done?

Yet there is hope. I have seen
Many changes since I began.
The web-footed beasts have been
(Dear beasts!)—and gone, being part of some wider plan.
Perhaps in his infinite mercy God will remove this Man!

Not of myself—I have no power of myself—
But out of you who read do I write these words;
And whether you understand them or not is nothing to me: I sort rather with those who do not read them.

Lo! I Open a Door

LO! I open a door.
   Through all suffering, through being an outcast myself, in prison and condemned,
   Lying on the floor of existence as one accursed and outlawed—
   Who shall not pass by me into joy eternal?

By this Heart

BY this heart sacred for you O children—for you a few years beating;
   By the deep yearnings of it, flowing, following you—and the world made holy wherever you have trod;
   By the firm pulse of it, and by its silent-dropping dark tears;
   By its weakness and by its immortal strength;
   By the love with which it encloses, in which it continually laves you;

By this Heart

By you greater yourselves; and by the love which I see flowing surely from you to me;
By these I put all evil aside
And I approach you, nearer, nearer—even so nearer than all thought—
And remain with you, doubting fearing nothing.

For fear I put away from you, and the wretched unrest of the world;
And from the Maya of appearances I deliver you: believe me here is deliverance;
[And not here only, in this inch of space and time, but wherever . .]—
And I show you the inheritance of the riches of all time.

Yet sorrow, the gift of gifts, revealer of eternal joy, I give you not;
But One shall come in the night-time, bringing it, to transmute the world for you,
Taking you by the hand, even while you live, through the great gate of Death into Elysian fields.
There as the nightingale through the night beside his mate sings,
In the soft dark—filled with the spirit of the stars and of the flowing river and the wafted fragrance of the fields: the sunlit memories of the day about him, and above him his own voice in the clear height poised unfaltering—
So in perfect contentment thro' all your mortal work
Shall your spirit sublimely sing.

As one who from a high cliff

I LOOK upon my life as from afar:
   I hear its murmur, mark its changeful sheen,
(As one who from a high cliff marks the waves
He just now rode on,)
Beautiful, gleaming, shot with hues from heaven,
With strange pale lustre—beautiful indeed,
O God, from this great eminence of Death.

To One in Trouble

THE Lord of heaven and earth, out of darkness, out of silence, by ways that thou understandest not, shall redeem thy soul.

These Waves of Your Great Heart

YOU battling with your own heart, speaking the words of peace in vain,—

The convulsive waves heave and break, do they not?
They go moaning down the dark shore, bitterly, unabating,
Heavily with weary thud falling falling—into the darkness falling.

O heart!

These Waves of your Great Heart

This is the ocean that is broken (on its surface) with measureless never-ending unrest.

O heart!

This is the wide and immense ocean: over which who shall sail?

O child!

You that shiver there in the night-wind by the dread white-lipped shore!

Do you guess how wide this Ocean is?

Do you know how it rolls its waters away beyond the farthest horizon that you have imagined?

Afar, afar—spreading blue beneath the sun by coasts of calm and tropic beauty, by coasts of tumbling laughing beauty, by bays and bars and river-narrow straits?—

This ocean of the heart?—

Afar, afar—or bearing on its breast the great white-sailed ships of the earth, or the broad disc of the moon, or the images of men's homes in unimagined lands?

Thought you, frail phantom roaming by the shore,

Gazing wide into the night—a stranger where you had fancied yourself most at home—

Thought you that this great Ocean was to be like an ornamental water in your garden?

Thought you that you knew whence these convulsive waves?—the winds that stirred them, the deeps where they were born?

Think you they weep your sorrows alone, or shake the ground only under your feet?

Not so! not so!
But ever flowing from afar,
From the immeasurable past, from the illimitable shores of human life for ever flowing—on its margin passionately breaking,
With strange uncipherable meanings, whose words are the myriad years,
With speechless terror and amazement to the children beside it,
With amazement of expanded identity, and the inflow of immortal swift-riding purposes, incontrollable, leading straight to death,
In living procession out of the deep—O child! to you they come,
These waves of your great heart, rolling flowing without end:
Through long long ages, under storm and sunshine, by day and night, in indomitable splendor rolling,
At your feet now mournfully breaking.

Thus as I Yearned for Love

THUS as I yearned for love,
    At length the clouds parted,
And I knew the old old vision:
Him with the sorrowful eyes (pain, unrelenting pain),
With the distant piercing unapproachable eyes, I knew,—
The face from the murky clouds disclosed, and withdrawn again.

O night, fold upon fold, impenetrable, with silent tears in the darkness falling—mute night, remover of all evidence!

O dawn, with early rising almost before it is light, and preparations for a long journey!

O day, with children playing by the roadside, and greetings exchanged, and cheery demeanor!

And somewhere, unseen, over all, the same unapproachable eyes looking as ever down.

Eternal Hunger

Eternal Hunger! O through the black night
    Rave, Winds. The forest fanes
Tremble, rock, crash, and ring incessantly
The cry of homeless spirits. Roar
Ye torrents from the mountains. Roar O Sea,
Rave under the pale stars. O gulf of Death
Yawn blackening beneath.
But O great Heart,
O Love greater than all,
Over the mountains the forests and the seas,
O'er the black chasm of death, in spectral haste
Thou ridest, and the hungry winds and waves
Are but Thy hounds: Thou the eternal huntsman!

Great heart and lonely, indomitable in pride
As the pale Titan! a storm-battling eagle
Art thou above the promontory of the world;

Aý, and ah me!
A tender little bird
Wind-blown and baffled from its nest for ever.

Pain, ah! eternal pain.
I hear Aeolian harpings wail and die
Down forest glades, and through the hearts of men,
Pain, pain, eternal pain!
High round the cloud-girt pinnacle of gaunt snow
I hear the wind moan Pain, eternal pain.

O man, O child of Man!
Thou frail and baffled bird, thou weary thing,
Thou strong to suffer, of satanic pride,
I take thee up into this height of pain,
And shew thee all the kingdoms of the earth,
Yea, all the kingdoms of the hearts of men—
The pure and light-strewn kingdoms of strong love:

Gaze long in silence, friend; gaze long for all are thine.

Child of the Lonely Heart

CHILD of the lonely heart,
    O clinging supplicating soul,
  Through thy chamber, thy prison, thy palace, the body, solitary roaming,
  The great world through the windows sadly, questioningly exploring.—

Child of the Lonely Heart

O love, love, love,
At thy feet,
By thy side,
My hand if only resting in thine:
See, I am so little, I ask so little—
If thou wilt take this little overflowing cup
Into thy great ocean.

O love, love, love,
Thee alone.
Always only thee: I find nothing beautiful but thee.
Lo! when I look forth, what is it all?
These lines of houses,
This sad interminable sky,
This gay life—which is my pretext—but underneath I am sick sick at heart
For one touch of true love.

O love, love, love,
Since I was a little child, and till I die, the same.
Nothing I reserve—
I am so little and I ask so little:
If thou wilt take this little overflowing cup
Into thy great ocean.

Child of the lonely heart,
O clinging supplicating soul,
Through thy chamber, thy prison, thy palace—
Ah! children, through the world, through the ages, by thousands and thousands, by millions and millions,

Unaware, unwhispered—in your own great fellowship uninitiate—
Blindly yearning, tentatively questioningly darkly exploring,
Through the great Mother-heart eternally ascending!

To One who is where the Eternal are

Pass friend pass:
    Lest body and soul with desire I be consumed,
Pass, pass from me.
Your eyes burn in upon me. Out of the night,
Out of the darks of time, flashing, out of the still
Still height I cannot attain to, solemnly
Stedfastly gazing—
Their light pierces my brain.

O this is cruel!
Knowing that I cannot attain,
Why do you mock me?—passing me like a shadow,
Passing, passing, and again returning;
In the night within me like a great star shining,
In the world without passing me like a shadow.

If I were the yellow sands your feet once trod,
By the deep blue where they were still delaying;
Were I the sea that clipped your body round,
The shores, the ships,—
Ah me!—
Were I the thing your hand most idly touched,

One who is where the Eternal are

The light that fell upon your Southern home,
The murmur of the forest in your ears,
Where you, friend, once walked, dreaming!

Time answers like the closing of a door,
I am an exile. The swift years have set
Their gulf between us—you are safe from me;
Torment me then no longer: pass O pass,
Kiss me with shadowy lips, and pass from me.

I see the deep gulf roll below me now—
The leaden-colored flood, the scum, the swirl,
The shadow-peopled banks.
I feel the cold dank wind: Death blows upon it.
I reel upon the edge—
Sickness comes o'er me, clammy faintness, death.

2

Now am I near to Death.
The world for me is changed. The noiseless wing
Sways over all. The mountains are unreal,
The stones I walk on are not stones, the air
Breathes from another world, the voices call,
The hands I grasp remind me. All is still,
Still as deep night within. Without, the world
Hangs beautiful and distant like a vision.

Hush! all is silent.—
Now it is very near.

Noiselessly through the darkness, noiselessly
Gliding—ah! nearer nearer!
Softly out of the night, with soft step stealing
Nearer, ah, nearer!
With faint breath over Ocean, fresh and cool,
Death! death! O friend,
O far-infolder, speak! Is it Thou indeed
Pouring faint fragrance, drowning drowning me
Out of the world at length?—at length O friend,
O hesitating long!

Ah! let me die!
Snatch me thou Wonderful,
Thou with Almighty arms, enfold me, crush me
Close through all creature-pain at length to Thee.

3

The passion is gone past.

Now know I that death has been near me all my life—that it is a part of my life.

[O beautiful Ocean! O dim fluid plains and aerial distances!

O headland where I stand for ever gazing!]

The passion is gone past.
O friend, pale friend, stay with me now I pray.
Your eyes no more
Out of the dark consume me—fitfully flashing
Where the great waves break, weary without end.

Swaying swaying, softly eternally swaying,
The flood lies calm now. Stay with me then I pray.
Dwell with me through the day;
And through the night, and where it is neither night nor day,
Dwell quietly. Pass pass not any more.

Thou canst not pass.
I too am where thou art: through all this life
I walk the quiet kingdoms of the dead
Fast hand in hand with thee.
Press now the sweet life of thy lips on mine;
I hold thee fast:
Not by the yellow sands nor the blue deep,
But in my heart thy heart of hearts—
A great star, growing, shining.

THROUGH THE LONG NIGHT

YOU, proud curve-lipped youth, with brown sensitive face,

Why, suddenly, as you sat there on the grass, did you turn full upon me those twin black eyes of yours,

With gaze so absorbing so intense, I a strong man trembled and was faint?

Why in a moment between me and you in the full summer afternoon did Love sweep—leading after it in procession across the lawn and the flowers and under the waving trees huge dusky shadows of Death and the other world?

I know not.

Solemn and dewy-passionate, yet burning clear and stedfast at the last,

Through the long night those eyes of yours, dear, remain to me—

And I remain gazing into them.

To a Stranger

O FAITHFUL eyes, day after day as I see and know you—unswerving faithful and beautiful—going about your ordinary work unnoticed,

I have noticed—I do not forget you.

I know the truth the tenderness the courage, I know the longings hidden quiet there.

Go right on. Have good faith yet—keep that your unseen treasure untainted.

Many shall bless you. To many yet, though no word be spoken, your face shall shine as a lamp.

It shall be remembered, and that which you have desired—in silence—shall come abundantly to you.

To a Friend

FAITHFUL eyes, fail not.

Though sorrows come upon you, though temptations try, though age and grief assault you—fail not, fail not.

How many hang upon you for your light,

Shining in darkness—as the stars that shine

Upon the mighty deep for mariners!
O eyes, be true, give all away for that—
Give all your days and all good name and honor,
If need should be, for that. That we may steer
Through the dark night by you.

Of the Love that you poured forth

OF the love that you poured forth, dear friend, in vain—like a cup of water in the wide and thirsty desert—but it was all your life to you,

Do you dream that it is lost?

Perhaps it is—it may well seem so just now to you—yet indeed I do not think so.

As a Woman of a Man

DEMOCRACY!
O sombre swart face, now thou art very beautiful to me!

O haughty brow, with glittering withdrawn eyes, not a little contemptuous,

Thou art very beautiful to me!

I am as a child before thee;
All that I have learned, all my fancical knowledge,
My familiarity with times and distances,
All my refinement is nothing—my delicate hands, manners,

My glibness is nothing;
I crave the touch of thy soul, thou strong one,
I crave thy love.

Come! who art no longer a name:
Gigantic Thou, with head aureoled by the sun—wild among the mountains—
Thy huge limbs naked and stalwart erected member,
Thy lawless gait and rank untameable laughter,
Thy heaven-licking wildfire thoughts and passions—
I desire.

All conventions, luxuries, all refinements of civilization, and tyrannous wants,
Acquisitions, formulated rules, rights, prescriptions, and whatever constitutes a barrier—
I discard.

All the cobwebs of science, and precedents and conclusions of authority,
All possessions, and impedimenta of property, all rights of bundles and baggage—
I disown.

I stand prepared for toil, for hardship—this instant if need be to start on an unforeseen and distant journey—
I am wholly without reserve:
As a woman of a man so I will learn of thee,
I will draw thee closer and closer,
I will drain thy lips and the secret things of thy body,
I will conceive by thee, Democracy.

O Love—to whom the Poets

O LOVE—to whom the poets have made verses—
　　Whom the shepherds on the hills have piped to, and maidens sighed within their lonely bowers,
　　Whom the minstrels have sung, handing down their songs from one generation to another—
　　To thy praise over the world resounding
　　I add my strain.

　　Not because thou art fair;
　　Not because thine eyes glance winningly, nor because of the sly arch of thine eyebrows;
　　Not because thy voice is like music played in the open air,
　　And thy coming like the dawn on the far-off mountains;
　　Not because thou comest with the dance and the song, and because the flashing of thy feet is like the winds of Spring;
　　Nor because thou art sweetly perfumed,
　　Do I praise thee.

　　Not because thy dwelling is among knights and ladies —afar from all that is common or gross;
　　Not because thou delayest to the sound of playing fountains on marble terraces,
　　And white hands caress thee and clip thy wing-feathers,

And meek thoughts and blameless conversation attend thee;
Not because thy place is among the flowers and the wine-cups in spacious halls,
And because the sight of Death appals thee;
Nor because, love, thou art a child:

But because as on me now, full-grown giantesque out of the ground out of the common earth arising,
Very awful and terrible in heaven thou appearest;
Because as thou comest to me in thy majesty sweeping over the world with lightnings and black darkness,
[And the old order shrivels and disappears from thy face,]
I am as a leaf borne, as a fragrance exhaled before thee—
As a bird crying singed by the prairie-fire;
Because Thou rulest O glorious, and before thee all else fails,
And at thy dread new command—at thy new word Democracy—the children of the earth and the sea and the sky find their voices, and the despised things come forth and rejoice;
Because in thy arms O strong one I laugh Death to scorn—nay I go forth to meet him with gladness;
Ay, because thou takest away from me all strength but thine own,
Because thou takest all doubt and power of resistance,
Because out of disallowed and unaccepted things—and always out of these—full-armed and terrific,

Like a smiting and consuming flame, O Love, O Democracy,
Even out of the faces and bodies of the huge and tameless multitudes of the Earth,
A great ocean of fire with myriad tongues licking the vault of heaven,
Thou arisest—
Therefore O love O flame wherein I burning die and am consumed, carried aloft to the stars a disembodied voice—
O dread Creator and Destroyer,
Do I praise Thee.

WHO YOU ARE I KNOW NOT

WHO you are I know not, but I have it before me that you shall know.

For a certainty you are not greater or less than me: I neither look upon you with envy nor with pity, with deference nor with contempt.

Endowments and dignities and accomplishments are of no account whatever; but honesty, and to stand in time under the great law of Equality—after which you will be satisfied, and joy will take possession of you.

Till then, farewell. Do not follow me, but go your own way voyaging—and then haply some time we shall meet.

Have Faith

Do not hurry: have faith.

Remember that if you become famous you can never share the lot of those who pass by unnoticed from the cradle to the grave, nor take part in the last heroism of their daily life;

If you seek and encompass wealth and ease the divine outlook of poverty cannot be yours—nor shall you feel all your days the loving and constraining touch of Nature and Necessity;

If you are successful in all you do, you cannot also battle magnificently against odds;

If you have fortune and good health and a loving wife and children, you cannot also be of those who are happy without these things.

Covet not overmuch. Let the strong desires come and go; refuse them not, disown them not; but think not that in them lurks finally the thing you want.

Presently they will fade away and into the intolerable light will dissolve like gossamers before the sun.

Do not hurry: have faith.

The sportsman does not say, I will start a hare at the corner of this field, or I will shoot a turkey-buzzard at the foot of that tree;

But he stands indifferent and waits on emergency, and so makes himself master of it.

So do you stand indifferent, and by faith make yourself master of your life.

For all things are possible, yet at any one time and place only one thing is possible;

And all things are good, yet at any one time and place can you extract the good only from that which is before you.

Have faith. If that which rules the universe were alien to your soul, then nothing could mend your state— there were nothing left but to fold your hands and be damned everlastingly.

But since it is not so—why what can you wish for more? —all things are given into your hands.

Do you pity a man who having a silver mine on his estate loses a shilling in a crack in his house-floor?

And why should another pity you?

3

Do not hurry.

As at the first day the clouds suffused with light creep over the edges of the hills, the young poplar poises itself like an arrow planted in the ground, the birds warble with upturned bills to the sun;

The sun rises on hundreds of millions of human beings; the hemisphere of light follows the hemisphere of darkness, and a great wave of life rushes round the globe;

The little pigmies stand on end (like iron filings under a magnet) and then they fall prone again. And this has gone on for millions of years and will go on for millions more.

Absolve yourself to-day from the bonds of action.

[Wait, wait ever for the coming of the Lord. See that you are ready for his arrival.]

Begin to-day to understand that which you will not understand when you read these words for the first time, nor perhaps when you have read them for the hundredth time.

Begin to-day to understand why the animals are not hurried, and do not concern themselves about affairs, nor the clouds nor the trees nor the stars—but only man—and he but for a few thousand years in history.

[For it is one thing to do things, but another to be concerned about the doing of them.]

Behold the animals. There is not one but the human soul lurks within it, fulfilling its destiny as surely as within you.

The elephant, the gnat floating warily towards its victim, the horse sleeping by stolen snatches in the hot field at the plough, or coming out of the stable of its own accord at the sound of the alarm bell and placing itself in the shafts of the fire-engine—sharing the excitement of the men; the cats playing together on the barn floor, thinking no society equal to theirs, the ant bearing its burden through the grass—

Do you think that these are nothing more than what you see? Do you not know that your mother and your sister and your brother are among them?

4

I saw deep in the eyes of the animals the human soul look out upon me.

I saw where it was born deep down under feathers and fur, or condemned for awhile to roam fourfooted among the brambles. I caught the clinging mute glance of the prisoner, and swore that I would be faithful.

Thee my brother and sister I see and mistake not. Do not be afraid. Dwelling thus and thus for a while, fulfilling thy appointed time—thou too shalt come to thyself at last.

Thy half-warm horns and long tongue lapping round my wrist do not conceal thy humanity any more than the learned talk of the pedant conceals his—for all thou art dumb we have words and plenty between us.

Come nigh little bird with your half-stretched quivering wings—within you I behold choirs of angels, and the Lord himself in vista.

Crooning and content the old hen sits—her thirteen chicks cheep cheerily round her, or nestle peeping out like little buds from under her wings;

Keen and motherly is her eye, placid and joyful her heart, as the sun shines warm upon them.

5

Do not hurry: have faith.

[Whither indeed should we hurry? is it not well here?

A little shelter from the storm, a stack of fuel for winter use, a few handfuls of grain and fruit—

And lo! the glory of all the earth is ours.]

The main thing is that the messenger is perhaps even now at your door—and to see that you are ready for his arrival:

A little child, a breath of air, an old man hobbling on crutches, a bee lighting on the page of your book—who knows whom He may send?

Some one diseased or dying, some friendless, outcast, criminal—

One whom it shall ruin your reputation to be seen with—yet see that you are ready for his arrival.

Likely whoever it *is* his coming will upset all your carefully laid plans;

Your most benevolent designs will likely have to be laid aside, and he will set you to some quite commonplace business, or perhaps of dubious character—

Or send you a long and solitary journey; perhaps he will bring you letters of trust to deliver—perhaps the prince himself will appear—

Yet see that you are ready for his arrival.

Is your present experience hard to bear?

Yet remember that never again perhaps in all your days will you have another chance of the same.

Do not fly the lesson, but have a care that you master it while you have the opportunity.

6

These things I say not in order to excite thought in you—rather to destroy it—

Or if to excite thought, then to excite that which destroys itself;

For what I say is not born of thought and does not demand thought either for comprehension or proof;

And whoever dwells among thoughts dwells in the region of delusion and disease—and though he may appear wise and learned yet his wisdom and learning are as hollow as a piece of timber eaten out by white ants.

Therefore though thought should gird you about, remember and forget not to disendue it, as a man takes off his coat when hot; and as a skilful workman lays down his tool when done with, so shall you use thought and lay it quietly aside again when it has served your purpose.

7

A veil of illusion hangs following the lines of all things,

Over the trees and running waters, and up the sides of the mountains and over the sea and the cities, and circling the birds in the air as they fly—

So that these themselves you see not, only the indications of them, and yourself you see not, only the indication.

As long as through the eyes of desire, and of this and that, you look—and of vanity; as long as you hurry after results and are overwhelmed with the importance of anything you can do or leave undone—so long will the veil lie close, do not be deceived.

On all sides God surrounds you, staring out upon you

from the mountains and from the face of the rocks, and of men, and of animals.

Will you rush past for ever insensate and blindfold—hurrying breathless from one unfinished task to another, and to catch your ever-departing trains—as if you were a very Cain flying from his face?

Resume the ancient dignity of your race, lost, almost forgotten as it is.

What is it surely that you are fretting about? Is it the fashions, or what men say about you, or the means of livelihood, or is it the sense of duty this way and that, or trivial desires, that will not let you rest?

Are you so light, like a leaf, that such things as these will move you—are you so weak that one such slender chain will deprive you of inestimable Freedom?

And yet the lilies of the field and the beasts that have no banks of deposit or securities are not anxious: they have more dignity than you.

As long as you harbor motives so long are you giving hostages to the enemy; while you are a slave (to this and that) you can only obey. It is not You who are acting at all.

Brush it all aside.

Pass disembodied out of yourself. Leave the husk, leave the long long prepared and perfected envelope.

Enter into the life which is eternal, pass through the gate of indifference into the palace of mastery, through the door of love out into the great open of deliverance;

Give away all that you have, become poor and without possessions—and behold! you shall be lord and sovereign of all things.

I Heard a Voice

I HEARD a voice say unto me :—
Now since thou art neither beautiful nor witty, it is in vain that thou hangest about the doors of the admired palaces;
For thou wilt not gain admission—thou!

But here outside is a plot of waste ground where canst build thee a little cabin—all thine own;
And since it is close by the common road and there is no fence about it,
Many a weary traveler parched with the heat of the day shall turn in unto thee for a cup of cold water.
And that shall suffice for Thy life.

I Know that you are Self-Conscious

I KNOW that you are self-conscious,
That you are troubled—haunted—tormented. It is not pleasant!

But how wonderful is the mere sense of space in the world—after the sick-chamber and days of illness!
And how wonderful is the sense of measureless space in the soul, and of freedom, thenceforth inalienable!

Look then in the glass once more, and satisfy yourself thoroughly about it:

Do you not see, this time, that there is some one else looking in it also,

Beside you, over your shoulder?

Who are You

WHO are you who go about to save them that are lost?

Are you saved yourself?

Do you not know that who would save his own life must lose it?

Are you then one of the 'lost'?

Be sure, very sure, that each one of these can teach you as much as, probably more than, you can teach them.

Have you then sat humbly at their feet, and waited on their lips that they should be the first to speak—and been reverent before these children—whom you so little understand?

Have you dropped into the bottomless pit from between yourself and them all hallucination of superiority, all flatulence of knowledge, every shred of abhorrence and loathing?

Is it equal, is it free as the wind between you?

Could you be happy receiving favors from one of the most despised of these?

Could you be yourself one of the lost?

Arise, then, and become a savior.

Among the Ferns

I LAY among the ferns,
   Where they lifted their fronds, innumerable, in the greenwood wilderness, like wings winnowing the air;
And their voices went past me continually.

And I listened, and lo! softly inaudibly raining I heard not the voices of the ferns only, but of all living creatures:
Voices of mountain and star,
Of cloud and forest and ocean,
And of the little rills tumbling amid the rocks,
And of the high tops where the moss-beds are and the springs arise.
As the wind at mid-day rains whitening over the grass,
As the night-bird glimmers a moment, fleeting between the lonely watcher and the moon,
So softly inaudibly they rained,
Where I sat silent.

And in the silence of the greenwood. I knew the secret of the growth of the ferns;
I saw their delicate leaflets tremble breathing an undescribed and unuttered life;
And, below, the ocean lay sleeping;
And round them the mountains and the stars dawned in glad companionship for ever.

And a voice came to me, saying :

In every creature, in forest and ocean, in leaf and tree and bird and beast and man, there moves a spirit other than its mortal own,

Pure, fluid, as air—intense as fire,

Which looks abroad and passes along the spirits of all other creatures, drawing them close to itself,

Nor dreams of other law than that of perfect equality;

And this is the spirit of immortality and peace.

And whatsoever creature hath this spirit, to it no harm may befall :

No harm can befall, for wherever it goes it has its nested home, and to it every loss comes charged with an equal gain ;

It gives—but to receive a thousand-fold ;

It yields its life—but at the hands of love ;

And death is the law of its eternal growth.

And I saw that was the law of every creature—that this spirit should enter in and take possession of it,

That it might have no more fear or doubt or be at war within itself any longer.

And lo! in the greenwood all around me it moved,

Where the sunlight floated fragrant under the boughs, and the fern-fronds winnowed the air;

In the oak-leaves dead of last year, and in the small shy things that rustled among them ;

Among the Ferns

In the songs of the birds, and the broad shadowing leaves overhead;
In the fields sleeping below, and in the river and the high dreaming air;
Gleaming ecstatic it moved—with joy incarnate.
And it seemed to me, as I looked, that it penetrated all these things, suffusing them;
And wherever it penetrated, behold! there was nothing left down to the smallest atom which was not a winged spirit instinct with life.

Who shall understand the words of the ferns lifting their fronds innumerable?
What man shall go forth into the world, holding his life in his open palm—
With high adventurous joy from sunrise to sunset—
Fearless, in his sleeve laughing, having outflanked his enemies?
His heart like Nature's garden—that all men abide in—
Free, where the great winds blow, rains fall, and the sun shines,
And manifold growths come forth and scatter their fragrance?
    Who shall be like a grave, where men may bury
Sin and sorrow and shame, to rise in the new day
Glorious out of their grave? who, deeply listening,
Shall hear through his soul the voices of all creation,
Voices of mountain and star, voices of all men,
Softly audibly raining?—shall seize and fix them,

Rivet them fast with love, no more to lose them?
Who shall *be* that spirit of deep fulfilment,
Himself, self-centred? yet evermore from that centre
Over the world expanding, along all creatures
Loyally passing—with love, in perfect equality?

Him immortality crowns. In him all sorrow
And mortal passion of death shall pass from creation.
They who sit by the road and are weary shall rise up
As he passes. They who despair shall arise.

Who shall understand the words of the ferns winnowing the air?
Death shall change as the light in the morning changes;
Death shall change as the light 'twixt moonset and dawn.

I Heard the Voice of the Woods

I HEARD the voice of the woods and of the grass growing silently and of the delicate bending ferns,
And it said:
For the dumb and for the generations of them that have no voice my speech is—
For them too help comes.

I am the spirit of the Earth.
Round me the woods and mountains roll, rising and falling to the far sea;

I Heard the Voice of the Woods

In the hollow below me roars the great river to its doom;
The clouds draw onward; and the voices of the generations of men are woven like thin gossamer through the air about me.
Yet here where I am there is peace—such as mortal yet on earth hath hardly known,
But which shall be known, and even now is known.

Where the stems stand dividing the winnowed sunlight,
Where the green floor is dappled with soft warm moss, and the swift hum of the bee is heard,
And the air glides through like a gracious spirit in-breathing beauty,
I walk—meditating the voiceless children, drawing them to myself with deep unearthly love.

Come unto me, O yearning and inarticulate (for whom so many ages I have waited),
Breathing your lives out like a long unuttered prayer,
Come unto me: and I will give you rest.
For I am not the woods nor the grass nor the bending ferns;
Nor any pale moonlight spirit of these;
And I am not the air;
Nor the light multitudinous life therein;
Nor the sun and its radiant warmth;
But I am one who include—and am greater—
One (out of thousands) who hold all these, embosomed,
Safe in my heart: fear not.

In your eyes deep-looking I will touch you so as to be free from all pain;
Where the last interpretations are, in the uttermost recesses, I will reach you;
Utterance at length shall your pent-up spirit have,
To pour out all that is in you—to speak and be not afraid.

Dear brother, listen!
I am no shadow, no fickle versemaker's fiction,
Many are the words which are not spoken, but here there is speech;
Many are the words which are not spoken, but in due time all shall be spoken:
There is neither haste nor delay, but all shall be spoken.

Come up into the fragrant woods and walk with me.
The voices of the trees and the silent-growing grass and waving ferns ascend;
Beyond the birth-and-death veil of the seasons they ascend and are born again;
The voices of human joy and misery, the hidden cry of the heart—they too ascend into new perpetual birth.
All is interpreted anew:
In man the cataracts descend, and the winds blow, and autumn reddens and ripens;
And in the woods a spirit walks which is not wholly of the woods,
But which looks out over the wide Earth and draws to itself all men with deep unearthly love.

Come, walk with me:
On the soft moss—though you guess not my arm is about you—
By the white stems, where the gracious air is breathing,
On the green floor, through the pale green winnowed sunlight,
Walk: and leave all to me.

The Wind Chants Well To-day

THE wind chants well over the world to-day;
It runs in waves up the slopes of the corn-fields, and sounds deep and distant, like the sea, among the firs;
The tall grasses in sheltered spots quiver on their wiry stems—for it is flowering time—
And shake faint clouds of pollen upon the air.

Strange purposes inhabit the woodland hollows and the high air to-day;
The long-legged spider threading the blades of grass, touching trying retreating, encloses strange purposes, the wind encloses strange purposes.

But I know you well O wind—you cannot escape me.
You are very subtle, you have innumerable disguises:
You are one thing to the grass with its beautiful hanging anthers and branched stigma,
And another thing to the birds, and another to the solemn swaying fir-trees.

You conceal yourself well, O wind, but I am level with you to-day—you cannot hide yourself from me.

I go arm in arm, I ride over the world with you. I visit a thousand spots and leave my messages—

And am as invisible as you.

I am a Voice

I AM a voice singing the song of deliverance—
Centuries long, centuries long, floating aloft in ecstasy.

Surprised at myself—to find myself looking out on this landscape here—to be engaged on these occupations and plans which people call mine, but which are not mine at all—to be living in this house which it is nothing to me whether I live in it or not—to be fretting myself with these and these anxieties and cares—to be this limited and foolish mortal that I am;

Yet again at intervals soaring aloft, going back again to my home in the sky,

To sing for all time
The song of joy—of deliverance.

O Sea, with White Lines of Foam

O SEA, with white lines of foam caught by the winter sun,

O pale blue transparent sky with wind, long stretches of coast faint-outlined, and waving grasses!

How often to seek you, out of the pent life of custom and brick perspective, a boy I came,

O Sea, with White Lines of Foam

Filled with vague desires, hardly knowing what or wherefore—like thine, O restless sea and ceaseless blowing wind—

Came to pour forth my soul to yours, ye beautiful creatures—sad, sad, longing yearning without end!

Say, great sea—whose music continues to-day the same as then; O wonderful illimitable sky, the same; O grasses shivering just for all the world as now—

Say, have you not given me, by strange ways, the thing that I sought?

For now returning,

Satisfied, filled to the full of all desires, grateful as a lake sparkling in the sunshine,

Filled to the full, desiring yearning no more—faint only with joy and the fragrance of the love which distils from you—

Upon you I look once more.

Changed are your words; changed are your words O grasses and pale blue flowing winds, and yours ye streets and faces that pass along them!

Changed are your words to me.

I heard you—but it was as one that hears an unknown tongue; I thought I saw you, but I see that you deceived me.

And now I do not know why I should ever make another move—what you say has entirely checkmated me.

But to those that go forward, go ye ever forward before them; and to them that listen let your strange vocabulary continue.

Home

AMONG all men my home is: I have seen them and there is no people, unto the ends of the earth, with whom I will not dwell.

I give my body to the sea and to the dust—to be dashed on the rocks, or to break in green spray in spring-time over the fields and hedge-rows—or to lie rotting in the desert for the sustenance of flies;

My soul, if it be so, to peregrinate all creature-kingdoms and every condition of man—with equal joy the lowest;

But I to return, to remain, to turn again to my old home, to dwell—as ever—where the prince of love once led me,

When he touched the walls of my hut with his finger from within, and passing through like a fire delivered me with great unspeakable deliverance from all evil.

Off Gaspé

A FEW small huts, a narrow strip of cultivated land; Behind, the frowning mountains of Gaspé, forest-clad; in front, the wide sea-mouth of the St. Lawrence.

How lost and ignorant! says one passing by on board ship—wondering that life can be supported in such a place,

So rude and so remote—no arts, no papers, telegrams—scarcely the ordinary commodities!

The monotonous sea, the brief summer, the sullen forests, the scanty products of land and water, the occasional visits of the priest from over the mountains!

Off Gaspé

A living death—he says.

Yet here too—and in winter snow and ice—here too the human heart, not dead at all, just the same as in the midst of great cities, lives and blooms;

Here lies close to the sky and the rocks and the sea, and is at home—as the star is at home in the sky, and the daisy in the grass;

Without communication with New York or London, and yet in the centre of the world as much as either, and with news and telegrams coming from a long way farther.

O human heart!

Neither lost nor ignorant—living at first hand from thy source,

I perceive that thy home and mine are the same—one house though the doors be different.

Not here or there; not here, O friend, in the centre of the world and there outcast and forlorn [rather outcast and forlorn and lost and ignorant he who thinks thus]—

But ever at home—to thee greetings and congratulations and love wafted over the water,

I send.

A thousand gulls and guillemots on the calm sea-bosom in the flooding sun-warmth basking!

This ship sailing for thee, like a sign through a gleam of summer—thou dwelling between the steep forests and the shore with joy in thy heart as I have!

By the Shore

ALL night by the shore.
The obscure water, the long white lines of advancing foam, the rustle and thud, the panting sea-breaths, the pungent sea-smell,
The great slow air moving from the distant horizon, the immense mystery of space, and the soft canopy of the clouds!

The swooning thuds go on—the drowse of ocean goes on:
The long inbreaths—the short sharp outbreaths—the silence between.

I am a bit of the shore: the waves feed upon me, they come pasturing over me;
I am glad, O waves, that you come pasturing over me.
I am a little arm of the sea: the same tumbling swooning dream goes on—I feel the waves all around me, I spread myself through them.
How delicious! I spread and spread. The waves tumble through and over me—they dash through my face and hair.
The night is dark overhead: I do not see them, but I touch them and hear their gurgling laughter.

The play goes on!
The strange expanding indraughts go on!

By the Shore

Suddenly I am the Ocean itself: the great soft wind creeps over my face.

I am in love with the wind—I reach my lips to its kisses.

How delicious! all night and ages and ages long to spread myself to the gliding wind!

But now (and ever) it maddens me with its touch: I arise and whirl in my bed, and sweep my arms madly along the shores.

I am not sure any more which my own particular bit of shore is;

All the bays and inlets know me: I glide along in and out under the sun by the beautiful coast-line;

My hair floats leagues behind me; millions together my children dash against my face;

I hear what they say and am marvelously content.

All night by the shore;
And the sea is a sea of faces.

The long white lines come up—face after face comes and falls past me—
Thud after thud. Is it pain or joy?
Face after face—endless!

I do not know; my sense numbs; a trance is on me—I am becoming detached!

I am a bit of the shore :

The waves feed upon me, they pasture all over me, my feeling is strangely concentrated at every point where they touch me ;

I am glad O waves that you come pasturing over me.

I am detached, I disentangle myself from the shore ; I have become free—I float out and mingle with the rest.

The pain, the acute clinging desire, is over—I feel beings like myself all around me, I spread myself through and through them, I am merged in a sea of contact.

Freedom and equality are a fact. Life and joy seem to have begun for me.

The play goes on !

Suddenly I am the great living Ocean itself—the awful Spirit of Immensity creeps over my face.

I am in love with it. All night and ages and ages long and for ever I pour my soul out to it in love.

I spread myself out broader and broader for ever, that I may touch it and be with it everywhere.

There is no end   But ever and anon it maddens me with its touch   I arise and sweep away my bounds.

I know but I do not care any longer which my own particular body is—all conditions and fortunes are mine.

By the ever-beautiful coast-line of human life, by all shores, in all climates and countries, by every secluded nook and inlet,

Under the eye of my beloved Spirit I glide:
O joy! for ever, ever, joy!
I am not hurried—the whole of eternity is mine;
With each one I delay, with each one I dwell—with you I dwell.
The warm breath of each life ascends past me;
I take the thread from the fingers that are weary, and go on with the work;
The secretest thoughts of all are mine, and mine are the secretest thoughts of all.

All night by the shore;
And the fresh air comes blowing with the dawn.
The mystic night fades—but my joy fades not.
I arise and cast a stone into the water (O sea of faces I cast this poem among you)—and turn landward over the rustling beach.

A MILITARY BAND

WITH open mouths and eyes intent they press around the stand,
A thousand listeners, in the flare of gas beneath the trees,
Young men and boys mostly, yet some older, and a few girls and women.

The red-coats sit in circle round their leader—solid and robust—their lips retracted, taking short quick breaths, their throats full-veined and swollen;

The first cornets ring out wild and clear, backed by the ripienos, the tenors and the trombones;

The euphonium takes its strong and leading part, the cry of the hautboy is heard—apart—like the cry of a wounded animal, the flutes and flageolets pipe merrily, and the drums resound.

But the circle of faces—pale in the flickering gas—scarcely moves.

Look! how intent they are, face after face, with eyes fixed, strained, as though they would pierce through brass and scarlet!

What is it you fix so intently, O faces, have you never seen a red-coat before?

But no, they hardly see the red-coats: though all eyes centre there they hardly see what is before them.

Lo! a great curtain hanging from the topmost sky right down to the bottom of creation—

Flat, enormous, without rent, covering the whole world (yet hardly half-an-inch in diameter)—

Before each listener it hangs, and on it all things are painted.

Wonderful, figured all over from top to bottom, from side to side, wonderful wonderful—and for each one different:

On it—for some—forms of lust displayed, the glory of limbs flame-girdled, floating from side to side, with fierce clutches of beauty—(O eyes no wonder you are intent!)

On it—for some—the battle-field mounting in smoke, the flag, the roar, the appalling roar of faced cannon, the certain death: the heroic the decisive the furious and disdainful act, the deathless figure of bravery—(O eyes no wonder you are intent!)

On it—see here!—a maiden at her window, peeping over her flowers: the pure, the sweet, the stainless starlike face, for the vow of true knighthood only—(O eyes no wonder you are intent!)

Lo there! even more beautiful, the face of year and year-long wife-hood: the friend, the trusted one without whom life cannot be imagined—dual love dividing and filling the universe—(O glistening eyes no wonder you are intent!)

On it—Ah! these are the eyes of the lost one, the departed mother: the tender watchful beseeching eyes, the sacred light—not God himself more sacred;

This is the glorious brow of comradeship, faithful unalterable, to heroic deeds arousing;

On it—here for this boy—scenes of the wild ocean and adventure, the ship in a storm, the raft, the lightning, and the rescue;

For another, ambition, the political arena, the debate, the crowded galleries, the centering of eyes;

The footlights of the stage, the murmured delight of the audience, the enthusiastic encore;

Scenes of travel, the lands of day-dreams and longing, the Andes, the Pacific, the Polar aurora and the ice, the trackless forests of Central America and Siberia and Western

Australia, and of the Amazon; the wild animals of Central Africa;

The ancient cities, the historical world-old sites, the birth-places of gods, the thrones of kings, the centres of civilisation, the churches, ceremonials, processions, pilgrimages, the markets, railroads, great feats of engineering;

Faces, costumes, forms, objects innumerable—all these figured, arabesqued,

Running in free lines over the curtain which hangs from the zenith to the nadir;

And on it besides with the rest arabesqued and running,

The band-stand with the scarlet and the brass, and the conductor energetic with his baton in the midst, and the swollen veins and lithe lips of the first cornet player;

And on it running waved and dazzling the lines of gas against dark shade-masses of foliage—shot through with the electric· scream of the flageolets and underborne with the deep thunder of drums;

And on it the faint blue evening sky and the faint faint stars behind it.

Wonderful, wonderful!

I too look upon the curtain: I see the figures, the symbols, the shining hieroglyphs written with free hand across it—I see the sun and moon;

I see the great dark background on which they are written—flat, enormous—falling from the zenith to the nadir.

See! how it flaps and sways in the cool night-air, as

if it were about to give way—surely there is something behind it!—yet no rent.

Holding yet well together, holding your secret faithfully,

Curtain of each soul, curtain of creation, tiny curtain, vast enveloping all the universe,

Veil of the imperfect creature, under which the wings form—growing thinner momently and more transparent—

Amnion-veil of the vast universe—growing thinner—

O shot through with the scream of flageolets and underborne with the deep thunder of drums! almost pierced with the fixed gaze and strain of innumerable eyes!

Ah, wonderful wonderful!

Gazed upon thousands of years, nearer nearer, fascinating, drawing ever drawing multitudes towards it;

Children sitting at a theatre thinking the drop-scene the real play itself—others older guessing somewhat how the matter stands—lights dimly seen moving behind, corners lifted or swaying;

The Andes and Pacific dividing down their middle line, the vast forests disclosing in their depths, ancient cities blossoming like huge flowers and fading away in fragrance; the faint-blue star-spangled sky of evening rolling swiftly and noiselessly together, the round earth floating for a moment in the sunlight—and then gone, like the last patches of gold and blue on a soap-bubble; faces of brothers and sisters, faces of the speechless animals, opening back, myriads myriads of years back in perspective to him who sits upon the throne—

Ah, wonderful wonderful!

In the great dark of the night swaying floating like a flag which a gentle wind dwells among the folds of—

Great mother Thou that foldest all creatures in thy folds—

Whom to explore, the children traveling from ages and ages back, by long pilgrimages and routes labyrinthine ever pressing on, to decipher, to unravel, to read the words that are written:

Once more and the stars shall fall showering from thee —the shining hieroglyphs shall fade; black for a moment thou shalt hang—then rolling swiftly together—

Lo! what mortal eye hath not seen nor ear heard—

All sorrow finished—the deep deep ocean of joy opening within—the surface sparkling—

The myriad-formed disclosed, each one and all, all things that are, transfigured—

Being filled with joy, hardly touching the ground, reaching cross-shaped with out-stretched arms to the stars, along of the mountains and the forests, habitation of innumerable creatures, singing joy unending—

As the sun on a dull morning breaking through the clouds, so from behind the sun another sun, from within the body another body—these shattered falling—

Lo! now at last or yet awhile in due time to behold that which ye have so long sought—

O eyes no wonder you are intent.

Wings

WINGS, wings!
    I beheld the young leaves breaking from the buds and poised on the tips of the branches;

I saw a squadron of anemones in the meadows all waving in the wind as impatient to take flight together;

I looked at the acorn buried in the earth, and lo! it divided and put forth two seed-wings; and the embryo plant resembled the penis and dual testicles of man and the animals;

And the starling like-shaped flew overhead through the trees, and the lark hung, a cross, in heaven;

And the butterfly flew by—emblem of the soul—and the bee hung downwards in the wind-flower cup;

And I stood by the hive in the garden and marked how from its lips the bees shot like arrows into the wide valley below;

And I stood in the great assembly and marked how from the decisive lips of the orator the winged words darted and transfixed the audience;

And I saw on the Central American savannahs the half-wild horses racing and bounding together down to the rivers or resting in the shade of the trees;

The light-footed tireless wolf I saw, and the eagle soaring over the mountains; and I watched the moth glide from the entrails of the caterpillar, and the gnat all perfect and stainless from its watery case;

And within myself and under the skin—deep down—I felt the wings of Man distinctly unfolding.

And as I lay on the great hill-side the kisses of the sun alighted on me after their long flight, and rested; and the birds warbled through the midday; and the flowers and the earth itself and the great tree-boles sent forth their incense-swarms of atoms;

And behold! beyond the mountains and the great clouds floating by I beheld dim vast and aerial the figure as of a man with arms outstretched over the universe;

And as I gazed—lo! slowly all these other things swam with me and became incorporate with that figure, and the clouds floated and the streams ran down from ledge to ledge within it;

And the trees with their square arms took on a new signification, and the little seeds with their twin cotyledons were for an emblem, and I saw whither the birds were hastening, and the direction of the index of all generation;

And the starlings flew through the spaces of its thoughts, and the anemone squadrons trembled along its flanks;

And the horses galloping over the plains could not escape the plains they galloped over, nor the light-footed wolf its quest;

And the eagle could not deny its own form as it soared over the mountains—nor I the knowledge of that which was unfolding within me:

And I understood the meaning of the wings.

ON AN ATLANTIC STEAMSHIP

MID-OCEAN, night—
The spars loom square and black against the sky, and the mast-head light sways slowly.

I hear as in a dream the never-ending lullaby, the continued surge of water off the bows, the vibration and smothered pulse of the engines.

Deep in the bowels of the great ship, half-naked huge-limbed grimy-eyed sweating, the firemen tend their thirty-six fires.

From time to time one slips on deck to enjoy the cool;

He lights his pipe. The moon along the high ridge of a pitch-black mass of cloud steals, peering over fitfully on the silent gulfs.

The ship glides on and on. Oily-surfaced heaves and sways the deep as far as eye can see.

Eight bells strike. The watch changes.

One bell—two bells. The deck is almost deserted. And still the ship glides on and on—the deep sways slightly rustling;

The look-out man in the bows cries 'All is well'—and the lamps are brightly burning.

2

In the morning as usual the deck is alive with passengers

[The great ocean-plains swelling sparkling for hundreds, thousands, of miles round us, the visible circle unbroken by island or any object]—

Of all nations languages degrees, of various habits trades traditions,

Strangers to each other and to the water—they look with curious eyes upon the novel scene.

An elderly Indian civilian, saloon-passenger, in grey check morning suit and tennis shoes, blameless and wealthy, looks down with curious eyes from the rail of the upper deck upon the crowded emigrant groups;

He turns to draw the attention of the young lady standing beside him.

It is a strange and varied scene—the sparkling waters, the rigging and cordage, the children in red hoods playing on the sunny deck, the basking groups, some playing cards, some smoking, chatting—the silent companionless ones, pensive far-away-looking over the waves;

The Irish, mostly sitting or reclining in knots, young and old, men and women, in gay colors, resting their heads on each other or wrapped in pairs under one shawl—joking laughing kissing screaming slapping;

Germans, Hungarians, Poles, Norwegians, Laplanders, Swedes—some with red shirts and jack-boots, boys with concertinas and pipes, rosy Dutch girls, and mothers with tribes of children.

Here walking up and down with their brother three English girls, fresh and bright as daisies—on their way to join their parents in the West;

Here a little lady from Dublin with clear low voice singing to a circle of companions;

There in a corner by himself unnoticed among the rest, in low musical chant by the hour reciting praying, sits an old Russian Jew.

Greybeard, with veined forehead, a tailor by trade—his son-in-law has sent for him to Texas;

Through Hamburg and Hull and Liverpool he has traveled, eating no Gentile food but dry bread.

The Hebrew text lies before him—but he knows it by memory mostly;

Prayers for the day he recites ["Abraham taught the morning prayer and Isaac the afternoon and Jacob the evening prayer"]—

Prayers for the captain and for the crew and the passengers and for all sea-travelers ["prayers for self alone God will not hear"]—

Prayers against storm, shipwreck, disease and famine, and all dangers of the deep—not forgetting the warning of Jonah; and for each man's ruach against the ruach of the ocean; and against the changes of clime and time—

All these he recites, sitting alone with his thoughts amid strangers.

It is a strange and varied scene.

The dark passion-eyed little Irish devil of a New York saloon-keeper with his blasphemous stories and unscrupulous confessions—takes it in from his point of view;

The long-headed long-twinkling-eyed elderly woman in her print hood, helpful and receptive, with broad mouth—enjoyer of jokes, not easily shocked—takes it in also from hers;

The gold-miner with slouch hat and easy dress leans with his back against the bulwarks—he has seen it all twice before;

He has been home just now to Cornwall to visit his wife and children, and is off again to the mountains of Idaho. By his side stands his seventeen-year-old son, silent, clear-eyed, loving well his father.

The cheerful elderly spinster brings her camp-stool on deck and chats to a companion—laughing hysterically over her own fears, and how she pushed against the side of her berth in the night when it was rough, to steady the rolling ship!

The American horse-dealer (he is bringing over some cart-horses from England) walks up and down—grey-eyed, with decisive chin and lips, easy careless sociable and 'cute.

Under the awning aft by the saloon gangway an elderly and well-to-do matron and her two daughters recline in easy chairs; the lean grey-haired ship's purser, proud of his gentlemanly manners, stops as he passes to say a few words to them;

And the ship glides on and on—the water breaks from the bows,

The spars stand square and black against the sky, and the masts sway to and fro slowly.

On an Atlantic Steamship

3

What a scene!

Here in this hollow cup a thousand souls floating on the unmeasured deep—

A little dust of humanity gathered at random on the shores of one continent, to be tossed at random to the winds of another.

The young clerk with wife and babe, from London, going out to try his fortune at farming in Manitoba:

The great big-boned steerage steward, so kindly to the children and sensible—native of Rome, proud of his Latin origin, member of the Carbonari and imprisoned by Austrians in his time—now serving out treacle and bread and butter to emigrants;

The spruce first-cabin waiters and brawny slipshod humored crew,

The cooks, officers, the clean red-whiskered little captain on the bridge, the smug decent doctor, the oily-jacketed look-out behind his screen in the bows;

The taking of observations at breakfast time and again at noon, the sun's limbs brought down to the horizon—the logarithms and tables, the charts and the log;

The long heave and gasp of the engines, the gulls slow floating behind or darting after waste slops;

The huge side of the ship, an iron wall 170 yards long to the waves, the flowers mirrors gilt and velvet of the saloon, the piano, the gossip, the elegant dinner, the mutual advances and recognitions, the parson who consents to read service on Sunday, the philanthropist interested in gutter children, the two self-possessed American girls, the young Englishmen doing the great tour;

The bare sanded boards of the steerage cabins, the crowded emigrant meals, the swinging watercan and electric lamp, the stretched arms with mugs and plates;

The berths with hundreds of sleepers at night, the family groups during the day;

The father, awkward and ox-like, with nine motherless children, caring for their little wants—the women pityingly helping him;

The narrow-eyed pale young basket-maker reading his Bible in his berth all day; the Lancashire laddie and his pals singing salvation-comics at meal-times;

The military-got-up old fellow (years and years ago he was in the regulars) so clean and spruce—brushing his boots carefully every morning; the little boy of twelve traveling all by himself, petted by the cook and peeling potatos for bits of dainties;

The love-making, bible-reading, card-playing, singing—the women sewing or washing baby-linen;

The captain's cabin, with charts and glasses, the crew's quarters in the forecastle—men smoking in their bunks—the stoke-hole, the bar, the engine-room;

The warm evenings with renewals of animation—

Jingles of music in the cabins, hymns and comic songs and dances on deck to the accordion;

The inquisitive-eyed priest, the same that read the service, looking out from the saloon door—peering fleshly at the better-looking boys and girls;

On an Atlantic Steamship

At dusk the crew running among the women-passengers —firemen, cabin and deck-hands—fingering and fooling; the women enjoying;

The incorrigible nigger cook's boy, with muscular developed frame, protruding his great lips at the girls and then drawing them back with a grin showing huge rows of white teeth;

The mean pudding-faced Swedish lad and Irish woman spitting at each other—with no other language in common;

The sickness, the smells, the refuse meat swept from floors and tables and thrown in bucketfuls overboard;

The coarse half-smothered lust, the gluttony and waste of food;

And the great ship gliding on and on—in her course pointed by the earth-pole and the stars and the sun—

The spars standing square and black against the sky, and the mast-head light swaying slowly.

4

The evening before last the water was oily-calm, floating blue flecked with yellow up to the western horizon.

Behind, the track of the great ship lay like white lace, with ridgy waves thrown off and rustling as they receded on each side; in the distance brooding the dappled clouds hovered 'twixt sky and sea—dove-color and grey and heavy with unformed rain.

After sunset there was preaching and singing forward on deck.

One or two ladies from the saloon distributed tracts, some from the steerage joined in praying, and called upon the Lord for safety during the voyage.

Quite a little crowd got round, some earnest, some jeering, some quiet spectators—(the cabin-boys mostly dancing in pairs round the corner in time to the hymns).

All the while the great masts kept swaying slowly to and fro in the sky—as though never moving forward from their place—the huge vault rising enormous with dappled moonlit clouds in the east;

While from the west the faint daylight still shone upon the worshipers, and the sound of their music melted and died on the vast sea-bosom.

Later on, when the deck was almost deserted—All faintest dove-grey and silver, the gleaming water passing up without distinction into the gleaming sky, with moon behind the clouds—

All one hue, in faintest silent perpetual movement, like no earthly scene,

Immaterial, transfigured, the huge wash of ocean two miles deep lying so calm below—

The moonlit ocean of air unsuspected above the clouds—suspended between—

Gliding on and on, as in a mirror or a dream . .

All so calm, large, undisturbed, vast in extent and power: the sea stretching out to the touch of the air—miles, hundreds, thousands of miles—

On an Atlantic Steamship

The sympathetic answer of the floating cloud-layer to the floating heaving water-layer below . . .

I saw a vision of my own intimate passing out over the waters, and between them and the clouds—the vessel going on and leaving us—

Liberated, identified, all pain stript off and left with the husk behind—senses of enjoyment strangely widened, lifted—

Moving on at will, passing along the waters, the slow air—catching the faint scent, the whispers, the coherent incoherent words,

The marvelous calm, peace, grandeur, vastness, the incommunicable joy—

Entering into it, and being at rest.

5

In the morning all was changed again.

Drizzly and grizzly chopped the grey water with leaden clouds and rain; the horizon was a circle of mist;

Coldly and flabbily the passengers looked out upon the world.

Sullen like a marble cliff just tinged with blue, a huge slab a quarter mile long and eighty feet rising over the water,

Scored, festooned, beetling, with cavernous hollows washed by the sea,

With mist trailing to leeward of it, and thin mist passing over its white flat top, with white fragments dotting the sea around it—

Sullen silent and lonely a great iceberg floated by.

For a few minutes the passengers were roused, and crowded the side of the vessel—some of the firemen running up from the stoke-hole to have a look.

But presently like bees stupefied with cold they dispersed to their cabins and to sleep, and the deck was clear again.

6

To-day, bright and fresh, with new warmth, as it were wafted from the approaching land—all is gay and cheerful.

The deep inky-blue of mid-ocean yields to a lighter tint, and the waves break merrily into flashes of turquoise light crowned with foam.

Six narrow-winged gulls pass by—flying low, serpentine —hunting across the water;

Every now and then shoals of porpoises appear—hundreds at a time—playing splashing swimming alongside, towards the wind, leaping half-a-dozen together out of the water—

[Bounding three or four yards, with evident enjoyment and commotion at the sight of the ship—their sharp back-fins and divided horizontal tails plainly visible;]

Then a whale is seen spouting, or a fleet of Portuguese men of war drifts by, rose-color and blue—or a real ship is sighted and spoken with.

So the day speeds on; and pleasant is basking on the sunny deck, and pleasant the new companionships and the confidences; and the food tastes sweet, and the air has a breath of land in it, as of most distant hayfields; and hope and expectation range high;

And the evening falls, and late on into the warm night the clustered wanderers on the fore-deck sing the songs of the old country,

While the spars loom square and black against the stars, and the mast-head light sways slowly.

By Lake Wachusett

THE night-breeze murmurs odorous through the wild chestnuts where Lake Wachusett lies embowered in trees;

The moon shines over the mountains not other than when the wild man walked them;

The crickets and frogs cry shrill, the bull-frog twangs his bass, and the firefly shines fitful among the bushes;

While solitary in his boat the fisher is known by his lamp gleaming over the water.

Murmured as in a dream I catch the import of creation.

Like a far-off sound which the attentive listener mistakes not:

Through the chirruping of the crickets and high fluting of the frogs, through the lull of the breeze and the voice of the fisherman singing across the lake—through the calls of the Indians faintly lingering still among the laurel and pine tangles—

Through the face of the moon leaning down from the sky, and the fitful bird-eluding flash of the firefly—

Nay, through the remembered faces and calls of the city, and all sights and sounds—

Still I catch the old old theme, the theme of birth and deliverance.

Tremble on O breeze overhead, tremble O prince of love, with thy wings the whole universe overshadowing,

Calling Thou from their hidden dwelling-places the souls of men to their deliverance:

Where they lie hidden in the waters calling, or fitful in the air flashing—or in all strange elusive forms hiding vainly their birth-marks, yet by Thy voice discovered;

Where by the solitary lamp upon the lake, after trout and pickerel, or upon the pavements of cities, or with the moon through the mild night, or on the gleaming water-surfaces with cool gurgling throats—

Eluding, grotesque—still to thy voice they answer unwitting.

Tremble on O breeze glittering dissolving all things transparent—tremble O prince of love with thy wings all things overshadowing:

Calling invoking out of chaos, out of the mad jumble and whirligig of the world, through all destinies and forms and long agelong preparations—

Souls winged and equipped for freedom.

O Mighty Mother

O MIGHTY Mother—in silence receive thy child. Weary, fainting, having traveled far and forsaken thee, having undertaken burdens too great to be borne—

Atlas of griefs and sorrows, well nigh borne down beneath the load—

Thy foolish child, wandering afar from thee, yet led by what divine madness?—

O mighty Mother receive.

Never again to stray.

Having circled the globe, having completed the many-thousand-year-long round which thou secretly appointedst for me—

Through what mystifications troubles delays, what returning on old tracks, what torments and inward suffering (thou knowest best)—

What entanglements and illusions—

O mighty Mother receive!

Outcast and friendless (for that was my necessary doom) and homeless on the verge of creation I first knew myself—sorrow was the wall which divided me from thee.

I beheld thee afar and knew thee not; I was a prisoner and guessed not that I was in prison.

But now at thy feet—thanks, thanks!

Pouring out my soul in gratitude to thee—thy child so foolish, to Thee, dear mother

Whilst thou one by one disentanglest the loaded heavy chains which I have dragged so far—

(One by one, for not all at once will they come off, and fast and eating into my flesh are they riveted)—

At thy feet I sit and sing, knowing thou hast sworn to give me Freedom.

Ages shall my song last, for not all at once can I disburden myself;

Ages will I sing for joy—warbling in thy presence—as the birds to the risen sun;

Then at last arising Thou mother shalt take me by the hand: we will leave the earth, and thou shalt learn me to fly through heaven.

AFTER LONG AGES

AFTER LONG AGES

Tired child, on thy way to Paradise:

Does the path seem long? Rest here and let us beguile a few moments.

Rest here, in mortal form Thou that I see advancing— Child of sin and sorrow and suffering rest close here.

Hast thou heard faintly between the clouds in the everlasting blue the music of voices and of wings? Hast thou gazed deep into the eyes of the animals?

Hast thou silent in the great secret caverns of thy own heart heard the awful footsteps of thy Lover advancing?

Be at peace. Fear not. Behold, thou shalt conquer all evil.

Clouds of gloom shall wrap thy soul; the long days without grace shall weary thee; the voice of whom thou lovest shall speak to thee as of old no more

Be at peace. Fear not. Behold, thou shalt conquer all evil.

Turn, lift up thine eyelids, to me, beautiful one; clear away the shadows of the lashes from those liquid deeps;

Turn full-orbed thy gaze against mine. Fear not. Serene serene as heaven is all that is between us.

After Long Ages

Who is it that I see sitting at her lattice window—far down those liquid deeps?

Who is it the voice of whose singing comes borne to me like the sound of a voice across the far sea?

What is this figure, dear child, that I see moving so mysteriously in those depths—

Vague-outlined, hinted, as of one moving behind a curtain?

Lo! the caged one, the solitary prisoner feeling around the walls of her prison!

Lo, the baffled beaten and weary soul! lo, the crowned and immortal god!

I

After long ages resuming the broken thread—coming back after a long but necessary parenthesis,

To the call of the early thrush in the woods, and of the primrose on the old tree-root by the waterside—

Up with the bracken uncurling from the midst of dead fronds of past selves:

As of morning, and to start again after long strange slumber and dreams,

Beholding the beautiful light, breathing the dainty sweet air, the outbreath of innumerable creatures,

Seeing the sun rise new upon the world as lovers see it after their first night,

All changed and glorified, the least thing trembling with beauty—all all old sights become new, with new meanings—

Lo! we too go forth.

The great rondure of the earth invites us, the ocean-pools are laid out in the sunlight for our feet.

For now, having learned the lesson which it was necessary to learn, of the intellect and of civilisation—

Having duly taken in and assimilated, and again duly excreted its results—

Once more to the great road with the animals and the trees and the stars traveling to return—

To other nights and days undreamt of in the vocabularies of all dictionaries

I inevitably call you.

II

Calm and vast stretches the sea as at the first day, in sheets of blue and white; a light ground-swell sends the transparent wash over a bank of shingle, where it lies in pools along the water's edge.

A lug-sailed fishing boat drifts lazily with the tide, and then comes to anchor in the glaze; three or four porpoises show their backfins, oscillating as they pass;

While to the westward, far in the haze, phantom-like and large with the early sun on their sails, two square-rigged brigs glide on.

The chrysanthemums stand crowded in the cottage garden—and the ships glide on and on in the offing;

The low sun sends his light streaming over the world,

and glows amid the myriad salmon-pink petals tipped with yellow.

Ho! the sweet autumnal air! the cool green leaves thick-waving!

O earth, naked in love, bulging sunwards, with rosy fingers clasped about your head, and feet at the opposite pole,

Smiling and proud and with raised head I see you glance at your own beautiful body—at the sea, at the ships, at the star-shaped flowers of autumn;

Smile for smile unashamed you return to greet the glances of your lord.

But when night comes and the stars appear,

Pensive, unobserved, up on one arm raising yourself, lo! now I see you gaze abroad in solemn wonder;

For a new life moves within you—yet what to be you divulge not.

III

Well-folded for man waits the word for which so many ages he waits; not one moment before its due time is it spoken.

The runnels of water tinkle downwards towards the sea;

Calling to their cattle over the hills the voices of the herdsmen sound very musically through the still air; from afar and down the galleries of Time come the sounds of all mortal occupations;

The axe rings hollow among the woods; high in great quarries facing the sun is heard the click of chisels and the helter-skelter of falling stone; the hammers of the riveters echo along the shipyards of numberless shores;

The great promontories stand out mute over the sea; not one moment before their due time do they speak;

And the ships glide past them to the coasts of all lands, the winged thoughts of the voyagers circle the globe.

Well-folded and concealed the purpose of the earth waits: innumerable are the arguments of the little creatures that run about on it; wonderful their designs, exemplary their tenacity; but this purpose puts all the arguments and designs aside in time—it overpowers and convinces the most tenacious.

[For all creatures that are on the earth have different designs, and their arguments and actions war against and destroy each other;

But if thou canst in thyself open the door to that purpose which all fulfil alike, then shalt thou be free from the bonds of action and of argument, and shalt be absolved from that time forward.]

IV

Sweet are the uses of Life.

The house is wreathed with holly boughs at Christmas; the shining holly—the smooth-leaved—out of the woods nods to the sparkling eyes of the children as they dance;

The candles are darkened, and they stand round the dragon-fire in the bowl, hushed, large-eyed, in the livid and flickering light.

After Long Ages

The sun rises magnificent in winter upon the vast concave of air—level bars of mist lie in the hollows; firs and evergreens adorn the bare and silent woodlands.

The horse in the stable purrs at the sound of the tread of his master, and turns his beautiful head, as much as to say, Why are you so late with my breakfast? He paws impatiently while his feed is being prepared.

Towards the city along all the roads in the early light the workers converge. They take wafts of the fresh morning with them to their work. Sorrow and joy accompany them and share their meals in the everyday old haunts.

In the house a Stranger waits for the children; he stands by in the dark and leans over them and watches their faces, as they watch the dancing blue flame;

He moves along the roads unseen, and waits in the great city, and in the woods at early dawn he waits. None but the woodman and He see the thin waned moon arising with stars in pale and silent beauty before the sun.

Sweet are the uses of Life.

The Stranger glides to and fro; hours and centuries and thousand-year stretches he waits.

Among the children of mankind he waits. He too takes his place with the rest; he is a king, a poet, a soldier, a priest, a herdsman, a fig-pricker, a pariah.

It is indifferent: he sees all and passes with all—joy surrounds him wherever he is.

He sees the down-trodden and outcast; he sees the

selfish and tyrannical—he looks them right in the face but they do not see him;

He sees the patient and heroic; but he utters no word either of praise or blame.

The tall ash-shoots aspire in the hedge-rows; the trees lift innumerable fingers towards the sky, the brooks run downward unceasingly, atoms that have remained for thousands of years sealed in the rocks arise and pass beyond the boundaries of the earth and go voyaging through space;

All else hastens onward towards some unknown accomplishment—unerring;

He waits secure, and sings the songs of praise.

The morning and the evening are his song, and the land and the sea are the words of it, and the voices of all creation heard in silence are the perpetual offering of it.

He needs not to arise, nor to go hither and thither—all is finished and perfect.

What he desires, what he alone dreams of, that all mortal things through all time and space never-ceasingly occupy themselves to perform.

His fingers, as he sits at ease among the other children, are the myriad sunbeams and the thicksown stars and the innumerable blades of grass;

The winds are his messengers over all the world, and flames of fire his servants; the icebergs break from their northern shores, the southern lands clothe themselves with green and yellowing crops, and the clouds float over the half-concealed dappled and shaded Earth—to fulfil his will, to fulfil his eternal joy.

V

Sweet are the uses of Life.

The morning breaks again over the world as a thousand and a million times before;

The light flows rippling in, and up to the window-pane, and passes through and touches the eyelids of the sleeper.

It says: "Come forth, I have something to show you."

And the sleeper arises and goes forth—and everything is the same as yesterday.

Then he says to the light, "You have deceived me, there is nothing new here"—so he goes back sullenly to his chamber.

But the light is not huffed, but comes again next morning (thinks nothing of the long journey across) and slips through the window-pane and touches the sleeper's eyelids as before, "Come forth, I have something to show you;"

And again the next morning, and the next, and the next.

And the sleeper wonders whatever the light would be at, but the latter says nothing—only fails not to keep his self-made appointment.

Then after many years, after many thousands of years—

After many times lying down to sleep and rising again, after many times entering again into the mother's womb, after often passing through the gates of birth and death—the sleeper says to him that awakes him:

"Ah! beautiful one, ah! prince of love, so many times with thy fingers in vain touching my closed lids!

Now at last thy love pouring in upon me has found an entrance, and filling my body breaks the bounds of it, and bursts forth back again into the regions whence thou comest.

Ah! prince of love, lord of heaven, most beautiful one, of thee I am enamored and overcome with love;

Beholding thy beauty, hearing the words that thou sayest to me, being touched with the nearness of thy breath and the divine odor which exhales from thee—being sick, constrained with love, rending the chains which detain me—

Henceforth the long chain of births and deaths I abandon, I arise and go forth with thee—to begin my real life."

VI

Sweet are the uses of Life.

The woodstacks stand in the woods, and the ground is strewn with chips amid the fluttering anemones; the woodman downs his felling axe and lifts the beer-can to his lips;

The sweat streams in his face and beard, the sun-warm odor of the pines is wafted, and the bee booms through the clearing.

At night, ready for the alarm bell of fire, round their table in the engine-room smoking and playing cards the firemen sit; preparing for sleep the innocent girl rose-bud pats and smoothes her hair admiringly in the glass.

After Long Ages

Sweet are the uses, sweet the calls;

Out of the glass which is ever opposite peers a face which is not to be denied;

The flame leaps up behind the city roofs, the beer in the can stretches out like a lake among the trees before the thirsty drinker, the table is spread for the hungry with delicious viands;

The tongue presses gently the palate, the freshly running blood leaps and pulses like a brook through the arteries, the swarming millions in it dance past the Stranger who sits upon the banks;

Fresh comes the call each morning; (who knows whether now or when he will arise?)

The deed of daring calls, ambition calls, revenge and hatred call; the sun calls peeping over the mountains in the morning, the stars call glancing in at the windows at night, the myriad dancing sights and sounds call, weaving their magic circle as of old;

Hardly can he resist the fetch; he is drawn forth whether he will or no;

The primrose on the tree-root calls, love calls glancing from eyes of depth unfathomed;

Sexual lusts and cravings call—sweet fever for other flesh which nought else will satisfy,

Bruised bitter-sweet passion, determined and desperate, falling swooned and breathless on beloved lips and limbs.

VII

Centuries long in her antechambers tarrying,
Lost in strange mazes, wandering, dissatisfied—in sin and sorrow, lonely despised and fallen—
At length the soul returns to Paradise.
(O joy! the old burden, passing words!)

The humble-bee among the currant blooms hangs centuries long suspended; the lark still carols a mere speck in the sky.

Centuries long in her antechambers tarrying,
Lost in strange mazes, wandering dissatisfied,
Out of the windows peering wondering longing,
Following the shadowy angel—by others unseen—that comes and beckons,
Leaving all, leaving house and home, leaving year-long plans and purposes, ease and comfort,
Leaving good name and reputation and the sound of familiar voices, untwining loved arms from about her neck, yet twining them closer than ever—
Through the great gates, redeemed, liberated, suddenly in joy over the whole universe expanding—after her many thousand year long exile,
At length the soul returns to Paradise.

Cinderella the cinder-maiden sits unbeknown in her earthly hutch;
Gibed and jeered at she bewails her lonely fate;

Nevertheless youngest-born she surpasses her sisters and endues a garment of the sun and stars,

From a tiny spark she ascends and irradiates the universe, and is wedded to the prince of heaven.

VIII

O let not the flame die out!

Hitherto with wayward feet, in ignorance as a child, with sweet illusions and shows like dancing fireflies, and hopes and disappointments, have you been led on;

Henceforth putting these aside, as coming of age and to your inheritance, deliberately looking before and after you shall measure your undertaking and your powers.

For as a traveler beholds a snow mountain on the distant verge, beautiful, with inexpressible longings through the hot summer air—so as belonging to another world shall you behold from afar the signal of the goal of your wanderings;

Rising, falling, lost in thickets wildernesses deserts, the untrodden summit shall yet gleam on you—its beauty shall never be forsaken of your love.

O let not the flame die out!
Cherished age after age in its dark caverns, in its holy temples cherished,
Fed by pure ministers of love,
Let not the flame die out!

Within thy body I behold it flicker,
Through the slight husk I feel the quick fire leaping—
Let not the flame die out!

Send forth thy ministers for fuel.

Send forth the sight of thine eyes and the reaching of thy hands and the wayward stepping of thy feet,

Teach thy ears to bring thee and thy tongue to speak—labor, and spend all that thou hast for love; faint not: be faithful.

Cast at last thy body, thy mortal self, upon it, and let it be consumed;

And behold! presently the little spark shall become a hearth-fire of creation, and thou shalt endue another garment—woven of the sun and stars.

Cinderella the cinder-maiden sits unbeknown in her earthly hutch:

Love sees her once and rests no more till he has rescued and redeemed her.

IX

O laughter, laughter!

Shake out O clouds and winds your hidden words over the earth—and you ye meadows rejoice with innumerable daisies!

All the songs and hymns of creation from the first day, all the carols of the birds and choiring of the sun and stars in the limpid and boundless aether!

What sang and fluttered in the leaves, and was heard between the clouds in the blue;

What poured itself out in sorrow and was exhaled in death, stumbling on in the dark over stocks and stones—

Weary and bruised yet faithful, determined and undaunted,

To become as that which is ever the same as itself, entering into the inheritance of beauty, the great veil lifted—

Beholding the original of all the things which move outside, the company of the immortal hosts, the rose of glory, radiant behind all mortal things—

Overcome, blinded with splendor, falling trembling on the threshold—

The long long journey is accomplished!

X

That day—the day of deliverance—shall come to you in what place you know not; it shall come but you know not the time.

In the pulpit while you are preaching the sermon, behold! suddenly the ties and the bands—in the cradle and the coffin, the cerements and swathing-clothes—shall drop off.

In the prison One shall come; and the chains which are stronger than iron, the fetters harder than steel, shall dissolve—you shall go free for ever.

In the sick-room, amid life-long suffering and tears and weariness, there shall be a sound of wings—and you shall know that the end is near—

[O loved one arise! come gently with me; be not too eager—lest joy itself should undo you.]

In the field with the plough and chain-harrow; by the side of your horse in the stall;

In the brothel amid indecency and idleness and repairing your own and your companions' dresses;

In the midst of fashionable life, in making and receiving morning calls, in idlesse, and arranging knicknacks in your drawing room—even there, who knows?—

It shall duly, at the appointed hour, come.

Ask no questions: all that you have for love's sake spend;

For as the lightning flashes from the East to the West, so shall the coming of that day be.

All tools shall serve—all trades, professions, ranks, and occupations.

The spade shall serve. It shall unearth a treasure beyond price.

The stone-hammer and the shovel, the maul-stick and palette, the high stool and the desk, the elsin and the clamms and the taching ends, the whipping-lines and swingle-tree, will do;

To make a living by translating men's worn-out coats into boys' jackets—that also will do.

The coronet shall not be a hindrance to its wearer; the robes of office shall not detain the statesman; lands, estates, possessions, shall part aside for him who knows how to use them; he shall emerge from the midst of them, free.

The writer shall write, the compositor shall set up, the student by his midnight lamp shall read, a word never seen before.

The railway porter shall open the carriage door and the long expected friend shall descend to meet him.

The engine-driver shall drive in faith through the night. With one hand on the regulator he shall lean sideways and peer into the darkness—and lo! a new signal not given in the printed instructions shall duly in course appear.

The government official shall sit in his pigeon-holed den, the publican shall recline on his couch in the back-parlor, the burglar shall plan his midnight raid, the grocer's boy shall take the weekly orders in the kitchen, the nail-maker shall put his rod back in the fire and take a heated one out in its place;

The delicate-bred girl shall walk the correct thing in her salmon-pink silk slashed with blue; the sempstress shall sit in her bare attic straining the last hour of daylight—and by every stitch done in loyalty of heart shall she sew for herself a shining garment of deliverance.

The mother shall wear herself out with domestic duties and attending to her children; she shall have no time to herself, yet before she dies her face shall shine like heaven.

The Magdalen shall run down to answer the knock at the door, and Jesus her lover himself shall enter in.

XI

Where the Master is there is paradise.

I know that nothing else shall satisfy you—nothing else has any real sense at all.

In the antechamber of the body it is vain to tarry; among the forms that belong to it and are painted upon its walls—beautiful as they all without one exception are—you shall look in vain for the master.

In the antechamber of the intellect (important as it is) it is vain to tarry; systems and philosophies, plans and purposes, proofs and arguments, shall please you for a time; but in the end they shall only contradict and destroy each other.

In the antechamber of art and morality (important as they are) you shall not tarry overlong. Here also as in the other chambers though you see the footsteps of the Master you shall not behold him face to face.

The trees grow in the Garden, but they are not the same as the lord of the Garden: out of them by themselves come only confusion and conflict and tangling of roots and branches.

This is the order of Man and all History.

Descending he runs to and fro over the world, and dwells (for a time) among things that have no sense;

Forgetful of his true self he becomes a self-seeker among shadows.

But out of these spring only war and conflict and tangling of roots and branches;

And things which have no sense succeed things which have no sense—for nothing can have any sense but by reason of that of which it is the shadow; and one phantasmal order follows another, and one pleasure or indulgence another, and one duty or denial another—

Till, bewildered and disgusted, finding no rest, no peace, but everywhere only disappointment,

He returns (and History returns) seeking for that which is.

After Long Ages

Toilsome and long is the journey; shell after shell, envelope after envelope, he discards.

Over the mountains, over the frowning barriers, undaunted, unwrapping all that detains him,

Enduring poverty, brother of the outcast and of animals, enduring ridicule and scorn,

Through vast morasses, by starlight and dawn, through dangers and labors and nakedness, through chastity and giving away all that he has, through long night-watches on the mountains and washings in the sunlit streams and sweet food untainted by blood, through praises and thanks and joy ascending before him—

All all conventions left aside, all limitations passed, all shackles dropped—the husks and sheaths of ages falling off—

At length the Wanderer returns to heaven.

Then all those things which have vainly tried to detain him—

When He comes who looks neither to the right nor the left for any of them,

Not being deluded by them but rather threatening to pass by and leave them all in their places just as they are—

Then they rise up and follow him.

Though thorns and briars before, in his path they now become pleasant fruits and flowers,

[Not till he has put them from him does he learn the love that is in them;]

Faithful for evermore are they his servants—and faithful is he to them—

And this world is paradise.

XII

Therefore I say unto you: Faint not;

Rest here awhile and forgive my foolish prating;

Turn from these words and look again at the world around you, the work you have to do.

Not for one year or two;

Not for a whim or a passing passion, or for after jealousies and recriminations, but for something more—

Something to grow in other spheres and to be more precious than the casket which contains it—

For sovereignty and freedom and the life which is not seen, do we exchange the ancient language of creation.

And I conjure you, if you would understand me, to crush and destroy these thoughts of mine which I have written in this book or anywhere;

And my body (if it should be our destiny to meet in battle) I conjure you faithfully to destroy—nor be afraid—as I will endeavor to destroy yours: so shall you liberate me to dwell with you.

Spare not, respect not, believe not anything that I have written. Rest not till you have ground it to smallest meal between your teeth.

And, looking me in the face, accept not anything that I do or say—for it does not call for acceptation.

After Long Ages

Me alone, when you have separated and rejected all these, shall you see and not reject.

XIII

What else (than this) are the dreams of all people and of eras and ages upon the earth?

What else are the glowing dreams of boyhood, and the toys of age, and the promises floating ever on before—dim mirages to wayworn travelers? (faint not, O faint not!)

What else the sound of Christmas hymns across the snow—the tender and plaintive songs of centuries, dreams of the Better Land—coming down from before all history?

What the obstinate traditions of races and explorations by sea and land; the instinct of the chase; searches for the Earthly paradise, Utopias of social reformers, Eldorados and fabled Islands, stirrings of adventure and conquest; pilgrimages, myths, and the tireless quest of the Sangreal?

The unquenchable belief in the elixir of life and the philosopher's stone; the feverish ardor of modern science, like a dog with its nose on the trail?

What else the marvelous dreams of the little creatures walking the earth—the dreams of religion—the skies peopled, and the vast cosmogonies of the gods, the huge and impending Otherworld, the mystic scroll of the Zodiac?

The dim-lit chambers of rock-temples and pyramids and cathedrals—the ark, the host, and the holy of holies?

The proclamations and gospels of all lands, the giving of fire from the mosque at Jerusalem, the lighting of innumerable candles; the far-away songs of the priests by the Nile-strand, standing by the empty sarcophagus with the words, "Osiris is risen"; the midnight naked dances of the Therapeutæ upon the sands, the processions of salvation armies and revivalists?

The daily life of each man and woman, the ever expected Morrow, the endless self-seeking, the illusive quests (faint not, O faint not!), the bog-floundering after fatuous wisps, the tears disappointments and obstinate renewals of hope—

All routes and roads and the myriad moving of feet to and fro over the earth—

What are they but Transparencies of one great fact—symbols of the innumerable paths

By which the soul returns to paradise?

XIV

I BEHELD a vision of Earth with innumerable paths; I saw the faces that go up and down—the world that each carries within.

I heard the long roar and surge of History, wave after wave—as of the never-ending surf along the immense coast-line of West Africa.

I heard the world-old cry of the down-trodden and outcast: I saw them advancing always to victory.

I saw the red light from the guns of established order and precedent—the lines of defence and the bodies of the besiegers rolling in dust and blood—yet more and ever more behind!

And high over the inmost citadel I saw magnificent, and beckoning ever to the besiegers, and the defenders ever inspiring, the cause of all that never-ending war—

The form of Freedom stand.

XV

I beheld a vision of Earth with innumerable paths;

And I saw, going up and down, the world-old faces of humanity—whom neither race nor clime nor time greatly alter;

Through barbarisms and civilisations, through agricultural and nomad and sea-faring, and dwelling in caves and dwelling in palaces, through all manner of crafts and cunning knowledge and out again, I saw the same old faces go.

The kingly face of duty loyal to the death, looking out upon the world before ever articulate words were uttered by tongue of man; the face of reason calm to deal with life;

Faces of tenderness and love, the quivering lips, the mother's breast among the animals;

The sturdy resolute face I saw, and the transparent eyes of candor like a stainless lake—when there was no other mirror to look in;

The dear homely ungainly face (before ever there was a tent door to sit by), the incisive and penetrating face, the laughing erring loving satyr-face of the child of nature among the woods; and open and unfenced as Nature herself the face of divine equality;

These I saw going up and down the paths which lead hither and thither from darkness to darkness:

I saw them in the street to-day, and when I looked beyond the farthest glimmer of history I saw the same.

And I saw, too, the menacing evil faces, creeping insincere worm-faces, faces with noses ever on the trail, hunting blankly and always for gain;

Faces of stolid conceit, of puckered propriety, of slobbering vanity, of damned assurance;

The swift sweep of self-satisfaction beneath the eyelids, set lips of obstinacy, wrinkled mouth of suspicion, swollen temples of anger—and the shamed shovel-face of self-indulgence;

These too I saw going up and down the paths which lead hither and thither from darkness to darkness:

I saw them in the street to-day, and when I looked beyond the farthest glimmer of history I saw the same.

O faces, whither whither are you going?

What are these paths innumerable leading from darkness to darkness?

Why under so many flags of disguise, under turban and fez and pigtail and sombrero, plaits of cow-dung and tufts of feathers, Greek arrow and Persian tiara, and cocked and chimney-pot hat, and head-dresses of gold pieces and straw and grass, do you (still the same) pass into light and out again—like ships across the pathway of the moon?

XVI

Through the narrow gas-lighted lanes of Florence the faces pass, and out of sight again.

After Long Ages

The old Campanile towers overhead into the yet lingering after-glow of sunset, the stars twinkle faintly already round its head—the memory of 500 years of Florentine life encircles it.

The tower of Galileo stands away off on the hills; but he from it watches the stars no more—his restless brain grinds no more at the problems of rest and motion;

The pilgrims of the Haj land in thousands at Jeddah, the route to Mecca is thronged with comers from all parts of the old world;

The children of the Roman Carnival pelt each other with confetti; the stream of worshipers into St. Peter's wait each in turn to kiss the toe of the statue which fell down from heaven; the sacred and bejeweled bambino is taken out of its altar-cradle and carried in procession through the streets;

By the mouth of the Kolima in the long arctic night while the moon circles round the sky the Russian exile stands and hungers without hope for the dear faces of wife and children; the features of the wild Siberyaks are hateful to his sight;

The Chinese woman—her baby slung on her back—rows and rows the ferry boat across the river: it is her home and she leaves it neither night nor day;

The furtive little Londoner with the bottle in her pocket slips back home from the public house—to drink while her husband is working; the carefully brushed and buttoned young man walks down Piccadilly;

The bulky red bus-driver shouts cheerily to his mates

as they pass; he cries "Cuckoo" in the warm April morning and looks innocently up into the empty sky;

Carriages with high-stepping horses crowd Regent Street; the policeman stops them and pilots—carries almost—a poor old woman across, very fragile, light as a little child;

The lame pinched old finder with grizzled hair and prowling eyes wanders the pavements all day, picking up oddments; he sees neither the houses nor the sky, neither men nor women; his eyes roll from side to side like one reading a book;

The lone mother sits in her dreary little shop, eyeing between the prints in the window the stupid gaping faces of the passers-by as they pause; in the chamber upstairs her boy lies ill; at long intervals a customer comes in and throws down a penny—which she puts duly in a teacup;

The country road-mender surveys his length of road with practised eye; he places marks on gate-posts and trees at intervals to indicate where the road-metal is to be shot;

The slip-shod old blacksmith prattles away as he rakes the cokes over his work and blows the bellows with his left hand; every now and then he stops to light his pipe with a few hot ashes;

On the hearth-side in the fitful glare sits the good-natured great farm-lad by the hour, enjoying his talk, obscene or otherwise.

XVII

At dusk the lamps are lighted in the great cathedral church—lines of gas fringe within the huge dusky dome mixing with the fading daylight. The hour of service approaches, the sound of footsteps becomes more frequent; around, the roar of the great city fades.

The commercial traveler comes in with his parcel and strap, deposits it on a chair and seats himself beside it; the city man comes with his bag; the country visitor gazes curiously aloft and around; the tired old piffler and newsroom loiterer slips in for half-an-hour's sleep; the young English girl, graceful as a kitten, and her brother sit reverently down; the prostitute also arrives and chooses her place with discretion.

The shaven-faced verger lights the candles of the great lectern, and the organ booms slowly forth its first notes—trembling through the spaces of roof and dome.

The music-teacher leaves her roll of music on the chair, and kneels downright upon a mat; and the lady with her little boy join in the service;

The ragged wandering-minded old man shuffles in and sits down, muttering to himself; the young man from the waterworks talks in a low voice to the girl with whom he is keeping company;

The middle-aged man sleeps, with his little girl huddled wide-eyed against his side; the young mason with clear eyes and stubbly unshaven chin looks round at the vast columns and carven capitals;

And the sleepy old canon stumbles on through the service, while the choir-boys wink at the tenors and basses.

In the morning, in the thick January morning, rows of

dirty tawny brick houses stretch all around through the fogs of London—here and there a light yet lingers in a window.

On the pavements are hurrying mortals with tall hats, bags, overcoats--depressed;

White-faced girls going to work, city men anxiously glancing at the papers as they go;

The postman with bag over his shoulders and bunch of letters in his hand, untidy servants sweeping the doorsteps, the butcher's boy in his cart, the governess going to her lessons;

The milk-carts, brewers' drays, hansom-cabs, the hurried self-absorbed crowd at the underground station, the skim downstairs, dash for the carriage doors, and train disappearing forthwith into the tunnel.

XVIII

O great city of millions scrambling backwards and forwards!—O toiling careworn millions of the earth!

Pursuing ever shadows shadows, laboring for that which seems to give so little return:

With tears tears, and short-lived laughter, and the black toad sitting ever in the heart.

O wanderers returning ever on your tracks—innumerable paths from darkness to darkness! O specks across the pathway of the moon!

You by the mouth of the Kolima regarding with pale face the great star-spangled sky—the glory all crossed and blotched with pain;

After Long Ages

You hurrying on in the foggy yellow dawn to the dressmaker's gas-reeking den—or in the filthy back slum dreaming of your childhood and the banks of primroses;

You lying anxious at night, weary and broken with business cares ever closing upon you—you prowling by day the crowded footways:

Come, sit down now at your ease and forget all. Sleep, weary children, and dream of peace and quiet.

Far have you yet to go, but there is no need to hurry;

What seems the end of your journey now, may-be it is only the beginning; what terrifies you so in prospect perhaps after all you will pass and hardly be aware.

You with black bag hastening to catch the train, hasten no more: the deed which you want—which shall declare you free—you will find not at your office;

Train disappearing into the tunnel, delude the passengers no more with the promise of reaching their destinations;

Cease prowling the streets, old man! I have seen what you are searching for: it is safe, and the reward is great—but now rest for a moment.

And you, tight-gloved and booted and with penciled eyes, be not so choice about your gloves and boots and where you will be seated—for while you are busy with all these things your lover waits solitary for you.

Lone mother in the dreary little shop, tired child on the way to paradise—now to thy boy lying dead upstairs

Does the path seem long?—rest here and let us beguile a few moments:

Rest here in mortal form thou that I see enveloped:
Child of sin and sorrow and suffering rest close here.

XIX

THE hills stand out in line against the yellow sunset, with snow in the hollows of their sides: in front stretch green undulating meadows, with trees and the sound of water, and smoke from cottage chimneys.

O cry aloud over the earth for the children of men, of immortal destinies!

The young farmer in gaiters and thick boots walks miles over the hills to see his sister at the lunatic asylum. In the visitor's room calm in neat attire she meets him; they are near the same age. Thankful, with tears, suffused, reading each other's eyes they sit together hand in hand.

Strange cobwebs cross and cross and cloud her face and mind, yet within her star-like burns her changeless love for him.

Praying, talking continually of the visions before them, pacing silent and mechanical up and down the ward, with disheveled hair, with narrow oblique eyes of suspicion, with animal postures and cries and chatterings and heavy stunned looks, the poor broken images and wasters of Humanity wait their time.

Now at evening from the meadows and the cottages and the familiar water-sides exhale tender regrets and memories

—compunctions of partings long past, and faces seen and voices heard no more.

With the odors of evening they arise—from the breast of mortal men and women exhaled.

By the door thou standest wondering tenderly of him or her who is gone; presently the doorway shall be empty of thy form, and another shall stand there wondering of thee.

As thou after thy mother, so she wondered to know of hers, and her mother again of her who gave her birth;

By chains of tender memory and love encircling the earth are the children bound to each other—there is not one that escapes.

Whither is the resort of them that pass, and where do the uncounted generations abide?

In what hollow do they dwell and what valley do they inhabit?—where do they sleep their invisible sleep, and does the light of the sun awaken them?

Of what they meditated on earth do they dream, and on us do they look with eyes innumerable as the stars?

XX

O cry aloud over the Earth!

Great ragged clouds wild over the sky careering, pass changing shifting through my poems!

Blow O breezes, mingle O winds with these words— whose purpose is the same as yours!

Ye dark ploughed fields and grassy hills, and gorses where the yoldring warbles—write ye your myriad parallel gossamers among my lines!

Lie out O leaves to the sun and moon, to bleach in their quiet gaze—whirl them O winds—float them away O sea, to drift in bays with the sea-smell and with odors of tar among the nets of fishermen!

Open O pages in all lands! Let them be free to all to pass in and out, let them lie like the streets of a great city!

Let them listen and say what the feet of the passengers say, and what the soughings of the fir trees say. Let them be equal—no more, no less—writing the words which are written as long as the universe endures.

XXI

O cry aloud over the Earth for the children of men, of immortal destinies!

The great orator stands upon the platform,
Careless of approval and careless of opposition he speaks from himself alone.
He is determined and will not abate one tittle of his determination.
The arguments, the pros and cons, he treats lightly—after a time he dismisses them;
Traditions of science and literature he discusses for a while, and then—somehow—quietly puts them aside;
Flowers and figures of rhetoric he uses, but presently they fail and fall away.

From the great rock-bases of his own humanity, of his

own imperious instinct and determination, he appeals with uplifted arm to God and eternal Justice—

And from a thousand eyes flash the lightnings of tears and joy, from that vast sea of faces breaks a roar of terrible and deep-throated accord.

The arguments, the pros and cons, fly high in the air like leaves in a gale;

The tradition of centuries loses its form and outline—like melting ice in water.

From her deep-implanted seat in the human breast, from behind all reasoning and science and arguments,

Humanity speaks her Will, and writes a page of History.

XXII

As a meteor glides silent for a moment among the fixed stars and is gone—so among the words of this book glides eluding that other Word which reveals their significance;

Wonderful, eternal—when these words perish and fall apart from each other that word shall not perish but return thither whence it sprang.

To see the old sight—and to dream the old dream—the theatre is crowded.

The stout matron comes from behind the bar, the clerk slips down from his half-furnished fireless garret, the lady and gentleman lounge in from their five-course dinner:

The joiner's apprentice slips off his apron and hurries over his tea and bread and butter; the dressmaker's girl and the private soldier and the blasé from the club are all there—

Amid the blaze of light and color, between the music and the jokes, the strange haunting clinging dream is there.

The young buck with coat-sleeves turned up with fur cannot but wait for it outside the stage door;

The improver goes back next morning to her work, but she cannot rightly see the box-plaits (as she runs them previous to putting them in the machine); when she hurries home through the streets at evening she keeps looking to see if what she caught sight of is there.

On the pavement in the flare of gas the motley crowd goes by; the policeman stands backed against the gin-shop at the corner, marshaling the buses or quietly gossiping with cronies.

Off the curb, by her tray of cork and felt socks, weary-eyed, wrapping her thin shawl close, the elderly woman stands, or tramps to and fro to keep her feet warm.

Under the great roof in the dockyard slip, amid incessant din, deep in the bowels of the iron ship, the riveters hammer day by day their red-hot iron rivets.

Brown-backed partridges fly across the ploughed land; far above them motionless the quick-eyed hawk discerns their moving shadows.

White-tunicked Albanian soldiers march across the hills above the beautiful city and lake of Janina.

Down beside a rippling stream over-shadowed by trees, at midnight the rapt watcher stands motionless. The stars in slow procession glide westward. They pass behind the dark tree-boles and emerge again; but he moves not—his thoughts move not.

Absorbed, the world circles round him, the shackles of existence fall off, he passes into supreme joy and mastery.

Lo! the rippling stream and the stars and the naked tree-branches deliver themselves up to him. They come close; they are his body, and his spirit is rapt among them: without thought he hears what they and all things would say.

XXIII

Ah! the good news so long sought—the ancient indestructible Gospel!

The little boat sways on the great calm deep, the clouds hang in haze on the edges—faint and far is the land.

Faint and far are the mountains, and the forests where the sun sleeps at midnoon.

Ah! the good news desired of men—the dreams of so many ages!

Who has seen that land? who has floated on that ocean?

For the earth is round and many ships sail its seas and innumerable feet traverse its lands, and great are its thunderclouds piled in the air:

But who yet has truly walked its lands and who has floated on its seas and who has been the worthy companion of those its clouds piled so magnificent in the air?

The ships lie in the harbor, behind them stretches the far sea-horizon and the round ocean curving into other latitudes;

The breeze floats gently off shore bearing the clouds on its bosom, and feeling among the folds of the flags;

The chrysanthemums stand crowded in the cottage garden, and the promontories rear their heads mute over the sea—not one moment before their due time do they speak.

Being transformed, being transformed into Thy likeness —passing the boundaries;

Passing the boundaries of evil, being delivered, being filled with joy;

Drinking out of the great lake that can never be emptied —having come to its shores—of the great inland ocean of joy that laves all mortal things;

Sitting down there under the trees, watching the birds that fly a little way out over it, watching the wild creatures that come down to drink also of it;

Sitting on the quay among the bales and spars, and taking stock of the ships that are waiting to sail, and the travelers that leave and arrive, seeing the breeze also floating gently the folds of the flags;

Content, overjoyed, knowing that I have yet far to go; but that all is open and free, and that Thou wilt provide—

Gladly O gladly I surrender myself to Thee.

XXIV

Lo! the stress, the immortal passion, the dashing against the barriers of self, the ever-widening of the bounds;

The endless contest, the melancholy haughty Titanic and lonely struggle of the soul;

The ecstatic deliverance, the bursting of the sac, the outrush and innumerable progeny!

Lo! the healing power descending from within, calming the confused mind, spreading peace among the quivering nerves;
Lo! the eternal Savior, the sought after of all the world, dwelling hidden (yet to be disclosed) within each;
The haunting clinging dream, the theme and long refrain of ages, O joy insuperable!
Casting out types through all creation, tentative, loose notes and motifs,
Sleeping in the bosom of the hills before ever the naked foot of man trod among them,
Dwelling in mighty fir and oak, giants of the forest, and in the tiny life which springs about their roots,
Time out of mind immeasurable, standing behind the night and stars—inhabiting the wheeling earth—
Lo, all as at random, thrown forth!

[The old Red Indian walks the silent-wooded wildernesses—hundreds and scores of hundreds of miles are familiar to him;
Like an ancient rock full of lines, weatherworn impassive is his face—the stars are his well-known friends.
The young Zulu with feathers on his head and wildcat tails around his loins, and carriage erect and proud as an emu, joins the gathering of warriors—he seems to push the earth from beneath him as he walks.]

XXV

I behold the broad expanse of life over the earth—

I see the stalwart aborigines straying naked through the primal woods, light-footed amid the grass; I hear their powerful cries and calls to each other, resounding from cliffs and gullies;

I see the civilised man in his study among his books, or driving with his lady along the boulevards; I see the well-dressed crowds of Paris and New York; I see the famished and raging mobs of incendiaries;

The long vain fight of man against Nature I see, not traveling hand in hand with but setting himself in opposition to her: the necessary prologue and apprenticeship—as of a wayward boy against his mother—yet vanquished, finally and surely vanquished;

All well; and I see there is no need to hurry.

I behold well-pleased the broad expanse of life over the earth; I see the great factories, with smoke in the early morning—the hands coming in to work; the lines of shops along the principal streets of cities—the piers and wharves with those who toil on them;

I see the great broad pleasure of life among the millions, the energy, the scheming, planning, and the solid execution of plans;

The ties of marriage, friendship, heroic actions, dreams, adventures;

I see also the sufferings, the hardships, the hatred,

the sin and misery, the clenched teeth, the evil of everything that is established and exists, and the need that it should be overthrown;

I take part in these too—they are well. I see the incessant change in society, the gaunt desperate problems which attend it in every stage,

And the great problem which for each man stands behind these problems—the open secret which unlooses them, dissolves them at a touch, as a drop of water dissolves a flake of snow.

XXVI

I behold well-pleased the broad expanse of life over the earth—nor is there anything in it which is not good.

All results in the great constitution of things are provided for, nor is it possible in all the fantastic freaks of Nature and of Man for anything to surpass its proper boundary or to fail of its due fruition.

Water does not lie level by a more inevitable law; into this great ocean (of the soul) all things at length return.

Free, free is the going and coming of so many feet; the kid-gloved fur-mantled lady sitting bible in hand among the poor is free to come and go;

So is the young thief—with his heavy burden of concealment, his weary eluding eyes yet not eluding, his face unlighted with laughter—free to come and go; (I do not scorn, I do not blame you—you are the same to me as the others are, and what you can take of me that you are free to;)

The selfish, the brave, the vain, the foolish, may come

and go, but whether they come or whether they go the results are secured to them of all they do.

For a long time walking the earth, threading an immense and seemingly endless labyrinth, returning on our own tracks as in dreams and sleep-walking, with eyes open but seeing not, following some mirage, something ever receding and eluding—always about to clutch it;

Occupied in business, with affairs—thinking this important and that important, vexed to compass this or that end—caught by the leg in the trap which we ourselves have laid;

Caught by ambition, envy, greed; owners of wealth and lying awake at night with anxiety over it, driving herds of cattle and swallowing the dust thereof, planning houses and building us our own prisons—

We go.

There is no bar. The paths are all open, the sign-posts few—each must find the clue for himself, the exit from the labyrinth.

For a long time walking the earth as in a dream there is no clue, only bewilderment,

Then presently also as in a dream it all clears up; the insoluble and varied problems which constitute ordinary life disappear entirely leaving no traces—and Life in every direction is navigable as space to the rays of the sun.

XXVII

O come with me, my soul—follow the inevitable call, follow the call of the great sky overarching you.

Disentangling the cobwebs of all custom and supposed necessity—the ancient cocoon in which humanity has lain so long concealed—

Pass forth, Thou, into the serene light: along the hills, by the clumps of overhanging trees, through the doorways of all mortal life, pass thou redeemed, enfranchised.

XXVIII

SO after many wanderings, after long ages resuming the broken thread,

After wandering over the earth for many years—with the Red Indian from mountain to mountain, from river to river;

With the Tartar and Malaysian, the Teuton and the Celt; with the emigrant and the exile and the settler wandering; with the Norsemen in their ships to the shores of Iceland and America;

Embracing new climates, customs, times—being constrained by none, hindered by none;

After many times lying down to sleep and rising again —after many times entering into the mother's womb;

The Sleeper says to him that awakens him:—

"Ah! beautiful one—ah! prince of love, so many times with thy fingers touching in vain my closed lids!

Now at last thy love pouring in upon me has found an entrance, and filling my body breaks the bounds of it and bursts forth back again into the regions whence thou comest.

Ah! prince of love, lord of heaven, most beautiful one, of thee I am enamored and overcome with love;

Here amid the grass once more a child sitting—watching the trembling stamens sway against the distant landscape;

Beholding all life and finding it good—being satisfied;

Pouring out the wine of my life to Thee—being transformed into thy likeness;

I depart—never again thus and thus to return.

Henceforth when summer burns on the high ground where the breezes play—where Thou passest as a flame, transforming the trees yet not consuming them, I will follow thee.

When night hangs crowded with stars I will ascend with Thee the unknown gulfs and abysses.

Spread, O earth, with blue lines of distant hills—stretch for the feet of men and all creatures!

Sing, chant your hymns, O trees and winds and grass and immeasurable blue!

Being transformed being transformed into Thy likeness —lord of heaven and earth!

Being filled with love, having completed our pilgrimage, We also pass into peace and joy eternal."

*E. C., age 43,
from a photograph
taken in 1887.*

Part
AFTER CIVILISATION

We are a menace to you, O civilisation!

We have seen you—we allow you—we bear with you for a time;

But beware! for in a moment and, when the hour comes, inevitably,

We shall arise and sweep you away!

Part III
AFTER CIVILISATION

We are a menace to you, O civilisation!
We have seen you—we allow you—we bear with you for a time,
But beware! for in a moment and, when the hour comes, inevitably,
We shall arise and sweep you away!

AFTER CIVILISATION

IN the first soft winds of spring, while snow yet lay on the ground—
Forth from the city into the great woods wandering,
Into the great silent white woods where they waited in their beauty and majesty
For man their companion to come:
There, in vision, out of the wreck of cities and civilisations,
I saw a new life arise.

Slowly out of the ruins of the past—like a young fern-frond uncurling out of its own brown litter—
Out of the litter of a decaying society, out of the confused mass of broken down creeds, customs, ideals,
Out of distrust and unbelief and dishonesty, and Fear, meanest of all (the stronger in the panic trampling the weaker underfoot);
Out of miserable rows of brick tenements with their cheapjack interiors, their glances of suspicion, and doors locked against each other;
Out of the polite residences of congested idleness; out of the aimless life of wealth;
Out of the dirty workshops of evil work, evilly done;
Out of the wares which are no wares poured out upon the markets, and in the shop-windows,
The fraudulent food, clothing, drink, literature;

After Civilisation

Out of the cant of Commerce—buying cheap and selling dear—the crocodile sympathy of nation with nation,

The smug merchant posing as a benefactor of his kind, the parasite parsons and scientists;

The cant of Sex, the impure hush clouding the deepest instincts of boy and girl, woman and man;

The despair and unbelief possessing all society—rich and poor, educated and ignorant, the money-lender, the wage-slave, the artist and the washerwoman alike;

All feeling the terrible pressure and tension of the modern problem:

Out of the litter and muck of a decaying world,

Lo! even so

I saw a new life arise.

The winter woods stretched all around so still!

Every bough laden with snow—the faint purple waters rushing on in the hollows, with steam on the soft still air!

Far aloft the arrowy larch reached into the sky, the high air trembled with the music of the loosened brooks.

O sound of waters, jubilant, pouring pouring—O hidden song in the hollows!

Secret of the earth, swelling sobbing to divulge itself!

Slowly, building lifting itself up atom by atom,

Gathering itself together round a new centre—or rather round the world-old centre once more revealed—

I saw a new life, a new society, arise.

Man I saw arising once more to dwell with Nature;

[The old old story—the prodigal son returning, so loved,

The long estrangement, the long entanglement in vain things]—

The child returning to its home, companion of the winter woods once more,

Companion of the stars and waters, hearing their words at first hand (more than all science ever taught),

The near contact, the dear dear mother so close, the twilight sky and the young tree-tops against it;

The huts on the mountain-side, companionable of the sun and the winds, the lake unsullied below;

The daily bath in natural running waters, or in the parallel foam-lines of the sea, the pressure of the naked foot to the earth;

The few needs, the exhilarated radiant life—the food and population question giving no more trouble;

[No hurry more, no striving one to override the other:

Each one doing the work before him to do, and taking his chance of the reward,

Doubting no more of his reward than the hand doubts, or the foot, to which the blood flows according to the use to which it is put;]

The plentiful common halls stored with the products of Art and History and Science to supplement the simple household accommodations;

The sweet and necessary labor of the day;

All these I saw—for man the companion of Nature.

Civilisation behind him now—the wonderful stretch of the past;

Continents, empires, religions, wars, migrations—all gathered up in him;

The immense knowledge, the vast winged powers—to use or not to use—

He comparatively indifferent, passing on to other spheres of interest.

The calm which falls after long strife, the dignity of rest after toil;

Hercules, his twelve labors done, sitting as a god on the great slope of Olympus,

Looking out over the Earth, on which he was once a mortal.

The word Democracy

UNDERNEATH all now comes this Word, turning the edges of the other words where they meet it.

Politics, art, science, commerce, religion, customs and methods of daily life, the very outer shows and semblances of ordinary objects—

The rose in the garden, the axe hanging behind the door in the outhouse—

Their meanings must all now be absorbed and recast in this word, or else fall off like dry husks before its disclosure.

Do you not see that your individual life is and can only be secured at the cost of the continual sacrifice of other lives,

And that therefore you can only hold it on condition that you are ready in your turn to sacrifice it for others?

The law of Indifference which must henceforth be plainly recognised and acted upon.

Art can now no longer be separated from life;

The old canons fail; her tutelage completed she becomes equivalent to Nature, and hangs her curtains continuous with the clouds and waterfalls;

Science empties itself out of the books; all that the books have said only falls like the faintest gauze before the reality—hardly concealing a single blade of grass, or damaging the light of the tiniest star;

The form of man emerges in all objects, baffling the old classifications and definitions;

[Beautiful the form of man emerges, the celestial ideal—

The feet pressing the ground, the supple strong ancles and wrists, the cleave of the loins, the shoulders, and poised head aureoled by the sun;]

The politician turns round upon himself—like the scientist he acknowledges his brain baffled by the problems; he reaches his hand for help to the hand of the People;

The commercial man turns round—the firm ground gives way beneath his feet also; to give now seems better than to get—and what sort of a trade-motto is that?

All the customs of society change, for all are significant; and the long-accepted axioms of every day life are dislocated like a hill-side in a landslip;

The old structures can no longer stand—their very foundations are shifted—

And men run forth in terror from the old before they can yet find firm ground for the new.

In all directions gulfs and yawning abysses,

The ground of society cracking, the fire showing through,

The old ties giving way beneath the strain, and the great pent heart heaving as though it would break—

At the sound of the new word spoken—

At the sound of the word Democracy.

No volcano bursting up through peaceful pastures is a greater revolution than this;

No vast mountain chain thrown out from ocean depths to form the primitive streak of a new continent looks further down the future;

For this is lava springing out of the very heart of Man;

This is the upheaval of heaven-kissing summits whose streams shall feed the farthest generations,

This is the draft and outline of a new creature,

The forming of the wings of Man beneath the outer husk—

The outspread pinions of Equality, whereon arising he shall at last lift himself over the Earth and launch forth to sail through Heaven.

The Meaning of it All

AGES and ages back,
Out of the long grass with infinite pain raising itself into the upright position,

A creature—fore-runner of Man—with swift eyes glanced around.

So to-day once more,
With pain pain and suffering—driven by what strange instinct—who can tell?

Out of the great jungle of Custom and supposed Necessity, into a new and wonderful life, to new and wonderful knowledge,

Surpassing words, surpassing all past experience—the Man, the meaning of it all,

Uprears himself again.

These Populations

THESE populations—
So puny, white-faced, machine made,

Turned out of factories, out of offices, out of drawing-rooms, by thousands all alike—

Huddled, stitched up, in clothes, fearing a chill, a drop of rain, looking timidly at the sea and sky as at strange monsters, or running back so quick to their suburban runs and burrows,

Dapper, libidinous, cute, with washed-out small eyes—
What are these?

These Populations

Are they men and women?
Each denying himself, hiding himself?
Are they men and women?
So timorous, like hares—a breath of propriety or custom, a draught of wind, the mere threat of pain or of danger?

O for a breath of the sea and the great mountains!
A bronzed hardy live man walking his way through it all;
Thousands of men companioning the waves and the storms, splendid in health, naked-breasted, catching the lion with their hands;
A thousand women swift-footed and free—owners of themselves, forgetful of themselves, in all their actions—full of joy and laughter and action;
Garbed not so differently from the men, joining with them in their games and sports, sharing also their labors;
Free to hold their own, to grant or withhold their love, the same as the men;
Strong, well-equipped in muscle and skill, clear of finesse and affectation—
(The men, too, clear of much brutality and conceit)—
Comrades together, equal in intelligence and adventure,
Trusting without concealment, loving without shame but with discrimination and continence towards a perfect passion.

O for a breath of the sea!

The necessity and directness of the great elements themselves!

Swimming the rivers, braving the sun, the cold, taming the animals and the earth, conquering the air with wings, and each other with love—

The true the human society!

ANDROMEDA

NOW over the Mediterranean shore, fronting the sun,
In the great woods where only the peasant comes
And brings his bottle of wine, and figs, and goat-milk cheese—
The Gods yet dwell, but are not seen of men.

Steeply the ground slopes from the chestnut woods above,
Through tangles of pine and arbutus, myrtle and rosemary,
Down to the sea.
The tasseled evergreen oak grants densest shade—the acacia showers its fragrance on the air;
In open spots the rock-rose blooms,
And the green lizard's little heart beats fast in the sun.

Here all day long mindful of times gone by
The sun yet lingers; from the slumbering sea
(On whose clear sands the yellow and hornéd poppy loves to stray)
Sometimes fair Aphrodite lifts an arm
Unseen of mortals.

The Dryads in the aspen branches wave
Their trembling fingers, and young Hyacinth
Droops earthward once more wounded by his lover.

But none resume their ancient human form.
He, the great Liberator, with the wand of love so wonderful
(Who dwelt on earth, and dwells not, but must dwell again),
He comes not—whom they wait.
The rocks, the trees, the flowers, the loving animals,
The sea, the heavenly winds,
The human form that chained within them all
Pleads for deliverance—
He comes not whom they wait.

Only the train shrieks by with monkey faces staring out of the windows;
Hotel and villa desecrate the land;
Wealth trails its slime; the Greek has fled; and Civilisation like a dismal dragon guards its prey.

The Triumph of Civilisation

ON the outskirts of a great city,
A street of fashionable mansions well withdrawn from all the noise and bustle;
And in the street—the only figure there—in the middle of the road, in the bitter wind,

Red-nosed, thin-shawled, with ancles bare and old boots,
A woman bent and haggard, croaking a dismal song.

And the great windows stare upon her wretchedness, and stare across the road upon each other,
With big fool eyes;
But not a door is opened, not a face is seen,
Nor form of life down all the dreary street,
To certify the existence of humanity—
Other than hers.

THE DEAD CHRIST

(After the picture by Fra Bartolomeo)

ONCE more the dead Christ lies—borne down the ages.

O precious head, still fragrant with the box of ointment broken,
O feet for kisses,
Thin shrunken knees, and hands yet worn with toil,
Dear Mother bending over, breathing clouds
Of love and pity!
Ah! the cruel fate!
Sweet lips she suckled, hands that pressed so small
Against her breasts—pierced now with shameful wounds!
The dead-pale face so gentle, the dear god
She brought forth on the Earth!

O People crucified in every land,
Mothers in all the earth weeping your sons!
Sisters and lovers kissing the feet of love,
Poor way-worn feet, gross toil-disfigured hands,
So loved, so loved!

Once more the dead Christ lies—borne down the ages.

Christmas Eve

Hark! the bells ringing!
In the deep night, in the depth of the winter of Man,
Lo! once more the son is born.

O agelong, not in Nazareth alone,
Nor now to-day—but through all ages of the past,
The bells of Christmas ringing:
The Savior-music like a dream from heaven
Touching the slumbering heart.

Sweet promise which the people with unerring instinct cling to!
O winter sun arising never more to set!
O Nature slowly changing, slow transforming to the hearts of men,
Shrine of the soul, shrine of the new-born god—of Man himself.

Little heart within thy cage so many years—year after year—
Beating, still beating, so tenderly yearning
For Comrade love, the love which is to come:
Often near stopping, or wounded like a bird, so full of pain—thy thread of life almost snapt—
Yet with joy so wonderful over all and through all continuing:

Soon altogether shalt thou stop, little heart, and the beating and the pain here shall cease;
But out of thee that life breathed into the lips of others shall never stop nor cease.
Through a thousand beautiful forms—so beautiful!—through the gates of a thousand hearts—emancipated freed we will pass on:
I and my joy will surely pass on.

When I am near to You

Now when I am near to you, dear friend,
    Passing out of myself, being delivered—
Through those eyes and lips and hands, so loved, so ardently loved,
    I am become free;
    In the sound of your voice I dwell
    As in a world defended from evil.

What I am accounted by the world to be—all that I leave behind:
    It is nothing to me any longer.
Like one who leaves a house with all its mouldy old furniture and pitches his camp under heaven's blue,
    So I take up my abode in your presence—
    I find my deliverance in you.

Cradled in Flame

Cradled in flame,
    Or like a tiny charm-figure within an agate reclining, from that which encloses it inseparate, indivisible—
    So, deep in my heart, through all that chances,
    Thy form, thy form, indelible remains.

All Night Long

ALL night long in love, in the darkness, passing through your lips, my love—
Breathing the same breath, being folded in the same sleep, losing sense of Me and Thee,
Into empyreal regions, beloved of the gods, united, we ascend together.

Then in the morning on the high hill-side in the sun, looking down upon the spires of the larches and Scotch firs,
Mortal, we tread again the earthy floor.

O Earth, the floor of heaven—
O Sun, shining aloft in the sky so pure—
O children of the sun, ye flowers and streams, and little mortals walking the earth for a time—
And we too gazing for a time, for a time, for a time, into each other's eyes.

Of the Past

OF the Past—of those that come no more—
Of the feet that tread the door-sill no more, of the eyes we no more can look into—
The sound of the voice so longed for, but it is not heard,
The one human form sought for over all the world, in all the throngs of cities, by sea-coasts and bays, over far continents and islands,

Among all the habitations of the stars, but it is not there—

Of the self swooning down, dying utterly,
Of love, love, without end and without beginning,
Visiting all mortals, the sum of human life,
With wings like a vast bird passing in the night—veiled awful form so close, yet impossible to detain:
Why dear face so white in the night—so white in the moon's faint light as it steals along the hill-top—
Dear face gazing up into mine, dost thou remind me?

Love's Vision

AT night in each other's arms,
Content, overjoyed, resting deep deep down in the darkness,
Lo! the heavens opened and He appeared—
Whom no mortal eye may see,
Whom no eye clouded with Care,
Whom none who seeks after this or that, whom none who has not escaped from self.

There—in the region of Equality, in the world of Freedom no longer limited,
Standing as a lofty peak in heaven above the clouds,
From below hidden, yet to all who pass into that region most clearly visible—
He the Eternal appeared.

Nearer than Ever Now

IF I should be taken up into Thee, O blue blue sky—to pass the bounds of myself, to share thy life, O Nature:

Pouring pouring upon all the words which now are distilled only painfully from me—pressed out, expressed—

To mingle my breath with Thy breath, my body and its liquids with the earth and the sea—losing my mortal outline in Thine:

Ah! unto those that I love swiftly running I would become their life,

Nearer would I touch them then, than ever now that I am prisoned in this form.

O Thou Whose Form

O THOU whose form is ever in my heart,
    O flesh that holds me pent with terrible force,
Dear limbs and lips that seize upon my life
And in your fire consume it—O sweet love:
Lo all I see—
The clear and sunny hills, the woods, the streams,
The orchards, fields, the lines of poplars tall,
The belfried towns, the river at my feet,
The great blue sky, yea He who stands behind it—
Are mine for thee, to lose themselves in thee.

THE ELDER SOLDIER IN THE BROTHERHOOD TO THE YOUNGER

DEAR comrade, at whose feet thus now I kneel,
    Of you perhaps so soon to be seen no more—
Here I give you my charge, that afterwards remembering and desiring me,
You may find me again in these others.

Slowly out of their faces I will emerge to you—lo! I swear it,
By the falling rain and dimpled thunderclouds in the East I swear it—
[To become your life whom I have loved so long]
With love absorbing, joy and blessedness enclosing,
I will emerge to you.

That you now to other comrades, and these again to others,
Over the whole world may bear the glad covenant, perfected, finished—
To form an indissoluble union and compact, a brotherhood unalterable,
Far-pervading, fresh and invisible as the wind, united in Freedom—
A golden circle of stamens, hidden beneath the petals of humanity,
And guarding the sacred ark.

Through heroisms and deaths and sacrifices,

Always for the poor and despised, always for the outcast and oppressed,

Through kinship with Nature, and the free handling of all forms and customs,

Through the treasured teaching of inspired ones—never lost and never wholly given to the world, but always emerging—

Through love, faithful love and comradeship, at last emancipating the soul into that other realm (of freedom and joy) into which it is permitted to no mortal to enter—

Thus to realise the indissoluble compact, to reveal the form of humanity.

To you, dear comrade, I transmit this charge—bequeathed also to me—

In love remaining faithful to you, as now, never to change,

Through all times and vicissitudes faithful faithful to you.

Here now at your feet, leaning on your knees, in your eyes deep-looking,

All that I have said I confirm.

INTO THE REGIONS OF THE SUN

So at last passing (the great sea stilled, the raging ocean)—passing away,

All sorrow left behind, the great intolerable burdens which men vainly try to carry,

All all abandoned, left there lying—

Into the Regions of the Sun

Suddenly lightened, like a bird that shakes itself free from the limed twigs,
Soaring, soaring, into joy supernal passing,
Lo! the dead we leave behind and pass to the realms of the living.

And not we alone.
By our love poured out, by the manifold threads and strands of attachment to others — which cannot now be severed;
By not one inwardly refused or disowned whom we have ever met;
By the dear arms of lovers circling each other all night long, by their kisses and mingled breath,
And love by night and day—thinking of each other when absent, rejoicing so to be near;
By tramps over the hills, and days spent together in the woods and by watersides;
By our life-long faithful love—(ah! what more beautiful, what in all this world more precious!)
By the life-long faithful comradeship now springing on all sides, the Theban band henceforth to overcome the world—its heroisms and deaths—
And him who gave the calamus-token first;
By all these—
Not alone, no longer alone—

But drawing an innumerable multitude with us,
Into the regions of the sun, into the supernal æther,

With love perfected, bodies changed, and joy—ah! joy on earth unutterable—

Lo! the dead we leave behind, and pass to the realms of the living.

As it Happened

CROSS-LEGGED in a low tailor's den, gasping for breath—

The gas flaring, doors and windows tight shut, the thick sick atmosphere;

The men in their shirt-sleeves, with close heat from the stove, and smell of sweat and of the cloth;

Stitching, stitching, 12 hours a day, no set time for meals—

Stitching, cross-stitching, button-holing, binding,
Silk twist, cotton twist, black thread, white thread,
Stouting, felling, pressing, damping,
Basting, seaming, opening seams, rantering,
With sore eyes, sick sick at heart, and furious,
In the low tailor's den he sits.

All day in his mind—like a hunted criminal—he revolves: How shall I escape?

How change this miserable pittance for Freedom, and yet not starve?

At night after some brief dream of joy he wakes to tears, tears, tears—

Drenching his bed with tears.

As it Happened

No God, no Truth, no Justice—and under it all, no Love.

[This is what is slowly killing him—no Love.]

A little fire burns in his heart, burns night and day; The slow pain kills—no Love.

O the deep deep hunger!

The mean life all around, the wolfish eyes, the mere struggle for existence, as of men starving on a raft at sea—no room for anything more.

All that he has read in books, all the stories of other times and lands—Mignon, Eloise, Eros the beautiful boy wandering over the world—so wonderful a world, and he in this prison, this filthy den!

O the deep deep hunger of Love!

All the obscene talk of the shop is neither here nor there: it cannot fill the void:

The shallow laughter of his companions and the bought kisses of the street-girls are the mere husks that the swine did eat.

O little heart, beating, beating!

Heart once so strong, full-pulsed; now often at night out of some dream of Splendor—

[Dream of Love—some shining form within a garden and at the gate stands a bearded man, dagger in hand, saying "Thou canst not enter here, except thou pass the Ordeal."

And he in his dream, beholding Love beyond, bares

his breast gladly to the knife, and feels the sharp point turn within his heart]—

　　Waking thus oft to pain and sick sick powerless days,
　　At last little heart thy strength gives way indeed.
　　Stumbling, with strange uncertain motion, like one confused—now hurrying on,
　　Now halting in thy pace as near to stop,
　　That something's wrong with thee is past a doubt.

　　And the grave doctor comes and says the valves are weak, and recommends rest and good food and fresh air and other things that are not to be had: but says nothing of that which lies nearest to the patient.
　　And he, the patient, half misdoubts himself—thinks likely the doctor knows best—feels only strangely dull and indifferent; and after a while rises and goes back to his den and takes his place once more cross-legged amongst the rest, stitching, stitching; and the horns on his heel and ancle grow again, and the air seems closer and more suffocating than ever; but he drags through the days, ever more lethargic growing, caring not much whether he die or live—thinking perhaps to die on the whole were better.

　　When, as it happened—and this was the strangest of all—quite suddenly, the most unexpected thing in the world,
　　To a casual little club, which once a week he was in the habit of attending, there came one night a new member,
　　Of athletic strength and beauty, yet gentle in his manners,

And with a face like a star—so stedfast clear and true that he the sufferer felt renewed by merely looking on it.

But what was even more strange, the newcomer turning spoke friendly to him, and soon seemed to understand,

And from that time forward came and companioned and nursed him, and stayed whole nights and days with him and loved him.

And out of his despair there grew something so glorious that he forgets it not, night nor day;

Great waves of health and strength come to him—as to a man who after the long Arctic night bathes in the warmth and light of the re-arisen Sun;

Even the wretched tailor's den is transformed; but soon leaving that he accepts by preference the poorest work in the open under heaven,

And breathes again, and tastes the sweet air afresh;

And watches a new sun rise in the mornings and a new transparency among the stars at night;

And the body grows strong and hardy, and the little heart gathers and knits itself together,

And sings, sings, sings:

Sings all day to its friend whether present or absent.

PARTED LIPS

PARTED lips, between which love dwells—
    Only a little space of breath and shadow,
Yet here the gate of all the world to me

SUMMER HEAT

SUN burning down on back and loins, penetrating the skin, bathing their flanks in sweat,
    Where they lie naked on the warm ground, and the ferns arch over them,
    Out in the woods, and the sweet scent of fir-needles
    Blends with the fragrant nearness of their bodies;

    In-armed together, murmuring, talking,
    Drunk with wine of Eros' lips,
    Hourlong, while the great wind rushes in the branches,
    And the blue above lies deep beyond the fern-fronds and fir-tips;

    Till, with the midday sun, fierce scorching, smiting,
    Up from their woodland lair they leap, and smite,
    And strike with wands, and wrestle, and bruise each other,
    In savage play and amorous despite.

A RIVEDERCI

ONCE more in dreams, wandering along the road by the sea,
    I tarry a moment leaning my elbows on the wall beside you—
    I look out over the blue waves with your eyes, and feel the sun on me as you that feel it;
    My mother it is that sits in the balcony among her

pots of oleander in the little narrow street, my boat that lies half-heeled upon the sand;
> These are my mountains that I love,
> This is your face and mine clear-cut upon the air,
> Your life-warm lips I kiss and mine you kiss again,
> And laughing part with bright *a rivederci*.

WHO WILL LEARN FREEDOM?

WHO will learn Freedom?

Lo! as the air blows wafting the clinging aromatic scent of the balsam poplar, dear to me,

Or the sun-warm fragrance of wallflowers, tarrying here for a moment, then floating far down the road and away;

Or as the early light edging the hills, so calm, unprejudiced, open to all;

So shall you find what you seek in men and women—your passage and swift deliverance.

As when one opens a door after long confinement in the house—so out of your own plans and purposes escaping,

Out of the many mirror-lined chambers of self (grand though they be, but O how dreary!) in which you have hitherto spent your life—

In these behold once more the incommunicable freedom of the sky, the green hills, the woods and the waters,

To pass in and out for ever, having abandoned your own objects, looking calmly upon them, as though they did not exist.

Now who so despised and lost, but what shall be my Savior?

Is there one yet sick and suffering in the whole world? or deformed, condemned, degraded?

Thither hastening I am at rest—for this one can absolve me.

O I am greedy of love—all all are beautiful to me!

You my deliverers every one—from death, from sin, from evil—

I float, I dissolve in you!

O bars of self you cannot shut me now.

O frailest child, O blackest criminal,

Whoe'er you are I never can repay you—though the world despise you, you are glorious to me;

For you have saved me from myself,

You delivered me when I was in prison—

I passed through you into heaven,

You were my Christ to me.

After all Suffering

AFTER all suffering, after all weariness and denial—
The heart almost stopped, food ceasing to nourish, grief making the tongue dry,

All pleasure in life ceasing, unable to rouse interest in any object or pursuit,

But love—and that gone far away!

After all,

Nearer to thy heart, O humanity,

By this of suffering we come.

I know that thou canst not deny me:
I know that each pain is a door by which I approach one degree nearer to thee.
What sorrow is there but I have shared it?
What grief but it has removed an obstruction between me and some one else?
Look in my face and see. You cannot bar me now.
I pass all doors, and am where I would be.

When a Thousand Years have Passed

THINK not that the love thou enterest into to-day is for a few months or years:
The little seed set now must lie quiet before it will germinate, and many alternations of sunshine and shower descend upon it before it become even a small plant.
When a thousand years have passed, come thou again. And behold! a mighty tree that no storms can shake.

Love does not end with this life or any number of lives; the form that thou seekest lies hidden under wrapping after wrapping;
Nevertheless it shall at length appear—more wondrous far than aught thou hast imagined.
Therefore leave time: do not like a child pull thy flower up by the roots to see if it is growing;
Even though thou be old and near the grave there is plenty of time.

A Message Committed to the Waves

I SEE the waters flowing as of old—dancing, rippling, O so light and beautiful;
The river-banks, and pollard willows leaning, and bulrushes where as boys we used to linger.

All transmuted, turned into words and tongues, licking me round like flames—unearthly, scorching;
All transmuted—the soft water-depths, the weeds below, the dimples of sunlight dancing,
The shrill piping of the lark, the kine knee-deep in grass, and the piled thunderclouds floating in the summer haze—
Like flames, unearthly, scorching.

For here on this water and round these banks we came floating—troops of friends—yet not on this water; by these banks, yet not by them.
And the dimples glanced, and the birds sang—as now, yet O how different!

Mystery, mystery!
O wonderful orb of creation!
O frame, beauteous ever-living twining frame of human love, chalice of precious drops poured out, mystic scroll on which our lives in blood are written,
Great great awful indivisible Nature—birthplace and grave of Humanity!

A Message to the Waves

Tremble tremble, O waves—bear my love too on your breasts to generations yet unborn;

(Lo! to you I commit it!)

Hear me ye perennial tongues and flames, ye fields and skies speak speak what I command you!

Ye hieroglyphics stand untampered to remotest time!

O grasses growing so lush about my feet and the feet of those who pass, while ever you grow on earth forget not the bleeding drops wherewith you have been watered!

Waft, O breezes, our love and the love of all true lovers, and fail not while you blow to bring glad messages to those who faint;

For we are borne upon you—

I am borne upon you. From this body, broken and useless, from this mortal here and there, I fade, I fail utterly; I cannot remain, it is no use;

Pouring pouring out, losing my name and place, flowing abroad, surrendering myself to all—I depart, to join the invisible.

Ah heaven! Ah sounds of harmony ineffable!

Ah tears, and deeps of sorrow dread and soundless!

Ah love! ah precious love including all!

So still to all—

To those lingering in prison,

To the aged and forsaken, stranded like wrecks on the bleak shore of life,

To the heartbroken and weary, to those stunned with despair;

To the wife awaking to the treachery of her husband;

To the exile leaving his dear ones, and probably for ever; to the crippled and incapable and diseased;

To the pinned workers in back streets oscillating drearily between the home and the workshop;

To those of the hopeless sad mechanical days over all the earth—the outcast, the shunned, the persecuted;

The closing days, the narrowing grooves, the heart touched no more by the sweet illusions, no more to hope responding, no more to the call of religion;

Ah to all in the mighty brotherhood sufferers—

Dearest, most precious ones,

Corner-stones of human life, hidden bearers of burdens, under-girders of the great ship with its incalculable freight!

Dearest and most precious of all—ah, sufferers, sufferers,

To you we give our love—

Arise! for great is your triumph!

Rest at Last

AH! love—having journeyed through all of life, having become freed even from thee—there remains nothing glorious but thee.

Exhaled out of all frailty, out of this little tenement of flesh, so ephemeral,

Out of these hands and feet which are and are not

—out of these eyes through which I look, on which I look—

Thou hast taken possession of earth and heaven: the sun is thy right hand and the moon thy left:
In Thee all forms, of all I seek, are mine,
And I in them attain at last to rest.

The Wind of May

O GLORIOUS wind, that in my lover's face blowest,
    Even as now in mine—though the deep sea part us—
Fragrant wind, with heart so tenderly laden,
Tell him, my lover, against whose face thou goest,
In his ears and nostrils and eyes and thick hair rippling—
Whose passion-fountain he too, nightlong, daylong,
Drinks at, inbreathing thee—sweet wind, O tell him
My love like thine for ever endures, and fails not.

Great cloud-wet wind, through the thick woods heavily trailing,
Mid millions of flowers their sex-life's sweetness exhaling,
Hyacinth-bell and May-bloom in countless beauty:
Feed him, body and soul, with secrets fairest,
Disclose thy heart, O wind, and the love thou bearest.

O Earth, scene of what toil and anguish!
Century after century, thousands thousands of years,
What reek of battles, smoke of vast wilderness-cities,
Going up from age to age, losing itself in the calm immeasurable blue.

O wonderful unutterable secret! the moon gliding through the trees!
The soul of man slowly transforming itself, growing bursting through the sheaths—the stars looking on!
The new creature born anew, in travail and in suffering, ascending into heaven;
Ah! songs and harmonies angelic sounding—ah! joy the mortal frame can scarce sustain!

A Voice over the Earth

THE sound of a voice floating round the Earth, saying:
Lo! I float over the world and over all cities and lands—wherever men and women are at home I am at home

The snowy peaks, in ranges, that guard the cradles of the human race—rising over their rocky cliffs, out of their valleys full of trees—the wind fluctuating the forests, the clouds swift-flying over the topmost jags;

The great plains, and lower lands, dotted with farms and villages and cities, for scores, hundreds, thousands, of miles;

The winding rivers and the islands, and the broad seas;

All these I see, and those that inhabit them,

Over the world I float, I range all human experience.

II

The broad Italian landscape spreads below me—the lands of the upper Po and Bormida;

I see the wave-like congregated hills terraced with vines to their very tops, the pink or yellow painted homesteads dotted here and there, the arched stone barns, and villages clustered on the hill tops with belfries high against the sky.

The old woman, my mother, with walnut brown skin

haunts the lonely farmhouse all day while the others are in the field;

She wanders from chamber to chamber, hardly knowing what she is doing. Her memory carries her back to the far past—she lives not in the present.

Sometimes into the great attic overhead she climbs, with its huge roof-beams and brick floor, and spreads the grapes to dry or leisurely picks them over.

The haymakers work barefoot in the clover patch, turning the clover and loading the low-wheeled waggon in the fragrant transparent evening;

The peasant plows with his one-stilted plow, or creaks along the road with his cart and yoke of cream-colored oxen;

The girls and women with red or yellow kerchiefs stand among the branches of the mulberry trees by the roadside, picking leaves for the silkworms;

The country folk congregate on the steps of the village church, looking out over the hills—the women passing in by ones and twos;

The men play *mora* over their wine in the little hostelry; the boys play at ball down the narrow by-streets, using the roofs and buttresses to baffle their opponents' strokes;

The old play of daily life goes on—the centuries-long play;

The ruins of the Roman aqueduct still cross the bed of the river, the ruins of Roman words and customs still lie embedded in the life of to-day;

The old blood still runs in the veins, the water runs

A Voice Over the Earth

in the rivers, the crops grow in the fields—the light of youth, of love, of old age, of death, shines in the eyes.

From the accident of here and now,
From this hill whence for a moment I overlook the fair garden of human life, from this few feet of human flesh which I inhabit,
From these fierce desires which hem me in, these defects, these limitations, these mortal sufferings,
This little creature-dom, this brief emprisonment of life,
I descend, I pass, I flow down,
[O words so vain to tell—O strange incredible transformation!]
I pass, I flow down, into the freedom of all times, into the latitude of all places.

I work on the hills once more with the slave and the freedman among the vines, I mix the mortar for them that build the aqueduct;
The lover and his girl lean against my breast in the moonlight long ages back as now;
The face of the mother understands my face a thousand and ten thousand years ago, as it does to-day;
I am the cream-colored ox with mild eyes, and I am the driver who curses and goads it;
I am the lover and the loved—I have lost and found my identity.

III

The Piedmontese peasant takes me again into his little cottage of sun-dried bricks among the vineyards, and gives me a glass of cool wine in the shade;

I see again the scantily furnished interior, the floor of native rock, the rickety ladder which serves for staircase to the chamber above, the table and chairs and one or two cooking utensils;

And the great frame of sticks and canes, big as a four-poster bedstead, where he breeds his thousands of silkworms.

But here too, alas! there is grief; for the poor son, so passionately loved of his mother, is wasting away apparently in a decline;

All day with shawl thrown over him he squats in the sun by the door, or walks feebly to and fro, unable to help his father in the field—at night he lies awake and hears the wearisome rustle of the silkworms eating their food;

The mother prays the good God, but knows not whether anything comes of it—the little figure of Mary in the niche of the wall looks just the same though hearts are breaking.

IV

Ah! fragrance of human love exhaled!

Great clouds from frail and perishable forms escaping silently,

Into the night, into the vast aerial night of Time!

The little flash of youth, the reaching of hands to hands, of hearts to hearts, of lips to lips,

The closing in of the outer shell, the chrysalis-death, and the terrible struggles for liberation;

The larvæ crawling the earth for a time—on hill-sides and in valleys, in huts and palaces—chained to their little plots of earth, their few frail feet of flesh;

The great thunderclouds passing over from snowy range to range, touching the little creatures with their shadows;

The great sun out of the unfathomable touching them too with his finger—breeding slowly but surely within them the life which must destroy their mortality.

V

Onwards, onwards, I float.

The smoke and glare, the confused roar and tumult of a manufacturing town spread all around; sounds of voices ascend past me into the silent supernal blue.

In the tobacco factory amid rows of girls, with my little bit of mirror or comb concealed in a nook of my bench— I sit—or photograph placed where I can see it as I work;

Or in the printing office of the daily paper—printing reports of law-courts and cricket-matches—I scramble with five or six others to the boxes for a fat take.

The long trial is over, and I am the prisoner on whom sentence has been pronounced.

The judge in scarlet and ermine, preceded by liveried heralds blowing trumpets, strides down the corridors and through the crowd thronging the steps of the Town Hall, into his blue and silver paneled coach;

Hustled and thumped and buffeted by the police, I am fetched from the dock by underground passages to the prison van, and bumped through the streets to the gaol—there to await my execution.

Pale and desperate in the cutlery buffing shop boys and girls bend over their wheels;

In squalor and monotony the winter daylight through dirty windows dawns and dies away again upon them;

In squalor and monotony the light of youth and of hope dawns and dies away again from their eyes;

The master looks round with his hands in his pockets, well satisfied;

The cheap goods ready to fall to pieces as soon as used are duly packed and despatched to African and Pacific Island traders.

Civilisation plays its part in the history of each nation and each individual,

Unerringly the time of its unfoldment to each arrives, and again the time of its dismissal and departure.

Brawny figures move to and fro in the iron works, half-seen through clouds of flying steam or against the glare of furnaces;

The flame of the Bessemer cupola roars, with showers of sparks, and rattling of cranes, and shouts of men;

A Voice Over the Earth

The foreman stands calmly aside, spectroscope in hand, or gives a signal with uplifted arm;

I see the reversing of the cupola, and the outpour of molten steel, lilac with yellowing vapor around it;

The rose-colored shafts of sunlight through the high roof, the terraces and platforms, the glints and halos amid the vapor;

The balcony where the men stand with their hydraulic handles controlling the huge lifts and cranes beneath them;

The groups steadying with iron poles and hooks the great lifted ingots of steel, or regulating the outflow of liquid stuff into the moulds;

The man in a corner washing his shoulders and head in a bucket of water;

The steam-hammers, the blocks of yellow-hot iron shimmering in the heated air;

The steel-melter's men around the crucibles with their tongs—their feet and legs swathed in rags to keep off the heat, their sweat-handkerchiefs held between their teeth;

The daring, recklessness even at times, the delight in the power and endurance—the drink, gross talk, rough jokes—throwing the great pressures upon the novices or shamming to pick quarrels with them;

The planing and cutting of armor-plates, the huge resistless steam-driven machinery, the gouges and drills,

The shaping of the plates (each one numbered) to the lines of the ships they are intended for—the careful drawing and planning, and following out of the plans;

The transporting of them to the sea-coast, the riveting of them each in its place;

And the floating away of these thousands of tons over the ocean and round the bend of the world.

And he at the forge streaming with sweat, the striker, with bared breast, turning out claw-hammer heads by the score,
Keeps dreaming and dreaming all day between the strokes, of love which is to come and change our earth into heaven;
But his brother who works with him laughs at his dreams—and the spring comes in the woods to all alike:
The gnarled oak breaks into pale yellow buds against the blue, the mouse stirs under the dry grass, and the corn-crake runs with head erect among the young green blades of corn.

VI

Each morning anew the mist rests on the hills; the sun rises on fresh clouds to be dispersed;
It splinters its shafts against the great rock face, and brings out in bold relief the figure of the quarryman in his loose blue-checked shirt;
Where on a projecting angle he stands, with mighty hammer-stroke driving the brods and wedges;
Now he splits off a great mass and displaces it with the crowbar,
While overhead among the tree-roots, in a sunny niche of the barings,
A sparrow chirps cheerfully to him.

Meanwhile the scythe-smith goes to see what he can do for his brother in prison;

He takes the train and finds out the public-house to which the turnkey goes, and gives him half-a-sovereign to get his brother something to eat.

The turnkey is a mild old man and would not willingly harm anybody;

He says nothing to the prisoner, but when he leaves his cell each day he quietly drops a good-sized tommy behind him.

And this is the Hogarthian interior of the Lincolnshire dancing chamber: the gas, the smoke, the fiddle-scrape, the slopped drink;

The great projecting bay-window with seats in it, the twilight fading on the groups in the market-place without;

The Dutch-looking ramshackle rooms lighting into one another—farmers' men and girls tumbling and sitting on each other's knees;

Fat women gyrating together; the young man pressing his comrade to him in the dance;

The middle-aged farmer slipping off into a barn at the back with a great wench: she cries, "How good, how good it is, O come again!"

In the Chamber of Birth

IN the chamber of birth,
　　Calm and joyful the exhausted mother, with disheveled hair, lies obliquely across the bed—the little primitive conical-skulled god rests snug on the pillow in front of her:

The baffling infant face, with closed eyes and flexible upper lip, and storms and sunshine sweeping across its tiny orb, and filmy clouds of expression!

But for her O the rest, the rest and the peace now it is all over—no desire to move, only to lie and rest for joy!

While the bustling cheerful midwife is full of praises and congratulations, and the good anxious husband comes to the door smiling again at last.

A Cottage among the Hills

OUTSIDE, the winter moonlight shines so peacefully upon the little cottage far away among the hills—
Where within the old human drama repeats itself.

The aged grandmother sits in the ruddy glow by the chimney-corner—her little grandson leans against her knee;

The other children (for some have come in from a neighboring cottage, and Christmas is now approaching) sing hymn after hymn in tireless trebles, and the old grand-dad tones the bass in now and then with still melodious voice;

While silent, with tired and suffering face (thinking of the week's work, and of her runaway drunken husband) the mother strips her youngest naked in the firelight.

Ah! the tender dreams, the griefs, the passions, and the shattered hopes!

The long culminating experience!

The slow change of the words the children sing—to meanings unimagined!

The flickering light on joists and rafters of the low ceiling;

The old man bent with toil (road-mending now these fifty years);

The rosy children with wide open mouths; the dear god whom they sing of—ever-coming, ever-expected;

The rose-bud black-eyed boy against his granny's knee;

And she—her white white hair, high brows, and pale transparent face—so sacred, calm,

Most like the moonlight shining there without.

ALICE

WITH little red frock in the fire-light, in the lingering April evening—

(The moonlight over the tree-tops just beginning to shine in at the cottage door)—

Her big brown eyes and comical big mouth for very gladness unresting, like a small brown fairy—

She stands, the five-year-old child.

Then, so gentle, with tiny tripping speech, and with a little wave of the hand—

"Good-night" she says to the fire and to the moon,
And kissing the elder wearier faces,
Runs off to bed and to sleep in the lap of heaven.

Baby Song

Croonie croonie, Baby baby, up and down,
  Sing song, all day long—
Father's gone away for many a day, but he'll come back again,
Over the waters, before long.

Croonie croonie, Baby baby, up and down,
Sun shine, winds blow—far behind baby the waters flow;
Winds and sun round him run, peep in his eyes and off they go—
All in fun.

Croonie croonie, Baby baby, O what tears!
Little heart break, little breast shake—fie such tears!
Mother's arms so tired with dancing,
All day long;
Baby baby—always baby—fretting crying all day long.

Baby baby, come to Mammy,
Stifle sobs upon her breast—
Little blunt gums on the nipple,
That's the feel we both love best;
Sleep will soon come after titty,
Sobs will cease and baby rest.

Croonie croonie, Baby baby, sleeping sound:
By the door we stand a moment—moonlight dappled on the ground:
Winds are sleeping, waters calm,
Keep our little babe from harm.

The great Earth shall be his cradle,
Rocking rocking day by day;
Star-bespangled curtains spread
Every night above his head;
Suns on suns shall gild his brow:
Baby baby, What art Thou?

Early Morning

THE thrush sings meditative high in the bare oak-boughs—while the still April morning just drops with faint rain, and the honeysuckle climbs snakelike with green wings among the underwood;
The voice of the ploughman sounds across the valley, and the cackle of the farmyard mingles with the rumble of a distant train on its way to the great city:

Where, in her boudoir, by the light of the dying fire—the shutters yet closed and the candles guttered and gone out—she lies, the Paris beauty, naked on her low tiger-skin couch;
And he, her lover, naked too, on the floor beside her has slipped—his head bent forward, and asleep—with her hand in his dark short hair.

The Golden Wedding

NOW fifty years through wind and sun and rain,
    Through the sweet heyday of youth, through life's maturity and age,
    We've bloomed and withered, dearest, side by side,
    Two trees upon one root.

Rememberest thou
How hand in hand schoolwards we ran, we two,
With tiny feet? Yes, we two, is it not strange?
Or later how the merry pealing bells rang us to Church (no music I thought like them);
    Then we reared five children, fell on troublous times, and toiled and suffered till we tired of life.
    And they went one by one, and launched upon the world and sailed away,
    Proud, with all canvas set, while we are left,
    Old battered wrecks—here in this cottage of the hills—and wondering
    Which the great waves of time will first wash down.

    And now dearest one, through all this lapse of years I look into your eyes,
    And see them deep as ever;
    Their beauty is to me a passion just as ever,
    Voiceless, unfathomable, that no time can touch.

If the great gulf should come and swallow me in sheer oblivion—still it is good to have known thee;
But that thou should'st die,
That thou should'st perish from thyself and cease to be,
I cannot credit. Somewhere nearer God,
When this thick mortal slumber has gone by,
We shall perchance awaken.

THE MOTHER TO HER DAUGHTER

BEAUTIFUL child that launchest out on the great sea of life,
Soon I, thy Mother, must leave thee: soon the dark shall close me in, and leave thee alone in the bright sunshine.

And thy lovers shall come and make love to thee: they shall lay their fortunes at thy feet, and their strength and the glory of their manhood;

They shall desire thee, for thou art beautiful as the silver sickle moon arising in heaven before the dawn.

Yet when they come forget not me, O my child: be not deceived by their words;

For none ever again shall love thee as I love thee, none ever again shall know, as I know, thy hidden thoughts—none shall read the light that plays upon thy face as I can read it.

These shall love thee for themselves: they shall seek thee in order to possess thee; but I have given all that I have to thee.

All the years that we have been together since thou

first pressed thy tiny palm upon my breast to look into my face, until now;

I have given myself to thee.

Before thy feet, or ever thou couldst walk, my love has walked, my thoughts have circled thee, my desire has made thee very beautiful.

If I might pray, I pray that when thou hast known the love of man

Thou, too, may'st become a mother, and so even through travail and suffering may'st know the greater love.

Then far away down the years thou shalt remember me;

As when one ascends a mountain the opposite mountain lifts itself higher and higher, so as thou goest farther from me I will grow upon thee clearer and closer even than now.

A Sprig of Aristocracy

Browned by the sun, with face elate and joyous,
Pitching hay all day in the wide and fragrant hayfields,

Frank and free, careless of wealth (preferring to do something useful, and to champion the poor and aged)—

O splendid boy, with many more like thee,

England might from her unclean wallowing rise again and live.

A Scene in London

Both of them deaf, and close on eighty years old;
She stone blind, and he nearly so;

Side by side crouching over the fire in a little London hovel—six shillings a week—

Their joints knotted with rheumatism, their faces all day long mute like statues of all passing expression (no cloud flying by, no gleam of sunshine there)—lips closed and silent:

But for that now and then taking his pipe out of his mouth,

He puts his face close to her ear and yells just a word into it,

And she nods her blind head and gives a raucous screech in answer.

S. JAMES' PARK

AN island ringed with surf—
A cool green shade and tiny enchanted spot of trees and flowers and fountains—

The ocean raging round it.

The roar of London interminably stretching, interminably sounding,

Great waves of human life breaking, millions of drops together, torrents of vehicles pouring, business men marching, gangs of workmen, soldiers, loafers, street hawkers;

Shopkeepers running out of their shops to look at their own windows, a woman seized with birth-pangs on a doorstep, ragamuffins and children swirling by eddies and rapids of fashion;

The everlasting tide, ebbing a little at night rising again in the day—with fierce continuous roaring—
Yet infringing not on the little island.

Here only a little spray, a dull and distant reverberation;
In the soft shade a pleasant drowsy air, the willows hanging their branches to the water;
The drake preening his feathers in the sun, or swimming among the flags by the pond side, regardless of Nelson peering over the tree-tops from his column, taking no note of the great clock-face of Westminster.

Only a little spray, broken water.
Drop by drop, one by one, or here and there in twos, Specimens, items out of the deep.
The baker's man, working 15 hours a day, leaves his handcart in a convenient spot outside and puts in a quiet quarter of an hour here with a novel;
The old woman—her thumb gathered and disabled by incessant work on crape—now as a matter of course thrown out of employ—goes along moaning and muttering to herself;
The pursy old gentleman who has made his money out of the mourning warehouse also goes along;
The footman on an errand walks leisurely by, the French nurse plays with the little English children;
The rather elegant young lady meets her man by appointment at one of the garden seats; they study Bradshaw together in an undertone, revolving plans;

The middle-aged widower comes along—thin, so thin, dressed all in black, seeing nothing, hearing nothing—sitting down for a moment, then up again—resting only in constant movement;

The tramp, with dead expressionless face—the man who is not wanted, to whom every one says No—comes along, and throws himself listlessly down under the trees.

Only a little spray, broken water.
The summer sun falls peaceful on the grass,
The tide of traffic rises a little during the day and ebbs again at night,
But the great roaring bates not—breaks the surf
Of human life forever on this shore.

The Twin Statues of Amenophis III at Thebes

THOUSANDS of years—
As now with the light of evening on their heads and featureless faces, their bases wrapt in gloom—

All the hours before dawn or after sunset, in the clear circling of the moon and stars, or through the long cloudless day, braving the terrific heat,

While the caravans of camels go by below, and the peasant ploughs with his ancient plough, or reaps his clover and lupins—century after century;

And the flood-waters of the Nile wash up and recede

again, and the sun darkens in the occasional sandstorm or rarer shower of rain—

Thousands of years:

Like great rocks, human, colossal, part of the Earth itself,
Cosmic, wondrous, far-back allegories of the human soul,
They sit looking out over the world while the generations pass.

And the travelers come and gaze—and go away again, wondering what they meant who made such things;
The philosophers of Greece come, and Alexander comes, and the Roman Emperors come; and the Christian fathers and monks (fit successors of the Egyptian), and the Mahomedan conquerors, and Napoleon, and the scientific men, come—and go away again;
And the wandering Arabs come and light their campfires—and go away again; and the Cook's tourist comes and goes away again;
And the river changes its course, and the mountains crumble in the heat of the sun, and the sandhills shift, and villages are built and are buried;
But of him who placed the figures there these words do survive:—

"I, Amenhotep, have made the name of the king immortal, and no one has ever done as I have in my works;
I made these two statues of the king—wondrous huge and high, forty cubits, dwarfing the Temple front—

In the great sandstone mountains I made them, one on each side, east and west;
And I caused eight ships to be built, whereon they were floated up the river;
And placed them here—to last as long as heaven."

'Artemidorus, farewell'
(inscribed on a mummy case in the British Museum)

ARTEMIDORUS, farewell.
No more no more thy dear lips shall I touch,
Nor kiss thy hands—those clinging hands in mine;
Thy gentle eyes—ah! shall we never gaze
Again upon each other?
Artemidorus, dearest, dearest one,
Leave me, O leave me not.

All the sweet hours that by the Nile we sat
In palm-tree shade, and watched the swallows dip;
Or when we first met at the sacred tank
Deep in the garden grounds of Arsaphes,
And told our secrets (heed'st thou?) to the fishes!
The lotus filling all the air with scent,
The pigeons wheeling, hundreds, overhead—
By our sweet love and laughter, then and since,
A thousand times, and all thy quips and pranks,
Leave me O leave me not.

Where shall I go? what do? why live? O why
Remain when thou art gone? There's nothing left.

The nights so long, with pain pain at my heart;
The days, the staring Sun, and every sight
Shooting an arrow at me.
Could I but see thee once, or hope to see—
One hair of thy head, one finger of thy hand,
To hear one little word more from thy lips—
'Twere more than all the world. But now the priests
Have got thee in their clutches; and already
They wrap the sacred linen o'er thy head,
Thy features and thy hair they cover up,
And round thy arms thy fingers and thy hands
They wind and wind and wind and wind the bands,
And I shall see thee nevermore, my own.
And then they'll paint
Thy likeness on the outer mummy case,
And stand it by the wall, as if to mock me,
Throwing my arms around a lifeless shell,
Breaking my heart against it.

And in a hundred years stray folk will come
And ask, "Who was Artemidorus pray?"
Nor listen for an answer—if in sooth
There's any that can give one. And in time
Strangers perhaps will overrun our land
And violate thy coffin, and unbind
With sacrilegious hands the rags, and find
Only a little dust—Ah! nothing else. . . .
And I shall be a little dust too then . . .
And whether lord Osiris, the good God,

Will hold our twin souls safely in his hand
Three thousand years through internatal forms
Of bird or beast or serpent, in reserve
For that new day they say has yet to dawn;
Or whether He too will chance fade to dust
Forgetting and forgotten of all men—
Behold I know not . . . Only this I know
Of all the words we said in joke or earnest,
And vows we vowed, and solemn troth we plighted,
And all the multitudinous chatter and idle tales
And laughter that we got through, like two streams
That babble for mere gladness down the lands,
Artemidorus dear,
Dearest of all things either in earth or heaven,
For the long silence but one word remains,
Remains but this—"Farewell."

From Turin to Paris

Tireless, hour after hour, over mountains plains and rivers,
The express train rushes on

The shadows change, the sun and moon rise and set;
Day fades into night, and night into day,
The great cities appear and disappear over the horizon.

On through the hot vineyards of Piedmont the express train rushes;

The great-limbed Ligurian peasant sprawls asleep in the third-class carriage which has been put on for a portion of the course;

The calm grave country girls droop their lids to slumber;

The huge unwieldy friar with elephantine limbs, small eyes, and snout like an ant-eater—not a particle of religion in his whole body—gazes blankly out of the window;

And the young mother with black lace on her head looks after her little brood.

On through the hot vineyards in the fierce afternoon the express train rushes—the villages on the hill-tops twinkle through the blaze—the fireman opens the furnace-door of the engine and stokes up again and again.

The first-class passengers dispose themselves as best they may, with blinds down, on the hot and dusty cushions;

The respectable and cold-mutton-faced English gentleman and his wife and daughters, the blasé Chinaman with yellow fan, the little Persian boy so brown, lying asleep against the side of his instructor,

The deeply-lined large-faced shaven old Frenchman, the Italian artist, bearded, nearing forty years old, with expressive mouth and clear discerning eyes,

Dispose themselves as best they may.

The sides of the carriages lie open, like glass.

The young priest fresh from College recites his evensong, then addresses himself to the conversion of his Protestant fellow-traveler—I see his winning manners at first, and then his intimidatory frowns followed by threats of hell-fire;

The group of laughing girls in one compartment are talking three or four languages;

In another an Italian officer leans close in conversation to a yellow-haired young woman, and touches her lightly every now and then on the arm;

In a third sits a bedizened old hag, purveyor of human flesh—with great greedy clever eyes (once beautiful under their still long lashes), deep wrinkles (yet not one of wisdom or of sorrow), and thin cruel lips;

On a frequent errand from London to Italy she travels;

I hear her pious expressions as she talks to the lady sitting opposite to her—I note her habit of turning up her eyes as of one shocked;

And still the train rushes on, and the fields fly past and the vineyards.

2

Dusk closes down, and the train rushes on and on;

The mountains stand rank behind rank, and valley beyond valley,

Towering up and up over the clouds even into broad day again.

Lo! the great measureless slopes with receding dwindling perspective of trees and habitations;

Here at their foot the trellised gardens, and rivers roaring under the stone bridges of towns,

And there the far ledges where the tumbled roofs of

tiny hamlets are perched—the terrace after terrace of vine and wheat, the meadows with grass and flowers;

The zigzag path, the lonely chalet, the patches of cultivation almost inaccessible,

The chestnut woods, and again the pinewoods, and beyond again, where no trees are, the solitary pasturages;

[The hidden upper valleys bare of all but rocks and grass—they too with their churches and villages;]

And beyond the pasturages, aye beyond the bare rocks, through the great girdle of the clouds—high high in air—

The inaccessible world of ice, scarce trodden of men.

3

There the rich sunlight dwells, calm like an aureole of glory, over a thousand forms of snow and rock clear-cut delaying.

But below in the dusk along the mountain-bases the train climbs painfully,

Crossing the putty-colored ice-cold streams again and again with tardy wheel;

Till the great summit tunnel is reached, then tilting forward,

With many a roar and rush and whistle and scream from gallery to gallery

It flies—rolls like a terror-stricken thing down the great slopes into the darkness—and night falls in the valleys.

4

Here too then also, and without fail, as everywhere else,

The same old human face looking forth—

Whether in the high secluded valleys where all winter comes no sound from the outer world, or whether by the side of the great iron road where the plate-layer runs to bring a passenger a cup of cold water, or whether loafing in the market-place of the fourth-rate country town—the same.

Here too from the door of her little wooden tenement the worn face looking forth—fringed with grey hair and cap —the old woman peering anxiously down the road for her old man;

[Saw you not how when he left her in the morning, how anxiously, how lovingly, with what strange transformation of countenance—Death close behind her—she prayed him early to return?]

The little boy with big straw hat and short blouse bringing the goats home at evening, the gape-mouthed short-petticoated squaw that accompanies him;

The peasant lying in the field face downwards and asleep, while his wife and children finish the remainder of his meal; the bullock-faced workers on the roads or over the lands;

Ever the same human face, ever the same brute men and women—poignant with what divine obscure attractions!

And the dainty-handed Chinaman in the first-class carriage surveys them as he passes, with mental comparisons;

And the string of mules waits at the railroad crossing in the last dusk as the train thunders by, and the navvy with great shady hat and grey flannel shirt, and scarf round his waist, waits;

And the inhabitants of opposite hemispheres exchange glances with one another for a moment.

5

The night wears on—and yet the same steady onward speed—the draw of the great cities, Paris and London, beginning already to be felt;

The pause for a few minutes at a junction—the good coffee and milk, the warm peaceful air, the late moon just rising, the few poplars near, the mountains now faint in the distance behind;

The faces seen within the cars, hour after hour, with closed eyes, the changed equalised expression of them, the overshadowing humanity—

(The great unconscious humanity in each one!)

The old bedizened hag overshadowed,

The young priest and his recalcitrant opponent both equally overshadowed—their arguments so merely nothing at all; the beautiful artist-face overshadowed;

The unsafe tunnel passed in the dead of the night, the slow tentative movement of the train, the forms and faces of men within—visible by the light of their own lanterns, anxious with open mouths looking upward at the roof—all overshadowed;

The little traveler asleep with his head on the lap of his instructor—the Persian boy—traveling he too on a long journey, farther than London or Paris;

The westward swing of the great planets through the

night, the faint early dawn, the farms and fields flying past once more;

The great sad plains of Central France, the few trees, the innumerable cultivation, the peasants going out so early to work,

The rising of the sun, for a new day—the great red ball so bold rising unblemished on all the heart-ache and suffering, the plans, the schemes, the hopes, the desires, the despairs of millions—

And the glitter and the roar already, and the rush of the life of Paris.

TO THE END OF TIME

KNOW that to the end of Time and the remotest corner of Space there is nothing that you cannot take for your own—nothing without personal relation to yourself, body and soul: to this body, sweet, bitter, painful, pleasurable, fatal—to that, equal. Not the most fatal drug but feeds that one, not years of slow exile or of illness.

Through this life, that life—the two always conjoined; through failure, stedfastness; through the sight of the change and flow of things, immortality; through the magnificence and splendor of nature (I speak to you now seated on some wooded slope or hill—the birds, the buds, the sky after rain), yourself equal in magnificence and splendor.

On the Eve of Departure

ALWAYS on the eve of departure,
    Thy goods all packed, thy testament signed and witnessed,
    Touching with lightest touch all offerings life lays at thy feet:
    This is thy fate, O blest one!

    After the day's work leaving the papers behind on the desk, the tools on the bench,
    Letting the garden-line remain in the garden, leaving the newly sharpened pick in the hardening trough,
    Leaving the scissors and the sleeve-board on the floor where they fell, and the waistcoat-lining unfinished on the machine,
    Letting go all the plans and purposes of the day, forgetting about them as if they had never been:
    Lo! this is thy fate, O blest one!

    The chains of office round your neck, yet to uncoil and lay them quietly aside,
    The cares of state that have held you since morning holding you no longer, the axe-handle relaxing its grasp on you;
    Out of the old ever-passing, free as air,
    For the acceptance of all, and the praise and blame of men, alike without prejudice:
    Lo! this is thy fate, O blest one!

Arenzano

IN the great Church over the little fishing-village,
In the gloom of evening and of the spacious interior—only a few candles lighted over a side altar—
[The great doors wide open to the twilight over the bay, with silhouettes of figures entering, and continual tread of feet upon the stone floor]—
There in the dusk the fisher-wives kneel and pray:
Ave Maria, ave, ave.
A great throng, hardly visible, with shawls thrown over their heads—and men and children:
Ave Maria, ave, ave.

The long monotonous semi-savage refrain and wash of voices,
Unending, like the rhythm of the sea itself,
The untrained choir, the rise suspense and breaking of the wave of trebles, the answer of the basses in passionate iteration—the mesmeric influence—
The great Christ over the main altar, half lost in gloom, with arms outstretched, and crucified,
The faint sweet smell of incense,
The long Past:

The long Past from which it all comes—
Strange voices and refrains,
As from the coasts of Tyre, and the worship of Ashtoreth,

Or this is Isis the ever-virgin Madonna and her infant Horus—one with the Virgin of the stars—
Or this the antiphonal music of the psalms
Within the Jewish Temple.

The same great needs of human life all down the ages—
Each tiny drop to feel the living wave it forms a part of;
Dear Love; and Death; the narrow clear-cut bounded present, the dread Unknown, the children clinging to each other—
Not one that dies, not one the waves engulf,
But tears and agony to those remaining.

Ah! who can tell and who can see the end?
Man that art God yet perishest as grass!
I sit here in a corner of thy world-old temple—
(Here in this old fishing-village just as much as anywhere else)—
In the dark unknown unnoticed I sit,
And hear the ceaseless sounding of Thy Sea,
And join the *Ave Maria, ave, ave.*

O Tender Heart

O TENDER heart of our humanity,
    O bleeding sacred heart, with tears of ages.

Dear Mother, once on earth, now glorified—
Thy arms outstretched in love o'er all creation—

O Tender Heart

Thy husk lies by the sea-shore, which Thou once
Didst thus and thus inhabit (parted now,
For it could ne'er contain Thee).

O buds and blooms of Spring once more returning,
Bright waters flowing, O heavenly blue still shining,
And Thou still spreading over all and changeless,
O tender heart of our humanity,
O bleeding sacred heart, with tears of ages.

Arise Thou glorified,
Year after year—leaving thy mortal days behind—
Dear mother in the great unseen impending,
Slowly creation orbs about thy form.
I follow where thou walkedst. I behold
Where ages back on earth Thou still didst pass;
I see thee in the streets to-day disguised;
Thy spirit glides eternal—and I follow,
Kissing the sacred foot-prints as I go.

All suffering for thy dear sake is holy—
(O thorn-crowned brow, O bleeding sacred heart)—
Thou that didst bear me and thy children all
With bitter pangs and sorrow for thy cup
(Thy thin hands laid at last within the grave),
All suffering for thy dear sake is holy.

The Carter

SO in the dirt, amid the filthy smoke and insensate din of the great city,
Into my attic came my friend the carter and sat with me for a while.

Young and worn, these are the words he said:
"Never before could I have believed it, but I see it all now;
There is nothing like it—no happiness—when you have clean dropped thinking about yourself.
But you must not do it by halves—while ever there is the least grain of self left it will spoil all;
You must just leave it all behind—and yourself be the same as others;
If they want anything, and you want it, well it is the same who gets it;
You cannot be disappointed then.
I do not say it is not hard, but I know there is nothing —no happiness—like it;
It is a new life, and them that has never tasted it, they have no idea what it is."

Thus in the din and dirt of the city, as over the mountain tops and in the far forests alone with Nature,
I saw the unimaginable form dwelling, whom no mortal eye may see,

The unimaginable form of Man, tenant of the Earth from far ages, seen of the wise in all times—
Dwelling also in the youthful carter.

THE STONE-CUTTER

"AND men to-day—are they not always running about to do something?
But He says: *I have finished the work that Thou gavest me to do.*"

Thus to me the stone-cutter, with chisel and mallet in hand all the while dishing out a sump-cover,
Standing out there in the Sun, in the light July breeze so cool,
Spoke the words of Christ—the old indestructible words —which all down the ages,
Whether in the mouth of stone-cutter or carpenter,
Emerge time after time from the heart of the people.

THE VOICE OF ONE BLIND

BLIND, ah! blind—it has come upon me now—
A veil thickening between the world and me.
[I saw them move through it—saw the dear faces and figures as in a fluid haze,
And then they blurred, and then I saw them not.]

Alone? Ah no! who shall describe the joy that has come upon me?

The blow that should have crushed me broke my chains,
And I, that was the prisoner, am free.

Sweet—all of fever fled—all calm now and peaceful,
To feel the warm sun on my hands, or traveling along my forehead,
To hear the sounds—the rustling of the breeze or chirrup of the birds, the kettle singing or the turned page of the book my loved one reads—
The touches and the hands, the voices and the sweet caresses;
How they come nearer, now!
I go no more to seek, I stay at home, and let them come to me.

And sweet sweet visions—
Ah! forms I saw not when my eyes were clear—
Sons, daughters, brothers, sisters, mortal friends,
What gods are come about me?

And Thou above all:
Thou, gracious presence, sweet enfolding me
Far far within, touching me nearest of all,
As through so many ages men and women Thou with the sweetness of thy love hast ravished::
So I touch them through Thee—through Thee to all
I am come nearer now.

A Song of One in Old Age

WEARY and broken, old age, art thou now come upon me?
My faculties drying up like pools of water in summer,
My body dying, my brain rusting, my heart-beat dull and torpid—
Falling off like a dead leaf from the tree, unheeded, useless—
Is this old age then? lonely, ah! how lonely!

The world hurries by so light and glad and joyous—each man following his call: but I without any;
The spring returns with the budding leaves on the beech so fresh, and the virgin grass, and the foals and young calves in the fields: as it has returned so oft before; but I am old and must die—there is no place for me any longer;
At night in dreams the faces return to me—the faces that I loved, ah! dearest faces!—but when I wake the world is changed, all changed: there is no place for them any longer, but strangers are around me.
How should love come to me—what is there that any one should seek me? Who will pause for the empty husk of a man, and shall I be a supplicant for pity?
How could I ever have guessed when I was young that this would come upon me—and yet it has come upon me, as it has come upon so many millions before?
To die—that is it. This at last is what I have so often counted on—to die, to be effaced, to be made of no account—and now it is forced upon me whether I will or no.

O Death, I shall conquer thee yet.

Didst thou think to terrify me?—but lo! was I not dead before thou camest?

Long long years ago did I not abandon this frail tenement, all but in name?—was not my last furniture packed up and ready to be transported?

The virgin grass received me, and the beech trees so tenderly green in spring, and the bodies of my lovers that I loved:

They became my dwelling, and I forgot that I existed.

I passed freely and floated on the ocean of which before I had only been part of the shore,

I took up my refuge beyond the limits where thou couldst come.

———

Yet now once more confined,

Here in this prison cell while the walls grow thicker—of all I was a little spark waits yet its liberation.

Come quickly, Death, and loose this last remainder of me—shatter the walls,

Break down this body of mine, and let me go.

Or else,

In patience let me wait seeing fulfilled

That which I sought so long—to be effaced.

Hidden I wait—this old husk suits me well—for who will guess the likeness of me through it?

This is my invisible cap wherein I'll ramble yet through many byways of sweet human life.

And thou too, stranger, shalt pity me if thou wilt, and I will accept thy pity gratefully—
Yet after all perhaps the best gift of the two
I'll give to thee.

Old age, old age?—No! only there outside.
Here where I am 'tis everlasting youth.
This is where the virgin grass springs from, I see, and the loves that clothe the frame of humanity.
Out of this old shell passing I begin again—there is no death here, there can be no death,
Only perpetual joy.

In Extreme Age

UNTO Thee, O Nature, I abandon myself:
    Accept me, thou beautiful,
Marred and deformed and stunted take me from myself
Unto thy own great uses.

Lo, I outgrow this body! painfully
My life ebbs yet and flows again within it.
These hands and feet, these eyes and brain, these senses, faculties, have served their turn—
The dinted tools I render back to Thee.

As when a boy I sat upon the beach in the sun, and watched the sparkling waves,
So now in extreme age sitting here

I trace no change—scarce any change at all.
Some little work done, some formal knowledge gained, some passages of sweet or sad experience;
But all these only outworks, falling off,
Leave me the same that I have been through life.
(So little one life—so brief, slight, a thing.)

Till now at length, feeling Thee gather round me close,
Close, closer, closer yet,
At last the bounds dissolve which kept us twain,
And I and Thou are one, and I alone am not.

After the Day's Work

PASSING by, passing by all exteriors,
  Swimming floating on the Ocean that has innumerable bays—
I too at length nestle down in thy breast, O humanity;
Tired I abandon myself to thee, to be washed from the dust of life in thy waves.

I Saw a Vision

I SAW a vision of Earth's multitudes going up and down over the Earth—and I saw the great earth itself wheeling and careering onward through space.
And behold! here and there to one among the multitude a change came;
And to whomsoever it came continued onward apparently as before—yet as from the larva springs the perfect image,
So (as it appeared to me) from that mortal form a new

being, long long long in preparation, glided silently up unobserved into the breathless pure height of the sky.

Ah! Blessed is He

AH! blessed is he that hath escaped—
 Whom love hath opened the doors of his cage:
No more returning
Shall he be subject again to sin and sorrow.

The Great Leader

I USE my name and powers, I use my great prestige,
 As a joiner uses a tool: they serve my purpose well.
Nevertheless think not that I regard them
Except as things to be destroyed in using.

I Accept You

I ACCEPT you altogether—as the sea accepts the fish
 that swim in it.
 It is no good apologising for anything you have done, for you have never been anywhere yet but what I have sustained you—
 And beyond my boundaries you cannot go.

Sol

CORUSCATING flame I behold the soul,
 Mine, yours, whoever it may be—
Darting great tongues of flame thousands of miles long,
Thousands of years.

A Glimpse

HERE at last having arrived I take my rest, my long long fill of rest, no more to move;
The roaring subsides, the wheels cease to go round, a calm falls on all—the stars and the daisies shine out visibly from the bosom of God.

You cannot baulk me of my true life.
Climbing over the barriers of pain—of my own weaknesses and sins—I escape.
Where will you hold me? by the feet, hands? by my personal vanity? would you shut me in the mirror-lined prison of self-consciousness?

Behold! I acknowledge all my defects—you cannot snap the handcuffs faster on me than I snap them myself: I am vain, deceitful, cowardly—yet I escape.
The handcuffs hold me not, out of my own hands I draw myself as out of a glove; from behind the empty mask of my reputed qualities I depart, and am gone my way,
Unconcerned what I leave behind me.

Into the high air which surrounds and sustains the world,
Breathing life, intoxicating, with joy unutterable, radiant,
As the wind of Spring when the dead leaves fly before it—
I depart and am gone my way.

The Long Day in the Open

HOUR after hour passes by, the Sun wheels on, the clouds disperse and re-form;

On all I have to do thou lookest O Nature, I have nothing to conceal from thee; O Moon traveling so close over the hills,

Dost thou not say what I have to say, are not our purposes one?

The Idler

I AM he that beholds and praises the universe,
Singing all day like a bird among the branches,
And the leaves put forth and the young buds burst asunder—yet I myself do nothing at all,
But dwell in the midst of them, singing.

In the Deep Cave of the Heart

IN the deep cave of the heart, far down,
Running under the outward shows of the world and of people,
Running under geographies, continents, under the fields and the roots of the grasses and trees, under the little thoughts and dreams of men, and the history of races,
Deep, far down,
I see feel and hear wondrous and divine things.
Voices and faces are there; arms of lovers, known and unknown, reach forward and fold me;
Words float, and fragrance of Time ascends, and Life ever circling.

Fly messenger! through the streets of the cities ancle-plumed Mercury fly!
Swift sinewy runner with arm held up on high!
Naked along the wind, thy beautiful feet
Glancing over the mountains, under the sun,
By meadows and water-sides,—into the great towns like a devouring flame,
Through slums and vapors and dismal suburban streets,
With startling of innumerable eyes—fly, messenger, fly!

Joy joy, the glad news!
For he whom we wait is risen!
He is descended among his children—
He is come to dwell on the Earth!

THE COMING OF THE LORD

I HEARD a voice saying:
Son of Man stretch forth thy hand over the earth—and over the sea-coasts and seas and cities of the earth:

I, the King, am come to dwell in my own lands—I am descended among the children of men.

[Blessed art thou whosoever from whose eyes the veil is lifted to see Me;

Blessed are thy mornings and evenings—blessed the hour when thou risest up, and again when thou liest down to sleep.]

Here on this rock in the sun, where the waves obedient wash at my feet, where the fisherman passing spreads his net on the sands,

I the King sit waiting.

This mountain is my throne—I breathe the incense of the myriad-laden meadows;

The little white-washed cottages lie below me, and there my dwelling is also.

See you not Me? though I stand in the height of heaven,

Glorious in all forms, am I become as a nothing before you?

Though I walk through the street with a basket on my

arm, or leaning on a stick—or loiter in many disguises?

See you not Me,

Who have looked in your eyes so long for that glance of recognition?

Yet when you see me no form of maid or boy, or one mature or aged,

Or the truth of anything shall escape you.

In the streets of the cities, where the horses' hoofs sound hollow upon the asphalte, and the old woman sits by her tray,

And the babble of voices goes by as you stand at the corner,

I will pass with the rest—you shall see me and not mistake me.

The woods no more shall be merely a cover for wild animals, or so much value in timber, nor the fields for their crops alone,

For I have trodden them—they are holy—and my footprints are over all the land.

Who walks in singleness of heart shall be my companion—I will reveal myself to him by ways that the learned understand not.

Though he be poor and ignorant I will be his friend—I will swear faithfulness to him, passing my lips to his, and my hand to betwixt his thighs.

3

Where I pass, all my children know me;

My feet tread naked the grass of the valleys, the trees know me by name—they hear my voice—the brook with heaped up waters rushes past me.

[O voices breaking out over the earth, O singing singing singing!]

My sun shines glorious in heaven, and my moon to adorn the night;

They are my right hand and my left hand—see you not Me between?

[Hark! my children sing—all day and night they are singing!]

4

O child—you whom I touch now, having watched over you so long, so long—

Are you worthy to follow and behold me?

Leaving all, leaving all behind,

Caring no more for the world, for all your projects and purposes, than if you had been stunned by a blow on the head,

Leaving all to me, absolutely all to me,

Then may-be you shall see me.

For though you shall carry on where you are placed, and shall not forsake your post, though you shall be unwearied, giving all that you have out of love to the least capable of making a return, though you shall be active before the world,

Yet shall you not act at all, not one single thing shall you do—but I will do it for you.

After that the arrows shall not pierce you, nor the heavy rain wet you, the shafts of malice shall not penetrate to you, nor the fire though it consume your body shall consume you;

But the sun shall shine, and the faces glance each morning afresh upon you,

For joy, for joy—and joy.

I the Lord Demos have spoken it: and the mountains are my throne.

The Curse of Property

ARE they not mine, saith the Lord, the everlasting hills?

(Where over the fir-tree tops I glance to the valleys.)

The rich meads with brown and white cattle, and streams with weirs and water-mills,

And the tender-growing crops, and hollows of shining apple-blossom—

From my mountain terraces as from a throne beholding my lands—

Are they not mine, where I dwell, and for my children?

How long, you, will you trail your slime over them, and your talk of rights and of property?

How long will you build you houses to hide yourselves in, and your baggage? to shut yourselves off from your brothers and sisters—and Me?

The Curse of Property

Beware! for I am the storm; I care nought for your rights of property.

In lightning and thunder, in floods and fire, I will ruin and ravage your fields;

Your first-born will I slay within your house, and I will make your riches a mockery.

Fools! that know not from day to day, from hour to hour, if ye shall live,

And yet will snatch from each other the things that I have showered among you.

For I will have none that will not open his door to all, treating others as I have treated him.

The trees that spread their boughs against the evening sky, the marble that I have prepared beforehand these millions of years in the earth; the cattle that roam over the myriad hills—they are Mine, for all my children—

If thou lay hands on them for thyself alone, thou art accursed.

The curse of property shall cling to thee;

With burdened brow and heavy heart, weary, incapable of joy, without gaiety,

Thou shalt crawl a stranger in the land that I made for thy enjoyment.

The smallest bird on thy estate shall sing in freedom in the branches, the plough-boy shall whistle in the furrow,

But thou shalt be weary and lonely—forsaken and an alien among men:

For just inasmuch as thou hast shut thyself off from one of the least of these my children, thou hast shut thyself off from Me.

I the Lord Demos have spoken it—and the mountains are my throne.

Over the Great City

OVER the great city,
   Where the wind rustles through the parks and gardens,
   In the air, the high clouds brooding,
   In the lines of street perspective, the lamps, the traffic,
   The pavements and the innumerable feet upon them,
   I Am: make no mistake—do not be deluded.

Think not because I do not appear at the first glance—because the centuries have gone by and there is no assured tidings of me—that therefore I am not there.
Think not because all goes its own way that therefore I do not go my own way through all.
The fixed bent of hurrying faces in the street—each turned towards its own light, seeing no other—yet I am the Light towards which they all look.
The toil of so many hands to such multifarious ends, yet my hand knows the touch and twining of them all.

All come to me at last.
There is no love like mine;

For all other love takes one and not another;
And other love is pain, but this is joy eternal.

UNDERNEATH AND AFTER ALL

THERE is no peace except where I am, saith the Lord.

Though you have health—that which is called health—yet without me it is only the fair covering of disease;

Though you have love, yet if I be not between and around the lovers, is their love only torment and unrest;

Though you have wealth and friends and home—all these shall come and go—there is nothing stable or secure, which shall not be taken away;

But I alone remain—I do not change.

As space spreads everywhere, and all things move and change within it, but it moves not nor changes,

So I am the space within the soul, of which the space without is but the similitude and mental image;

Comest thou to inhabit me, thou hast the entrance to all life—death shall no longer divide thee from whom thou lovest.

I am the sun that shines upon all creatures from within —gazest thou upon me thou shalt be filled with joy eternal.

Be not deceived. Soon this outer world shall drop off—thou shalt slough it away as a man sloughs his mortal body.

Learn even now to spread thy wings in that other world —the world of Equality—to swim in the ocean, my child, of Me and my love.

[Ah! have I not taught thee by the semblances of this outer world, by its alienations and deaths and mortal sufferings—all for this?

For joy, ah! joy unutterable!]

Him who is not detained by mortal adhesions, who walks in this world yet not of it,

Taking part in everything with equal mind, with free limbs and senses unentangled—

Giving all, accepting all, using all, enjoying all, asking nothing, shocked at nothing—

Whom love follows everywhere, but he follows not it—

Him all creatures worship, all men and women bless.

It is for this that the body exercises its tremendous attraction—that mortal love torments and tears asunder the successive generations of mankind—

That underneath and after all the true men and women may appear, by long experience emancipated.

A Hard Saying

WHO loves the mortal creature, ending there, is no more free—he has given himself away to Death—

For him the slimy black Form lies in wait at every turn, befouling the universe;

Yet he who loves must love the mortal, and he who would love perfectly must be free:

Disentanglement

[Love—glorious though it be—is a disease as long as it destroys or even impairs the freedom of the soul.]

Therefore if thou wouldst love, withdraw thyself from love:

Make it thy slave, and all the miracles of nature shall lie in the palm of thy hand.

NOT FOR A FEW MONTHS OR YEARS

THINK not that that which is growing inside you as you battle with these words is for a few months or years,

Or that it will find its rest and satisfaction in the things for which the world is so busy striving.

Food ease lust knowledge fame—'twill pasture up as nonchalantly as a dog, and look in your face for more.

They shall not satisfy it. The list of all the things that can be named shall not satisfy it.

DISENTANGLEMENT

BE not torn by desire:

When burning clinging love assails thee—like a red-hot thing which sticks to the flesh it scorches—

Beware!

For love is good and lust is good—but not to tear and rend thee.

Slowly and resolutely—as a fly cleans its legs of the honey in which it has been caught—

So remove thou, if it only be for a time, every particle which sullies the brightness of thy mind;

Return into thyself—content to give, but asking no one, asking nothing;

In the calm light of His splendor who fills all the universe, the imperishable indestructible of ages,

Dwell thou—as thou canst dwell—contented.

Now understand me well:

There is no desire or indulgence that is forbidden; there is not one good and another evil—all are alike in that respect;

In place all are to be used.

Yet in using be not entangled in them; for then already they are bad, and will cause thee suffering.

When thy body—as needs must happen at times—is carried along on the wind of passion, say not thou, "I desire this or that";

For the "I" neither desires nor fears anything, but is free and in everlasting glory, dwelling in heaven and pouring out joy like the sun on all sides.

Let not that precious thing by any confusion be drawn down and entangled in the world of opposites, and of Death and suffering.

For as a light-house beam sweeps with incredible speed over sea and land, yet the lamp itself moves not at all,

So while thy body of desire is (and must be by the

law of its nature) incessantly in motion in the world of suffering, the "I" high up above is fixed in heaven.

Therefore I say let no confusion cloud thy mind about this matter;
But ever when desire knocks at thy door,
Though thou grant it admission and entreat it hospitably, as in duty bound,
Fence it yet gently off from thy true self,
Lest it should tear and rend thee.

3

And him thou lovest or her thou lovest—
If without confusion thou beholdest such one fixed like a star in heaven, and ever in thy most clinging burning passion rememberest Whom thou lovest,
Then art thou blessed beyond words, and thy love is surely eternal;
But if by confusion thou knowest not whom thou lovest —but seest only the receptacle of desire which inhabits the world of change and suffering—
Then shalt thou be whirled and gulfed in a sea of torment, and shalt travel far and be many times lost upon that ocean before thou shalt know what is the true end of thy voyage.

THE MORTAL LOVER

THIS is the little mortal lover in whose heart the low scorching flame of rejected love burns night and day, withering all his life.

In vain the great mountains and the sea, in vain the sun in heaven, in vain all faces offer themselves;

There is no rest: only death and annihilation for everything that is born;

Only a corpse swinging up-river with the tide among the mud-banks, and swinging down again with the ebb;

And the tide ebbing and flowing aimlessly for ever in a land where all are dead.

He lies awake all night and strains his eyes for a glimmer of light, but there is none;

Every pursuit, every hope, all of life, is a mockery—he has been gulled into existence.

We have been brought here (he says), a mass of sensitive capacities, to behold a possible satisfaction—then to be trampled underfoot like worms, without redemption, never again to know each other or ourselves.

The heart aches and burns in slow torture, the sounds of daily life are a mockery, the pursuits of men are like the laughter of maniacs playing on the brink of a precipice.

Millions and millions approach the edge—a vast body always moving on from behind;

The gulf is measureless in depth, but the young and those who are in the rear know not of it—they only feel the vast onward movement, and with loud chants and rollicking songs march gaily confidently on;

Then suddenly those who are older and nearing the edge behold the horrible and naked truth—they see the avalanche of human beings for ever going over into the abyss;

With shouts and cries of warning they turn upon those that are behind: but it is useless, they too are pushed on relentlessly;

Behind is a babel of sounds, cries of Forward, Progress, God, Immortality, and the like; around are shrieks and despairing threats, curses and plaintive unheeded warnings; before is the abyss of oblivion,

Into which countless generations before have gone, and we must go;

And this is the hell of existence.

He lies awake all night with pain gnawing at his heart, and strains his eyes for a glimmer of light, but there is none.

The End of Love

SEEK not the end of love in this act or in that act —lest indeed it become the end;

But seek this act and that act and thousands of acts whose end is love—

So shalt thou at last create that which thou now desirest;

And then when these are all past and gone there shall remain to thee a great and immortal possession, which no man can take away.

A New Life

HENCEFORTH I propound a new life for you—that you should bring the peace and grace of Nature into all your daily life—being freed from vain striving:

The freed soul, passing disengaged into the upper air, forgetful of self,

Rising again in others, ever knowing itself again in others.

The villa stands with its picturesque gables and garden, its rhododendrons all in flower, and exotic firs, with clumps of tulips;

The ploughman to his horses clicks and calls all day in the midst of the vocal landscape;

The rivers wind lazily about the land; the slow air floats on from the West and South, bringing on its bosom long-promised gifts.

Out of houses and closed rooms, out of the closed prison of self which you have inhabited so long;

Into the high air which circles round the world, the region of human equality,

With outspread wings balanced, resting on that which is not self,

Floating high up as a condor over the mountains in aerial suspense,

Or as an eagle flying screaming over the cities of the earth, with joy delirious—

So passing enfranchised shall you regain after long captivity

Your own your native abode.

THE LAW OF EQUALITY

YOU cannot violate the law of Equality for long.

Whatever you appropriate to yourself now from others, by that you will be poorer in the end ;

What you give now, the same will surely come back to you.

If you think yourself superior to the rest, in that instant you have proclaimed your own inferiority ;

And he that will be servant of all, helper of most, by that very fact becomes their lord and master.

Seek not your own life—for that is death ;

But seek how you can best and most joyfully give your own life away—and every morning for ever fresh life shall come to you from over the hills.

Man has to learn to die—quite simply and naturally—as the child has to learn to walk.

The life of Equality the grave cannot swallow—any more than the finger can hold back running water—it flows easily round and over all obstacles.

A little while snatching to yourself the goods of the earth, jealous of your own credit, and of the admiration and applause of men,

Then to learn that you cannot defeat Nature so—that water will not run up hill for all your labors and lying awake at night over it:

The claims of others as good as yours, their **excellence**

in their own line equal to your best in yours, their life as near and dear to you as your own can be.

So letting go all the chains which bound you, all the anxieties and cares,

The wearisome burden, the artificial unyielding armor wherewith you would secure yourself, but which only weighs you down a more helpless mark for the enemy—

Having learned the necessary lesson of your own identity—

To pass out, free, O joy!—free, to flow down, to swim in the sea of Equality—

To endue the bodies of the divine Companions,

And the life which is eternal.

To Thine Own Self be True

NOT by running out of yourself after it comes the love which lasts a thousand years.

If to gain another's love you are untrue to yourself then are you also untrue to the person whose love you would gain.

Him or her whom you seek will you never find that way—and what pleasure you have with them will haply only end in pain.

Remain stedfast, knowing that each prisoner has to endure in patience till the season of his liberation; when the love comes which is for you it will turn the lock easily and loose your chains—

Being no longer whirled about nor tormented by winds

of uncertainty, but part of the organic growth of God himself in Time—

Another column in the temple of immensity,
Two voices added to the eternal choir.

Abandon Hope All Ye that Enter Here

To die—for this into the world you came.

Yes, to abandon more than you ever conceived as possible:

All ideals, plans—even the very best and most unselfish—all hopes and desires,

All formulas of morality, all reputation for virtue or consistency or good sense; all cherished theories, doctrines, systems of knowledge,

Modes of life, habits, predilections, preferences, superiorities, weaknesses, indulgences,

Good health, wholeness of limb and brain, youth, manhood, age—nay life itself—in one word: To die—

For this into the world you came.

All to be abandoned, and when they have been finally abandoned,

Then to return to be used—and then only to be rightly used, to be free and open for ever.

To One Dead

You must look at your own body lying dead there quite calmly—

[If you have ever loved and quietly surrendered that love you will understand what I mean]—

The dear fingers and feet, the eyes you have looked in so often—they are yours no longer;

You are not bound to them, you are something else than you thought.

Now you see that these things are only a similitude:

A new and wonderful life opens out—so wonderful, O so wonderful!

· Those eyes whose answer once you forebore to ask for —do you remember how after all, how wide and wonderful at last they opened upon you, shining up for you (yes for you) from depths you saw not in them before?

And that body which now you have forsaken, so now for the first time do you understand it and its life (all the old passages in it so clear, so real, so wonderful, so transparent);

Now it radiates back upon you what you are—of whom it is only the similitude;

And even so it is only **one** of your similitudes.

OF ALL THE SUFFERING

OF all the suffering—
    (Think think of it, and learn what Freedom is)—
All the weary disappointed faces,
The lives narrowed down, the dark and joyless prospect,

Of all the Suffering

Capacities stunted that might have been developed, hope gone, the cross of anguish on the forehead;

Of the fair might-have-been, the lips so loved that Death has hid from view,
The dread inexorable past, the nothing left to live for,
Age empty purposeless—a mere cold husk—
Death coming slow, with pain and foul disease;

Of all the cruelty of one to another,
Slights that cut the heart's tenderest chords, words said that can never be unsaid;
Of the deliberate cruelty of savages and half-formed people, gloating in revenge, or amused by others' pain;
The victim staked out horizontally on the ground, the little fires built beside or under his arms and legs, or upon his breast,
The careful ingenious torture lasting for hours, the jeers, the diabolic laughter—the moaning of the deserted and half-charred remnant through the long night—the stars looking on;
Of the thousands languishing in prisons, slowly succumbing through all mental tortures into madness;
Of the millions over whom the dread night-mares hang —deaths, partings, exiles, illness, pain and persecution— the brief respite in sleep, the waking to despair:
Think think of these, and learn what Freedom is.

Of all the delusion of thinking oneself apart from others —and all the needless torment that springs from it;

Of the fear that one might somehow tumble out of the world of Existence—dying oneself while others lived on;

Of the lightning-flashes of love which fitfully and for a moment to dazed wanderers reveal the truth;

Of after pain endured the immense and widened outlook;

Of the poor little thing that shuts itself in its own cell, and then looks forth with anxious eyes upon the world—as though there were no escape—tossed by winds of Chance, subject to Death and Dissolution:

The little primitive cell that grows and differentiates and grows till that which was in it attains at last to Manhood and Deliverance;

Of all the beating about in the dark round the walls of one's prison, yet never hitting the secret door of exit;

Of all the sorrow and blindness that inveil for a time the unformed embryonic creature—

Inveil fatally and forethoughtfully for ends glorious beyond all mortal imagination:

Think think of these and learn what Freedom is.

A Long Journey

THE long insatiable yearning of the mortal creature, for absolute union—never accomplished;

Each mortal love the symbol, the promise, and the part-fulfilment of that for which all life exists.

Not this year or next, not this life or perhaps the next,

But day by day and day by day as long as thou art, pass thou nearer to that great joy.

Here too (as so often said before) it is no matter of chance :

It is not that these are lucky having found their mates, and thou art unfortunate standing alone (for they have not found their mates, and thou standest not alone);

But every day and every day (for thee as well as for them and all) the way lies on before—to be slowly accomplished—

To make thyself fit for the perfect love which awaits and which alone can satisfy thee.

Lo! that divine body which dwells within thy mortal body, slowly preparing its own deliverance—

What is all suffering before that? to surrender this is but to open the way for that—'tis but the law of Equality.

Begin to-day to walk the path which alone is gain;

In the sunshine, as the sunshine, calm contented and blessed, envying no one, railing not, repining not;

Receiving the message of the patient trees and herbs, and of the creatures of the earth, and of the stars above;

Possessing all within thyself, with showers of beauties and blessings every moment—to scatter again to others with free hand;

Neither hurrying nor slackening, but sure of thy great and glorious destiny, walk thou—

And presently all around thee shalt thou see the similitude of him whom thou seekest:

He shall send a multitude of messengers in advance to cheer thee on thy way.

The Secret of Time and Satan

IS there one in all the world who does not desire to be divinely beautiful?

To have the most perfect body—unerring skill, strength, limpid clearness of mind, as of the sunlight over the hills,

To radiate love wherever he goes, to move in and out, accepted?

The secret lies close to you, so close.

You are that person; it lies close to you, so close—deep down within—

But in Time it shall come forth and be revealed.

Not by accumulating riches, but by giving away what you have,

Shall you become beautiful;

You must undo the wrappings, not case yourself in fresh ones;

Not by multiplying clothes shall you make your body sound and healthy, but rather by discarding them;

Not by multiplying knowledge shall you beautify your mind;

It is not the food that you eat that has to vivify you, but you that have to vivify the food.

The Secret of Time and Satan

Always emergence, and the parting of veils for the hidden to appear;

The child emerges from its mother's body, and out of that body again in time another child.

When the body which thou now hast falls away, another body shall be already prepared beneath,

And beneath that again another.

Always that which appears last in time is first, and the cause of all—and not that which appears first.

2

Freedom has to be won afresh every morning,

Every morning thou must put forth thy strength afresh upon the world, to create out of chaos the garden in which thou walkest.

(Behold! I love thee—I wait for thee in thine own garden, lingering till eventide among the bushes;

I tune the lute for thee; I prepare my body for thee, bathing unseen in the limpid waters.)

3

Wondrous is Man—the human body: to understand and possess this, to create it every day afresh, is to possess all things.

The tongue and all that proceeds from it: spoken and written words, languages, commands, controls, the electric telegraph girdling the earth;

The eyes ordaining, directing; the feet and all that they indicate—the path they travel for years and years;

The passions of the body, the belly and the cry for food, the heaving breasts of love, the phallus, the fleshy thighs,

The erect proud head and neck, the sturdy back, and knees well-knit or wavering;

All the interminable attitudes and what they indicate;

Every relation of one man to another, every cringing, bullying, lustful, obscene, pure, honorable, chaste, just and merciful;

The fingers differently shaped according as they handle money for gain or for gift;

All the different ramifications and institutions of society which proceed from such one difference in the crook of a finger;

All that proceed from an arrogant or a slavish contour of the neck;

All the evil that goes forth from any part of a man's body which is not possessed by himself, all the devils let loose—from a twist of the tongue or a leer of the eye, or the unmanly act of any member—and swirling into society; all the good which gathers round a man who is clean and strong—the threads drawing from afar to the tips of his fingers, the interpretations in his eyes, all the love which passes through his limbs into heaven:

What it is to command and be Master of this wondrous body with all its passions and powers, to truly possess it—*that* it is to command and possess all things, that it is to create.

*

The art of creation, like every other art, has to be learnt:

Slowly slowly, through many years, thou buildest up thy body,

And the power that thou now hast (such as it is) to build up this present body, thou hast acquired in the past in other bodies;

So in the future shalt thou use again the power that thou now acquirest.

But the power to build up the body includes all powers.

Do not be dismayed because thou art yet a child of chance, and at the mercy greatly both of Nature and fate;

Because if thou wert not subject to chance, then wouldst thou be Master of thyself; but since thou art not yet Master of thine own passions and powers, in that degree must thou needs be at the mercy of some other power.

And if thou choosest to call that power 'Chance,' well and good. It is the angel with whom thou hast to wrestle.

5

Beware how thou seekest this for thyself and that for thyself. I do not say Seek not; but Beware how thou seekest.

For a soldier who is going a campaign does not seek what fresh furniture he can carry on his back, but rather what he can leave behind;

Knowing well that every additional thing which he cannot freely use and handle is an impediment to him.

So if thou seekest fame or ease or pleasure or aught for thyself, the image of that thing which thou seekest will come and cling to thee—and thou wilt have to carry it about;

And the images and powers which thou hast thus evoked will gather round and form for thee a new body—clamoring for sustenance and satisfaction;

And if thou art not able to discard this image now, thou wilt not be able to discard that body then: but wilt have to carry it about.

Beware then lest it become thy grave and thy prison—instead of thy winged abode, and palace of joy.

For (over and over again) there is nothing that is evil except because a man has not mastery over it; and there is no good thing that is not evil if it have mastery over a man;

And there is no passion or power, or pleasure or pain, or created thing whatsoever, which is not ultimately for man and for his use—or which he need be afraid of, or ashamed at.

The ascetics and the self-indulgent divide things into good and evil—as it were to throw away the evil;

But things cannot be divided into good and evil, but all are good so soon as they are brought into subjection.

And seest thou not that except for Death thou couldst never overcome Death—

For since by being a slave to things of sense thou hast clothed thyself with a body which thou art not master of, thou wert condemned to a living tomb were that body not to be destroyed.

But now through pain and suffering out of this tomb shalt thou come; and through the experience thou hast acquired shalt build thyself a new and better body;

And so on many times, till thou spreadest wings and

hast all powers diabolic and angelic concentred in thy flesh.

6

And so at last I saw Satan appear before me—magnificent, fully formed.

Feet first, with shining limbs, he glanced down from above among the bushes,

And stood there erect, dark-skinned, with nostrils dilated with passion;

(In the burning intolerable sunlight he stood, and I in the shade of the bushes);

Fierce and scathing the effluence of his eyes, and scornful of dreams and dreamers (he touched a rock hard by and it split with a sound like thunder);

Fierce the magnetic influence of his dusky flesh; his great foot, well-formed, was planted firm in the sand—with spreading toes;

"Come out" he said with a taunt, "Art thou afraid to meet me?"

And I answered not, but sprang upon him and smote him.

And he smote me a thousand times, and brashed and scorched and slew me as with hands of flame;

And I was glad, for my body lay there dead; and I sprang upon him again with another body;

And he turned upon me, and smote me a thousand times and slew that body;

And I was glad and sprang upon him again with another body—

And with another and another and again another;

And the bodies which I took on yielded before him, and were like cinctures of flame upon me, but I flung them aside;

And the pains which I endured in one body were powers which I wielded in the next; and I grew in strength, till at last I stood before him complete, with a body like his own and equal in might—exultant in pride and joy.

Then he ceased, and said, "I love thee."

And lo! his form changed, and he leaned backwards and drew me upon him,

And bore me up into the air, and floated me over the topmost trees and the ocean, and round the curve of the earth under the moon—

Till we stood again in Paradise.

BRIEF IS PAIN

("*Kurz ist der Schmerz, und ewig ist die Freude.*")

SLOWLY, out of all life unfolded, the supreme joy;
    Over all storms, above the clouds, beyond Night and the shadow of the Earth,

The Sun in the blue æther changeless shining.

Grief passes, sorrow endures for a moment;

To a certain stage belonging it dogs the footsteps of the individual;

Then fading and passing it leaves him free, a new creature, transfigured to more than mortal.

The myriad spindles of the grass reflecting the light, the long and level meadows waving to the breeze,

Brief is Pain

The faint haze of summer, blue in deep shadows of the foliage,
The toilers toiling in the fields, the bathers to the water descending or standing on the banks in the sunlight,
The secret that lies wrapt in the summer noon and the slow evolution of races,
The which what voice can utter, what words avail to frame it?

Not pleasure alone is good, but pain also; not joy alone but sorrow;
Freed must the psyche be from the pupa, and pain is there to free it.
Throes and struggles and clenchings of teeth—but pain is there to free it.

Lo! the prison walls must fall—even though the prisoner tremble.
Long the strain, sometimes seeming past endurance—then the dead shell gives way, and a new landscape discloses.
Curtain behind curtain, wall behind wall, life behind life;
Dying here, to be born there, passing and passing and passing,
At last a new creature behold, transfigured to more than mortal!

For brief after all is pain, but joy ah! joy is eternal!
And thin the veil that divides, the subtle film of illusion—
The prison-wall so slight, at a touch it parts and crumbles,

And opens at length on the sunlit world and the winds of heaven.

The Body and the Book

THE chambers are all in order, all the doors stand open.
Enter Thou—this is the house that I have stored for thee among the rest:
To all that is here thou art welcome.

But for me ask not.
Once when the house was closed I dwelt here—a prisoner;
But now that it is open—all open—I have passed out,
Into the beautiful air, over the fields, over the world, through a thousand homes—journeying with the wind—O so light and joyous,
Light and invisible,
I have passed, and my house is behind me.

Ask not for the prisoner, for he is not here;
Ask not for the free, for thou canst not find him.
Go back thou too and set thy house in order,
Open thy doors, let them stand wide for all to enter—thy treasures, let the poorest take of them;
Then come thou forth to where I wait for thee.

PART IV
WHO SHALL COMMAND
THE HEART

Because the starry lightnings and the life
  Of all this Universe which is our Home
Weave round each soul a web of mortal strife,
  Hard is its speech to hear and slow to come.

As to one waking from a lonely dream
  The friendly taper dwindles to a star,
So to each man men's faces distant seem—
  Their dearest words sound faint and very far.

Daily we pass, like shadows in dreamland,
  And careless answer in the old curt tone,
Till Death breaks suddenly between us, and
  With a great cry we know we have not known.

Ah! surely, to have known and to behold
  The beauty that within the soul abides,
For this Earth blossoms and the skies unfold,
  For this the Moon makes music in the tides;

For this Man rises from his mould of dust,
  Ranges his life and looks upon the Sun,
For this he turns and with adventurous trust
  Forsakes this world and seeks a fairer one.

Who shall Command the Heart

WHO shall command the heart, that wondrous Thing,
That wild love-creature, roaming the wilderness,
That none can tame?
Roaming the world, devouring with eyes of flame, eyes of desire,
All forms of heavenly Beauty?

Say, little heart, that beatest pulsest here beneath the ribs,
Who chained thee in this body? — what Titan ages agone? —
Who muzzled thee to drive this crank machine,
Thou wanderer of the woods, thou crimson leopard,
No better than a turnspit?

Nay, but thy 'prenticeship long enough surely thou hast served;
The time has come, and thy full age and strength;
The cage-bars hold no longer, and the body-machine breaks down;
But thou art young and beautiful as ever.

Wild pard who lovest thus to hunt with Man,
I bid thee loose.
Say, wilt thou come with me, and shall we ride,
Companions of the Chase, the universe over?

From Caverns Dark

BEHOLD, a hundred and a thousand lives,
And thousands more, in caverns dark within thee.
No secret wish that flits along thy fancy,
But lo! far back in some ancestral form
It dwelt, had eyes and feet, and ranged its life;
No thought, no dream, but long-dead men and women
Live in the quiet murmur of its wings
Far down, far down, and move about thy brain
And look on the Sun again.

Ah, silence! hearest not the whispering
In darkness, of those countless multitudes?—
That maiden fair who languished out her soul,
Long generations back, and spake no word;
That father whose young daughter to the grave
Bore down his heart with hers; that sturdy soldier
Who hacked and hewed in fervent piety
All who opposed him; that untiring mother
Who wore her life out for her children; aye,
And all the throngs that passed thro' city streets,
Centuries gone, 'neath overhanging gables,
Or toiled on rustic leas—the cleric youth

From Caverns Dark 371

    Who dreamed romance in manuscript and missal,
    Gurth herding pigs and whittling bow and arrows
    In beechen forests; haughty baron, and serf,
    And vain and timid and night-mare-ridden souls,
    And trustful, proud, ambitious—all are there!
    Hearest the whispering of multitudes?—
    All dead—yet all are there.

    And ages farther, born of the time before man walked the earth,
    Wild forms behold! and roaming spirits of animals,
    Hungering, thirsting, loving—beautiful beings
    That saw and wondered worshiping each other,
    And found their mates and fought their enemies,
    And sang and danced and hoarded, skulked and scolded,
    In passion's every mood; yet never once
    Turned eyes of consciousness upon themselves.
    Unwieldy beasts that bellowed through the tree-ferns for their young,
    And flying dragons and the roaring lion,
    And bats and moths just glimmering thro' the dark
    Like faintest memories—aye, all are there!
    Hearest the whispering of multitudes?—
    All dead—yet all are there.

    And in the ages yet to come the same:
    A hundred and a thousand lives within thee!
    And thousands more—which yet shall walk the Earth.
    Dreams, faint desires, scarce conscious of themselves,

Shall take swift shape and people the lands with forms
Of thy conceiving, strange similitudes
Even of thyself.
And, hungering thirsting loving, beautiful beings
Sprung from thy heart and brain and sexual part,
Half animal, half angel,
Shall see and wonder worshiping each other;
And find their mates and front their enemies
Onward through long processions of the Suns,
By shores of other continents than now,
In unimagined haunts and cities fair,
To where they fade from view and take at last
Their flight from Earth to homes beyond the Earth.

This mighty Life—past present and to come—
Enfolds thee. This thou art. This thou upgatherest;
And this Thou, tiny creature, pourest forth—
Where now thou standest—
Lord of the world, from caverns dark within thee.

THE LAKE OF BEAUTY

LET your mind be quiet, realising the beauty of the world, and the immense the boundless treasures that it holds in store.

All that you have within you, all that your heart desires, all that your Nature so specially fits you for—that or the counterpart of it waits embedded in the great Whole, for you. It will surely come to you.

Yet equally surely not one moment before its appointed time will it come. All your crying and fever and reaching out of hands will make no difference.

Therefore do not begin that game at all.
Do not recklessly spill the waters of your mind in this direction and in that, lest you become like a spring lost and dissipated in the desert.
But draw them together into a little compass, and hold them still, so still;
And let them become clear, so clear—so limpid, so mirror-like;
At last the mountains and the sky shall glass themselves in peaceful beauty,
And the antelope shall descend to drink, and to gaze at his reflected image, and the lion to quench his thirst,
And Love himself shall come and bend over, and catch his own likeness in you.

THE WANDERING PSYCHE

YOU, who un-united to yourself roam about the world,
Seeking some person or some thing to which to be united—
Seeking to ease that way the pain at your heart—
Deceive not yourself, deceive not others.

For united to that which you really **are** you are indeed beautiful, united to Yourself you **are** strong, united to **yourself** you are already in the hearts of those you love;

But disunited you **are** none of these things

And how shall **men** desire a mere shell, or how will you offer them a husk saying, There is fruit within, when there is no fruit—but only vacancy?

And these are the Gods that seek ever to come in the forms of **men**—the ageless immortal Gods—to make of earth that Paradise by their presence;

But while you bar the way and weave your own little plans and purposes like a tangle of cobwebs across the inner door,

How shall they make their entrance and habitation with you?

How shall you indeed know what it is to be Yourself?

I HEAR THY CALL, MYSTERIOUS BEING

I HEAR thy call, Mysterious Being;
In the dead of night, when the stars float grey overhead, and the Northern lights flicker faintly,

In the blazing noon when the sunlight rims with a luminous ring the wide horizon,

Flooding, enfolding all—

I hear thy call.

In the hollow depths below—I hear thee, Mysterious Being.

[I am swept out, as the tide to the call of the Moon is swept out from the shores it knows—to wonderful other shores;

I hear thy Call.

I am carried away, away, in a swoon to the ends of Creation.]

Deep, deep is Thy heart. As I sink in it, lo! there is nothing, nothing which is not held by thy love.

On the surface there is rejection and discrimination, but in the depth lo! everything is held by it.

Swift, swift is Thy flight. In an instant now here, now there—it is all the same to Thee.

As the lambent fire of sex within the body, as the Northern lights with luminous fingers over the sky—

So Thou through all creation.

As the great Sun blazing down at noon on the Himálayan forests, and bathing each leaf the same for hundreds, thousands, of miles—

So Thou through all creation.

[Flutter on little leaves—ye that break the light into a million beautiful forms!

Flutter on little worlds, that float in the ether of space!

Flutter on little hearts, whom the great Heart feeds and encloses!]

And thou, O stranger who dwellest perchance in yonder star, or globe that circles dark about yon star,

Or thou, dear lover that on this earth of ours holdest my heart in thine,

Can Death, I say, or Space or Time or Worlds avail in the end against us?

Take me, great Life—O take me, long-delaying,
Unloose these chains, unbind these clogs and fetters;
I hear thy call—so strange—Mysterious Being,
I hear thy call—I come.

So thin a Veil

SO thin a veil divides
Us from such joy, past words.

Walking in daily life—the business of the hour, each detail seen to;

Yet carried, rapt away, on what sweet floods of other Being:

Swift streams of music flowing, light far back through all Creation shining,

Loved faces looking—
Ah! from the true, the mortal self
So thin a veil divides!

The open Secret

SWEET secret of the open air—
That waits so long, and always there, unheeded.

Something uncaught, so free, so calm large confident—
The floating breeze, the far hills and broad sky,
And every little bird and tiny fly or flower
At home in the great whole, nor feeling lost at all or forsaken,

Save man—slight man!

He, Cain-like from the calm eyes of the Angels,
In houses hiding, in huge gas-lighted offices and dens, in ponderous churches,
Beset with darkness, cowers;
And like some hunted criminal torments his brain
For fresh means of escape, continually;
Builds thicker higher walls, ramparts of stone and gold, piles flesh and skins of slaughtered beasts,
'Twixt him and that he fears;
Fevers himself with plans, works harder and harder,
And wanders far and farther from the goal.

And still the great World waits by the door as ever,
The great World stretching endlessly on every hand, in deep on deep of fathomless content—
Where sing the Morning-stars in joy together,
And all things are at home.

THE SONGS OF THE BIRDS, WHO HEARS

THE songs of the birds, who hears? in the high trees calling,
All the long noon high calling?—
In the meadows below them the wind runs over the grass, the shadows lengthen.
Who sees, who hears?—

In the wonderful height of heaven the clouds are flocked like sails,
    Slow moving, floating, rounding from deep to deep.
    The light swims slowly, changing over the world,
    The distant peaks are touched; and the hills lie silent.
    Who sees, who hears?

    The fox-gloves tall out of the earth arise;
    They stand up out of green shadow;
    Out of night, out of seeds dim in the earth arising,
    They look forth on the blue and green wilderness, and are changed as it changes—
    Changed out of all recognition.
    Who sees, who hears?—

    For all things melt and run—if you only watch them long enough!
    And you cannot emprison anything in one shape—it will surely give you the slip.
    Nothing in essence dies, and nothing in mortal form remains. All is in movement, long calculated, long determined on, with regard to another kind of Form.
    The diamond that you wear in your hair, the gold piece you hold so solid in your hand—they are no more solid than a swarm of bees is solid, of which the units are in constant motion to and fro, some leaving and some joining the swarm.
    They have other business than yours to attend to—they have other spheres beside the market and the drawing-room—and they will surely give you the slip.

The Songs of the Birds

The rocks flow and the mountain shapes flow,
And the forests swim over the lands like cloud-shadows;
The lines of the seeming-everlasting sea are changed,
And its waves beat on unmapped phantom shores:
'Not here, not here!'
All creatures fade from the embraces of their names,
[And you and I, slow, slowly disentangling,]
The delicate hairbells quivering in the light,
The gorse, the heather, and the fox-gloves tall,
The meadows, and the river, rolling, fade:
Fade from their likenesses: fade crying 'Follow!
Follow, for ever follow!'

Who hears, who sees?
Who hears the word of Nature?
The word of her eternal breathing, whispered wherever one shall listen,
The word of the birds in the high trees calling,
Of the wind running over the grass,
The word of the glad prisoners, the tender footless creatures, the plants of the earth,
Rising too, bright-eyed, out of their momentary masks?
'Not here! not here!'

But over all the world, shadowing, shadowing:
The dream! the vast and ever present miracle of all time!
The long-forgotten never-forgotten goal!
Over your own heart, out of its secretest depths:

In crystalline beauty!
Out of all creatures, cloud and mountain and river:
Exhaling, ascending!
From plant and bird and man and planet up-pouring:
Thousand-formed, One,
The ever-present only present reality, source of all illusion,
The Self, the disclosure, the transfiguration of each creature,
And goal of its agelong pilgrimage.

A Child at a Window

I SAT in the dark, at night, outside a little cottage door,
And the light from within streamed through the casement and broke in spray upon the climbing ivy-leaves.
And presently, overhead, a chamber-window opened, and a child peeped silently forth,
And looked up into the vast night and at the all-trembling stars.

And at the same moment, in a far far globe wheeling unseen round a certain star, a child-face peeped forth from its habitation, and looked out into the night, even in the direction of the first child;
And in other globes other faces looked forth;
But they all shrank back and trembled, seeing nothing but vacancy, and saying, How dark, how vast, how awful is the Night!

Yet all the while it was the great Day of the universe into which they looked,
Lit by a million suns.

NIGHT

DARKNESS o'erhead, around,
A curtain closing down upon the earth,
Drowning the woodland tree-tops.
Stretching of hands, straining of eyes—to feel, to see,
To catch the faint faint glamor here and there amid the branches,
The wavering dubious forms and presences.
No floor, no sky, no sound. Only a soft warm moisture in the nostrils,
Folding and brooding all the land in silence.

APRIL

O APRIL, month of Nymphs and Fauns and Cupids,
Month of the Sungod's kisses, Earth's sweet passion,
Of fanciful winds and showers;
Apollo, glorious over hill and dale
Ethereally striding; grasses springing
Rapt to his feet, buds bursting, flowers out-breathing
Their liberated hearts in love to him.

[The little black-cap garrulous on the willow

Perching so prim, the crested chaffinch warbling,
And primrose and celandine, anemone and daisy,
Starring the tender herb which lambs already nibble.]

Month of all-gathering warmth,
Of breathless moments, hotter and hotter growing—
Smiles turned to fire, kisses to fierce earnest—
Of sultry swoons, pauses, and strange suspense
(Clouds and dæmonic thunder through the blue vault threateningly rolling);
Then the delirious up-break—the great fountains of the deep, in Sex,
Loosened to pouring falling rushing waters;
Shafts of wild light; and Sky and Earth in one another's arms
Melted, and all of Heaven spent in streams of love
Towards the Loved one.

Lucifer

Seest thou me pass—swift with my angels out of heaven propelled—
All stars and lightning in a fluid train?
Seest thou me pass, I say?

His brows, the Lord's, in heaven are glorious;
His eyes give light there, fashioning and beholding rapt all forms divine;
His mighty loins are plunged in night and shadow.

And I—
I am the lightning of the generations through them,
Seed of the worlds to be.

He is the Lord, in moment of creation, fixed everlasting,
The Universe entire—or little flower starred in ecstasy;
And I, orgasmic, fierce, His swift deliverance.

[Seest thou me pass—all stars and lightning in a fluid train?
From heaven down into chaos seest thou me pass, I say?]

The Ocean of Sex

TO hold in continence the great sea, the great ocean of Sex, within one,
With flux and reflux pressing on the bounds of the body, the beloved genitals,
Vibrating, swaying emotional to the star-glint of the eyes of all human beings,
Reflecting Heaven and all Creatures,
How wonderful!

Scarcely a figure, male or female, approaches, but a tremor travels across it.
As when on the cliff which bounds the edge of a pond someone moves, then in the bowels of the water also there is a mirrored movement,
So on the edge of this Ocean.

The glory of the human form, even faintly outlined under the trees or by the shore, convulses it with far reminiscences;

(Yet strong and solid the sea-banks, not lightly to be overpassed;)

Till may-be to the touch, to the approach, to the incantation of the eyes of one,

It burst forth, uncontrollable.

O wonderful Ocean of Sex,

Ocean of millions and millions of tiny seed-like human forms contained (if they be truly contained) within each person,

Mirror of the very universe,

Sacred temple and innermost shrine of each body,

Ocean-river flowing ever on through the great trunk and branches of Humanity,

From which after all the individual only springs like a leaf-bud!

Ocean which we so wonderfully contain (if indeed we do contain thee), and yet who containest us!

Sometimes when I feel and know thee within, and identify myself with thee,

Do I understand that I also am of the dateless brood of Heaven and Eternity.

As the Greeks Dreamed

O N the loose hot sands at foot of the cliffs—
The cloudless blue burning above in furious mid-day heats—
As I bask,
Bathing my brown-tanned body in the warm dry clean grit, or cooling it in the sea;
And the sea creeps up, spacious, in curves along the shore,
With fringes of tawny lacework, and green and blue, deepening into the loveliest violet,
And Aphrodite herself out of this marvellously beautiful robe, this liquid cincture, swiftly gliding, for a moment stands,
(Her feet on the watery plain, her head in the great height against the Sun,)
Vast, glorious, white-armed, visible and invisible;

As the sea stretches miles and miles, and the grey chalk cliffs and capes, fainter and fainter, run forward into it, looking on,
And the fisherman slumbers in the shade of his boat, impervious,
And fainter still and more slumbrous on the horizon, in haze and silence the far ships go by;

Through it all, meseems, I see
How the human body bathed in the sheen and wet, steeped in sun and air,
Moving near and nude among the elements,

Matches somehow and interprets the whole of Nature;

How from shoulder to foot of mountain and man alike the lines of grace run on;

How, as the Greeks dreamed, in rock and rill divinest human forms lie shrined, or in the wild woods lurk embosomed;

And how at length and only in the loving union and uncoveredness of Man with Nature may either know or understand the other.

In a Scotch-Fir Wood

IN a Scotch-fir wood—
Where the great rays of the low sun glanced through the trees, in open beauty under the shaggy green,

Lighting stem behind stem in lofty strength interminable;

And the wild sweet air ran lightly by, with warm scent of pine-needles—

I heard a voice saying:

O Man, when wilt thou come fit comrade of such trees, fair mate and crown of such a scene?

Poor pigmy, botched in clothes, feet coffined in boots, braced, stitched and starched,

Too feeble, alas! too mean, undignified, to be endured—

Go hence, and in the centuries come again!

THE DREAM GOES BY

THE dream goes by, touches men's hearts, and floats and fades again—
Far on the hills away from this nightmare of modern cheap-jack life:
The finished free Society.

Finished and done with so much that clogs to-day the weary spirit, weary body;
Finished and done with all the old cumbersome apparatus of Law and Authority, with the endless meanness of 'business' and money-making, with the silly paraphernalia of distinction and respectability, with the terrible struggle of each against all, and the trampling of the weak underfoot by the strong;
Done with the endless joyless labors for the bread that perisheth, for clothing which keeps not the heart warm, for possessions which only weigh their owners to the ground;
With envies, greeds, jealousies—loads and burdens of life too great to be borne—Sisyphus toils that bring no nearer to the goal.

The grown man hand in hand with his little girl, walking the woodland path,
With brown uncovered bodies, both of them, so glad, content, unconscious;
And all the wealth and beauty of the world is theirs;
The Sun shining on their limbs; and in their minds the long results of human culture.

The simple dresses of the public thoroughfare, used or not used with quiet sense of fitness;
The simple diet so easily won, so gladly shared;
The stores of human science, human knowledge, accessible to all—for all to use.
And Death no longer terrible, but full
Of poignant strange Expansion; Labor too
(Which is our daily death
And resurrection in the thing created)
An ever-abiding joy.—
A life so near to Nature, all at one with bird and plant and beast and swimming thing,
So near to all its fellows in sweet love—
In joy unbounded and undying love.

The dream goes by, touches and stirs men's hearts,
And floats, and waits, again.

Surely the Time will come

SURELY the time will come when humanity will refuse to be diseased any longer.
This list of filthy and hideous complaints,—too filthy to be calmly spoken of: these small-poxes, typhoids, choleras, cancers, tumors, tubercles,—dropsy, diabetes, uræmia—all preventible, and easy enough to prevent;
And yet—incredible though it seems—men and women still tolerating and condoning them;
Men and women who pride themselves on their culture,

refinement, punctiliousness of nose, and so forth—and who would turn up the latter at the sight of a pig and a few fowls in an Irishman's cabin—actually tolerating in their own persons the perpetual presence of the most disgusting organisms;

And other men and women, through sheer ignorance, believing such a state of affairs to be necessary.

Surely the time will come when to be diseased, to spread disease around one, or transmit it to descendants,

To live willingly in the conditions that produce disease, or not strenuously to fight against such conditions,

Will be looked on as a crime—both of the individual and of society.

For since a little self-control, since a clean and elementary diet, pure water, openness of the body to sun and air, a share of honest work, and some degree of mental peace and largesse, are the perfectly simple conditions of health, and are, or ought to be, accessible to everybody—

To neglect these is sheer treason;

While to surrender them out of fear (should one stick to them) of being robbed of other things far less precious, is to be a fool, as well as a coward.

Surely the time will come when people, seeing how obvious and simple is the problem of human life,

Will refuse (even at the bidding of the Parson, the Policeman, Mrs. Grundy, and the commercial Slave-drivers and Tax-collectors) to live the lives of idiots;

Will refuse to do other work than that which they like, and which they feel to be really needed;

Will cease to believe that their own well-being can only

be maintained at the cost of the Fear, Torment, and Slaughter of the animals, and the Hanging and Imprisonment of men;

And will waste the hours no more in elaborately preparing food which, when prepared, does but rot the vitals of those who consume it, and in schemes of money-making and 'business' which but destroy their souls.

The time will come surely when we shall cease to burden our limbs and becloud our skins with garments, the major part of which are useless, unless as a breeding ground of ill-health, deformity, and indecency;

Shall cease to build walls and fortifications of property and possession each round ourselves as against the others —deliberately confining so and crucifying the great god of love within us—

And shall at last liberate our minds and bodies from that funny old lazar-house of the centuries, of which none but ourselves, after all, are the warders and gaolers.

THE ONE. FOUNDATION

ONLY that people can thrive that loves its land and swears to make it beautiful;

For the land (the Demos) is the foundation-element of human life, and if the public relation to that is false, all else is of need false and inverted.

How can a flower deny its own roots, or a tree the soil from which it springs?

And how can a people stand firmly planted under the sun, except as mediators between Earth and Heaven—

The One Foundation

To dedicate the gracious fruits of the ground to all divine uses?

Think of it—

To grow rich and beautiful crops for human food, and flowers and fruits to rejoice the eye and heart,

What a privilege!

Yet this to-day is a burden and a degradation, thrust upon the poor and despised.

The Scotch farm-lad strides across the ploughed leas, scattering with princely hand the bread of thousands;

The Italian peasant ties his vines to the trellised canes with twigs of broom, and the spring sunlight glances and twinkles on him from the cistern just below;

The Danish boy drives the herds home from the low-lying pasture-lands in the sweet clear air of evening;

And the world which is built upon the labor of these disowns them, and they themselves sink earthward worn out with unheeded toil;

While the Politician and the Merchant who flourish on lies and fill the people's ears and mouths with chaff are publicly seated in the highest places.

And the Earth rolls on, with all her burden of love unheeded,

And sadness falls on the peoples divorced from the breasts that fain would suckle them.

Think of it—

To place a nation squarely on its own base, spreading out its people far and wide in honored usefulness upon the soil,

Building up all uses and capacities of the land into the life of the masses,

So that the riches of the Earth may go first and foremost to those who produce them, and so onward into the whole structure of society;

To render the life of the people clean and gracious, vital from base to summit, and self-determining,

Dependent simply on itself and not on cliques and coteries of speculators anywhere; and springing thus inevitably up into wild free forms of love and fellowship;

To make the wild places of the lands sacred, keeping the streams pure, and planting fresh blooms along their edges; to preserve the air crystalline and without taint—tempting the sun to shine where before was gloom;

To adorn the woodlands and the high tops with new trees and shrubs and winged and footed things,

Sparing all living creatures as far as possible rather than destroying them;

What a pleasure!

To do all this in singleness of heart were indeed to open up riches for mankind of which few dream—

So much, so infinitely more than what is now called Wealth.

But to-day the lands are slimed and fenced over with denials; and those who would cannot get to them, and those who own have no joy in them—except such joy as a dog may have in a fodderam.

And so, even to-day, while riches untold are wrung from the Earth, it is rather as a robbery that they are produced—without gladness or gratitude, but in grief and sadness and lying and greed and despair and unbelief.

Say, say, what would those riches be, if the Earth and her love were free?

But all waits. And the thunderclouds brood in silence over the lands, meditating the unlipped words of destiny; and the sky rains light upon the myriad leaves and grass, searching inevitably into every minutest thing;

And Ignorance breeds Fear, and Fear breeds Greed, and Greed that Wealth whose converse is Poverty—and these again breed Strife and Fear in endless circles;

But Experience (which in time to all must come) breeds Sympathy, and Sympathy Understanding, and Understanding Love;

And Love leads Helpfulness by the hand, to open the gates of Power unlimited—even for that new race which now appears.

And the blue sea waits below the girdle of the sun-fringed shores, and lips and laps through the millenniums, syllabling the unformed words which man alone can pronounce entire;

And the sunlight wraps the globe of the Earth, and dances and twinkles in the ether of the human heart,

Which is indeed a great and boundless ocean, in which all things float suspended.

A Mightier than Mammon

AT last, after centuries, when the tension and strain of the old society can go no further, and ruin on every side seems impending,

Behold! behind and beneath it all, in dim prefigurement, yet clear and not to be mistaken—the Outline and Draft of a new order.

When Machinery has made affluence possible for everybody, and yet the scramble for Wealth is keener than ever, the line between rich and poor as sharp;

When locomotion and intercommunication practically make the whole World one, and yet the Nations stand round armed tooth and claw, and glaring at each other;

When it is recognised that culture and manual labor are not only compatible but necessary in combination with each other, and yet society remains divided into brutalised workers and cultivated nincompoops;

When men and women everywhere are hungering for community of life, to pass freely, to love and be loved; and yet they remain frozen up, starched, starved, coffined, each in their own little cells of propriety, respectability, dirty property, and dismal poverty;

When the cells are alive and in pain, because the body is lifeless;

When thousands of pulpits preach religion, and there is not a word of religion in it;

A Mightier than Mammon

When the great web and framework of the old order, Law, is collapsing with its own weight—myriads and myriads of statutes, overlapping, overlying, precedents, principles, instances, tumbled buried one behind another in inextricable confusion—and yet never before in the history of the world was there such a rigid brute-pharisaical apparatus of police, military and prisons to enforce the 'heads or tails' of the Courts, and the cant of the 'superior' classes;

When the Millionaire appears on the scene—a new type of human being—as the Dinosaur may have appeared ages ago upon the Earth, gigantic, lumbering, fateful and dangerous; yet destined perhaps finally to break down the ancient jungle of 'Government,' and the barriers of the old Nationalities; and to be a link in the evolution of the future;

When Art is divorced from Life, Science from human feeling, Marriage from Love, Education from Affection;

When to work freely at one's own chosen trade and to interchange freely the products with others is what almost everybody really desires—and is obviously the indicated social form of the future; and yet when nearly everyone is a wage-slave or works at work which he detests!

When the longing for the life of Nature, for the Air and the Sun, for the freedom of the Earth and the waters, for liberation, wildness, spontaneity, is upon folk as perhaps it never was before; and yet they are mewed up more than ever in houses clothes, 'business,' and general asphyxia and futility;

When similarly the longing for freedom of Sex is upon

people, for purity of love, unashamed, unshackled, creating its own law—and yet love is everywhere shamed and shackled and impure;

When the Electric Tension in every direction, owing to this separation of polarities, is becoming so great that the luminous spark, the lightning, the vital flash, has become inevitable;

Then at last, not to be mistaken, the outline and draft of the new creature appears—

The soul that soon shall knit the growing limbs glides in.

A new conception of Life—yet ancient as creation (since indeed, properly speaking, there is no other)—

The life of the Heart, the life of friendship and attachment:

Society forming freely everywhere round this—knit together by this, rather than by the old Cash-nexus:

The love and pride of race, of clan, of family, the free sacrifice of life for these, the commemoration of these in grand works and deeds;

The dedication of Humanity, the wider embrace that passes all barriers of class and race;

And the innumerable personal affection in all its forms—

These, and a proud beautiful sane utterance and enduring expression of them, first; and the other things to follow.

The love of men for each other—so tender, heroic, constant;

That has come all down the ages, in every clime, in every nation,

Always so true, so well assured of itself, overleaping barriers of age, of rank, of distance,
Flag of the camp of Freedom;
The love of women for each other—so rapt, intense, so confiding-close, so burning-passionate,
To unheard deeds of sacrifice, of daring and devotion, prompting;
And (not less) the love of men for women, and of women for men—on a newer greater scale than it has hitherto been conceived;
Grand, free and equal—gracious yet ever incommensurable—
The soul of Comradeship glides in.

The young heir goes to inspect the works of one of his tenants;
[Once more the king's son loves the shepherd lad;]
In the shed the fireman is shovelling coal into the boiler furnace. He is neither specially handsome nor specially intelligent, yet when he turns, from under his dark lids rimmed with coal-dust shoots something so human, so loving-near, it makes the other tremble.
They only speak a few words, and lo! underneath all the differences of class and speech, of muscle and manhood, their souls are knit together.

The Cinghalese cooly comes on board a merchant vessel at Colombo, every day for a week or more, to do some bits of cleaning.

He is a sweet-natured bright intelligent fellow of 21 or so. One of the engineers is decently kind and friendly with him—gives him a knife and one or two little presents;

But the Cinghalese gives his very soul to the engineer; and worships his white jacket and overalls as though they were the shining garment of a god.

He cannot rest; but implores to be taken on the voyage; and weeps bitterly when he learns that the ship must sail without him.

[Ah! weep not, brown-bodied youth wandering lonely by the surf-ridden shore—as you watch your white friend's vessel gliding into the offing, under the sun and the sun-fringed clouds;

Out, far out to sea, with your friend whom you will never see again;

Weep not so heart-brokenly, for even your tears, gentle boy, poured now upon the barren sand are the prophecy of amity that shall be one day between all the races of the earth.]

And here are two women, both doctors and mature in their profession, whose souls are knit in a curiously deep affection.

They share a practice in a large town, and live in the same house together, exchanging all that they command, of life and affection and experience;

And this continues for twenty years—till the death of the elder one—after which the other ceases not to visit her grave, twice every week, till the time of her own last illness.

A Mightier than Mammon

And this is of a poor lad born in the slums, who with aching lonely heart once walked the streets of London.

Many spoke to him because he was fair—asked him to come and have a drink, and so forth; but still it was no satisfaction to him; for they did not give him that which he needed.

Then one day he saw a face in which love dwelt. It was a man twice his own age, captain of a sailing vessel—a large free man, well acquainted with the world, capable and kindly.

And the moment the lad saw him his heart was given to him, and he could not rest but must needs follow the man up and down—yet daring not to speak to him, and the other knowing nothing of it all.

And this continued—till the time came for the man to go another voyage. Then he disappeared; and the youth, still not knowing who or whence he was, fell into worse misery and loneliness than ever, for a whole year.

Till at last one day—or one evening rather—to his great joy he saw his friend going into a public house. It was in a little street off Mile-end Road. He slipped in and sat beside him.

And the man spoke to him, and was kind, but nothing more. And presently, as the hour was getting late, got up and said Goodnight, and went out at the door.

And the lad, suddenly seized with a panic fear that he might never see his friend again, hurried after him, and when they came to a quiet spot, ran up and seized him by the hand, and hardly knowing what he was doing fell on his knees on the pavement, and held him.

And the man at first thought this was a ruse or a mere conspiracy, but when he lifted the lad and looked in his face he understood, for he saw love written there. And he straightway loved and received him.

And this is of a boy who sat in school.

The masters talked about Greek accidence and quadratic equations, and the boys talked about lobs and byes and bases and goals; but of that which was nearest to his heart no one said a word.

It was laughed at—or left unspoken.

Yet when the boy stood near some of his comrades in the cricket-field or sat next them in school, he stocked and stammered, because of some winged glorious thing which stood or sat between him and them.

And again the laughter came, because he had forgotten what he was doing; and he shrank into himself, and the walls round him grew, so that he was pent and lonely like a prisoner.

Till one day to him weeping, Love full-grown, all-glorious, pure, unashamed, unshackled, came like a god into his little cell, and swore to break the barriers.

And when the boy through his tears asked him how he would do that, Love answered not, but turning drew with his finger on the walls of the cell.

And as he drew, lo! beneath his finger sprang all forms of beauty, an endless host—outlines and colors of all that is, transfigured ;

And, as he drew, the cell-walls widened—a new world rose—and folk came trooping in to gaze,
And the barriers had vanished.

Wonderful, beautiful, the Soul that knits the Body's life passed in,
And the barriers had vanished.

Everywhere under the surface the streamers shoot, auroral,
Strands and tissues of a new life forming.
Already the monstrous accumulations of private wealth seem useless and a burden—
At best to be absorbed in new formations.
The young woman from an upper class of society builds up her girls' club; the young man organises his boys from the slums. Untiring is their care; but something more, more personal and close, than philanthropy inspires them.
The little guilds of workers are animated by a new spirit; to have pleasure in good work seems something worth living for; the home-colonists turn their backs on civilisation if only they may realise a friendly life with Nature and each other; the girls in the dress-making shop stand in a new relation to their mistress, and work so gladly for her and with her; the employer of labor begins to doubt whether he gets any satisfaction by grinding the faces of his men—a new idea is germinating in his mind; even to the landlord it occurs that to create a glad and free village life upon his estate would be more pleasure than to shoot over it.

As to the millionaire, having spent his life in scheming for Wealth, he cannot but continue in the web which himself has woven; yet is heartily sick of it, and longs in a kind of vague way for something simple and unembarrassed. He is pestered to death by sharks, parasites, poor relations, politicians, adventurers, lawyers, company-promoters, begging letters and business correspondence, society functions, charitable and philanthropic schemes, town and country houses, stewards, bailiffs, flunkeys, and the care of endless possessions; and sees that to cast all these aside and devote his wealth if possible to the realisation of a grand life for the mass-peoples of the Earth were indeed his best hope and happiness.

The graduate from Cambridge is a warm-hearted impulsive little woman, genuine and human to the core. Having escaped from high and dry home-circles, she found curiously the answer of her heart in a wage-worker of an East London workshop—a calm broad-browed woman, strong, clearheaded, somewhat sad in expression, and a bit of a leader among her trade-mates.

Having got into touch with each other, the two came at last to live together; and immediately on doing so found themselves a focus and centre of activities—like opposite poles of a battery through which when in contact the electricity streams.

So the news and interests of the two classes of society streamed through them. Through them too, folk from either side, especially women, came into touch with each other, and discovered a common cause and sympathy amid many surface differences.

Thus by a thousand needs beside their own compelled, was their love assured, their little home made sacred.

Everywhere a new motive of life dawns.
With the liberation of Love, and with it of Sex, with the sense that these are things—and the joy of them—not to be dreaded or barred, but to be made use of, wisely and freely, as a man makes use of his most honored possession,
Comes a new gladness:
The liberation of a Motive greater than Money,
And the only motive perhaps that can finally take precedence of Money.

Men and women mate freely again;
The sacredness of sex in freedom is taught in schools and churches; the ulcer of prostitution slowly disappears; the wasted love that flows in a morbid stream through the streets, or desiccates in grand mansions, runs once more into the channels of free devotion and life.
One by one, here and there, in silence perhaps, unremarked, or perhaps the centre of a little cyclone of excited abuse, a couple, offstanding, exempt, determined, assert their right to the highest and best that life can give.
[Fear not, gentle girl, the sneers of the womenkind, nor thou, young man, the pointed fingers of who can credit not the truth of love.]
To lead their own lives, irrespective of all criticism and custom, and graft into the great Heart of the world and each other.

Wild as a raven, and a free lover of Nature, is the Irish squire's daughter. She hates all the conventions and proprieties with an instinctive hatred—she hardly knows why. She is loved by a man whom the family consider beneath them. He is not without his faults certainly. But when her parents turn fiercely on her and him, she determines at all costs to stick to him. Her sister, the dove, approved and admired by everybody, marries a young Earl just come into the title; and she on the same day goes off with her friend, and is forbidden to cross, and in fact never crosses, the threshold of her home again.

The newly-made wife, wedded to an army officer, finds almost immediately after marriage that their temperaments are wholly incompatible. Instead of sacrificing herself to 'duty' or propriety, she has the good sense to insist on leaving him: on leaving him his freedom, and herself the same, as far as may be, for the future.

And this is of a young man, a man about town and the clubs, and well up in the finesse of society, but of real affectionate nature—who was truly bored with his own pursuits and surroundings, and so for him too the barriers vanished.

He fell in with a girl of quite rustic birth and life, but bright-looking, and of sturdy almost stubborn common-sense and wit; and was charmed—partly by her contrast to all that he was accustomed to.

Ultimately—and after some obstinate and exasperating refusals on her part—he made her his wife; much to the disgust of his relatives—whose only consolation was to find he did not intend to bring her among them!

She in fact felt (and he knew) that she could not cope with 'society' ways and customs, and her true instinct was to spare herself the vulgarity.

They took a little house near London, and lived quietly and happily, allowing any of their friends, who had good sense enough, to come and see them—she meanwhile learning much about the great world, and he learning much which he had never known before about practical work and the needs of the people.

Then, later on, when he came into his estate, and they went down into the country, instead of living in the ancestral wigwam they agreed it better to build a decent-sized cottage in the grounds for their own use;

And the Hall and outbuildings they fitted up as Workshops; and gradually getting the village lads and girls together found them employment at various small trades and crafts;

Till with the output of good and artistic work, their market became assured, and the affair grew rapidly in extent and solidity.

And the larger rooms they adorned in every way for library and reading purposes, and music and entertainments of all kinds; and the grounds were partly for recreation and partly for the cultivation of produce;

So that before long the place became much known and sought after, and the employees (who all had a share in the concern) were mighty proud of it.

Certainly the old county society felt somewhat shocked and uncomfortable, and even the tenant-farmers thought things were being carried too far;

But the young couple stuck to their programme, and as years went on, and after various obstacles and opposition lived down, their lives became the centre of the love and affection of the whole neighborhood, great and small, but especially the small;

And they achieved a real distinction, and the finest kind of aristocracy.

O little sister Heart, without thy big brother the rude Brain what wouldst thou do?

So I see thee sitting in thy solitary chamber, poring over a figure in a cameo—

So yearning lost desirous, faint forgetful,
Failing almost thy daily service of the body.

Then comes thy brother and snatches thee by the hand, saying, "Come out here into the world:

See all these wonderful things, and all there is to do;"
And talks so eloquent, so persuasively,
Soon thou art busy with him and his affairs, and the great world outside there in the sun;

Till presently he rests or sleeps awhile—and thou returning
Gazest again on the cameo in thy chamber.

Forms Eternal as the Mountains

SO, when for an instant my friends (and I myself) appeared like insubstantial forms whirled to and fro in the world, now jostled against each other, now carried apart—the sport of the winds and the waves, and puppets moved by the tangled threads of chance:

All at once the heavens opened, and I beheld, magnificent, serene—

Like mountains in the morning towering over the earth, changeless, or changing only as the mountains change,

[And Time and all the years were but a mist which rolled against them,

Hiding, revealing, here an outline, there an outline,

Here a ledge of blooming flowers, there a black and lowering crag]—

That other world where the Sun shines for ever,

Those other Forms that move not from their place.

Spending the Night Alone

TO lie all night beside the loved one—how lovely!

To hold in one's arms something so precious, so beautiful,

Dear head and hair and lips and limbs that shrine eternity,

Through scent and sense and breath and touch and love—

Forgetting all but this **one**—all but this **one**.

And then again to spend the night alone, to resume oneself—
To sail out in the silent watches over the sleeping world, and drink of the intoxication of space,
Calm, self-centred, to the great first One united;
Over-looking the wide sleeping-grounds of Time—forms of the past, the future—comrades innumerable,
Lovers possible, all safely eternally embosomed;
Kissing them lightly on the lips, the forehead,
Leaving them sleeping,
Spending the night alone.

O Joy Divine of Friends

O JOY divine of friends!
To hold within the circle of one's arms
More than the universe holds:
So sweet, so rare, so precious beyond words,
The god so tenderly mortal!

Not kisses only or embraces,
Nor the sweet pain and passion of the flesh alone;
But more, far more,
To feel (ah joy!) the creature deep within
Touch on its mate, unite, and lie entranced
There, ages down, and ages long, in light,
Suffused, divine—where all these other pleasures
Fade but to symbols of that perfect union!

O Child of Uranus

O CHILD of Uranus, wanderer down all times,
    Darkling, from farthest ages of the Earth the same
Strange tender figure, full of grace and pity,
Yet outcast and misunderstood of men—

Thy Woman-soul within a Man's form dwelling,
[Was Adam perchance like this, ere Eve from his side was drawn?]
So gentle, gracious, dignified, complete,
With man's strength to perform, and pride to suffer without sign,
And feminine sensitiveness to the last fibre of being;
Strange twice-born, having entrance to both worlds—
Loved, loved by either sex,
And free of all their lore!

I see thee where down all of Time thou comest;
And women break their alabaster caskets, kiss and anoint thy feet, and bless the womb that bare thee,
While in thy bosom with thee, lip to lip,
Thy younger comrade lies.

Lord of the love which rules this changing world,
Passing all partial loves, this one complete—the Mother love and sex-emotion blended—
I see thee where for centuries thou hast walked,
Lonely, the world of men.

Saving, redeeming, drawing all to thee,
Yet outcast, slandered, pointed of the mob,
Misjudged and crucified.

Dear Son of heaven—long suffering wanderer through the wildernesses of civilisation—
The day draws nigh when from these mists of ages
Thy form in glory clad shall reappear.

One at a Time

A MILLION faces, loves, bodies, lives—a million souls,
    Pouring down Time—
As in a dream I see, and know my own.
All nations, classes, trades, ranks, temperaments,
[The soldier's cap, the felon's crop, the bishop's mitre,
Under the eyelids of the peasant woman, beneath the burnous of the Arab chieftain,]
A million souls, yet from the rest at once distinguished—by the first glance revealed—
I see, and know my own.

[Nay through the ages, loved ones, true to you,
Inseparable at heart I still remain,
Nor doubt you for an instant, nor myself.]

But here, to-day, may-be of all One only
The hour, the strict Eternity of Time,
Presents—and I accept.

May-be the least, unworthiest as the world would say,
Yet even so sufficient—for blest the hour
Which brings what, else, Eternity would miss!
Another day the worthiest may claim me;
To-day we two alone will be the world:
And Love, the Lord of all, shall dwell between us.

THE DEAD COMRADE

THERE among the woods, after the battle returning,
In a little open spot—how well I remember it—
Where the ground was red with the blood of my lover, my dead comrade,

[Him whom to save I would have died so gladly, O so gladly,

Whom I could not at any time bear to see suffer even a little hurt,

So tenderly we loved, so tenderly,]

There on the stained red ground, in the midst of the clotted precious blood, not even yet dry, stood a small yellow flower—

The little Cow-wheat they call it, with its slender yellow blossoms in pairs, and its faint-tinged lips.

And now in the woods each year—in the silent beautiful woods, so calm, so sweet—though the same flowers spring by hundreds—

Not a word do they utter of that awful scene, not a word of all that carnage,

Of the splintered trees, the blood-smeared corpses, the devilish noises and the sights and smells,
Or of the livid face and faint-blue lips of him I loved as never another I could love.

O how can you grow so careless, little flowers, and yet continue ages to grow under the trees the same—
And all the light gone out of the world for me?
Each year when summer comes and July suns,
To the woods I must go like one drawn by a fatal dread and fascination,
To see the sight I most abhor to see—
The patch of blood, and the unharmed flower in the midst,
And faint in death the lips I love so well.

PHILOLÄUS TO DIOCLES

HOW often at dusk, dear friend, when thou art absent,
Sitting alone I wonder of what thou doest,
And dream, and wait of thee.

All the sweet noons and moons we have spent together;
All the glad interchange of laughter and love,
And thoughts, so grave, or fanciful:
What can compare with these, or what surpass them?
All the unbroken faith and steadfast reliance—nigh twenty years twining the roots of life far down;
And not a mistrustful hour between us—or moment of anger:

What can surpass all this, or what compare?
Could riches or fame?
Or if the Thebans honor me for their law-giver,
Or thou, Diocles, in Olympic fields art victor beloved and crowned,
What are these things to that?

And still thou growest upon me, as a mountain,
Seen from another mountain-summit, rises
Clearer, more grand, more beautiful than ever;
And still within thine eyes, and ever plainer,
I see my own soul sleeping.

Say, did not Love, the Olympian blacksmith, find us,
Æons ago, in heaven,
And weld our souls together before all worlds?

II.

When thou art far, and the days go by without thee,
Strangely I suffer.
Perhaps even so in winter suffer the plants and the trees, when the Sun withdraws his life-ray;
Thin runs the blood in my limbs, sucked out of the arteries;
The heart shrinks closed and painful—I lose command and vigor;
At times like these, methinks, I too have strayed from my body,
Afar, in pursuit of thee, my sun and my savior.

III.

Thou art so beautiful to me, sweet friend,
Years bring no shadow between us;
Always I praise the very ground beneath thy feet,
That leads thee toward me,
And give my unbelieving hands free leave to hold thee,
For still to assure myself that thou art there
Is my first need.

Love, that entwined our souls before all worlds,
Binds the great orbs of heaven too in their courses,
But by no bond more lasting.

IV.

And sweeter far to suffer is it, dear one, being sometimes absent,
    Than (if indeed 'twere possible) to feel the opposite pain
    Of too much nearness, and love dying so
    Down to mere slackness.

Now, as it is, the harp is firmly strung;
A tender tension animates the strings;
And every thought of Thee, and all the winds which blow along the world,
    Wake a sweet áccord underneath the din,
    And harmonize life's wilderness for me.

V.

Therefore I say, stay, comrade, lover mine,
Nor wander far from me while life remains,
But let us rather, and if it may be, hand in hand,
Pass to that last strange change, therein perhaps to know each other
Nearer even than now.

VI.

Indeed, thou art so deep within my heart,
I fear not Death. And though I die, and fail,
Falling through stupors, senselessness, oblivion,
Down to the roots of being; still, thou art there.
I shall but sleep as I have slept before,
So oft, in dreamless peace, close-linked with thee.

Hafiz to the Cup-bearer

DEAR Son, that out of the crowded footways of Shiráz,
With hesitant step emerging,
Camest and laid thy life down at my feet,
Faint and ashamed, like one by some divine wine vanquished:

I take thy gift, so gracious and sparkling clear,
Thy naïve offering, as of a simple Nature-child,
Wondering, like one who sees a rose in winter blooming, or cypress 'mid a wilderness of rocks;

Or finds among the marl and clay beneath his feet
A ruby fair embedded—and stops and takes it.

[The Earth, so dead and gross, and yet to points of finest light
Still working in the silence of her unseen chambers!
And thou, great common People, slavish still and brute and ignorant, in alley and tavern,
Yet in thy rugged mass fair hearts of finest glow
Infallibly condensing!]

Come, son (since thou hast said it), out of all Shiráz
Háfiz salutes thee comrade. Let us go
A spell of life along the road together.

IN THE STONE-FLOORED WORKSHOP

THERE in the stone-floored workshop in the middle of a great dirty city—the windows half made up with dust—
Three men, astraddle on their horsings, and over their grinding wheels bending.

The drum that brings the power from the engine-room pounds and thumps, the belting slaps and crackles, whizz go the wheels so steady in their sockets, and the streams of sparks fly rustling.
All is so old-fashioned, perhaps much as it was four or five centuries ago;

The old stone trows half full of water, in which the wheels run; the puddles, the mud, the wheelswarf spattered and crusting the walls and even the clothes of the grinders with yellow dirt;

The rude wooden bearings for the axles, soused with water when they get too hot; the drawing-up stones, emery wheels, polishers, glazers;

The little wheels, made out of fragments of larger ones, for hollow grinding, and (more modern) the fan for drawing and expelling the dust.

There astraddle, in their rough clothes, with clogs on their feet, and faces yellow-splashed, hour by hour bending over, the men sit—

With careful grasp of one hand and pressure of the other, holding the blades to the stone—the pads of their finger-tips worn through to the very quick where they now and then and unavoidably touch it in its swift career.

Very careful and responsible is the work—the least slip may cause an accident.

A man comes in from the hardening shop, puts down a bundle of rough-shaped blades, and goes out again.

And still the heads sway rhythmically from side to side as eye and hand follow their work across the wheel.

Very careful is the testing and examining of a new stone and the fitting it on its axle: a single flaw and in the great speed it will fly, bringing danger to all around it.

Now and then one pauses and takes a swipe out of a can;

or throws his band off, to change his wheel for another; or goes to the fire to examine some blades which are heating in a tray over it.

Curt is the talk (of fancy-backs, rattlers, sours and wasters, tangs and heels and shoulders), for the noise is too great, and the strain, for much beyond monosyllables.

Dingy the den and dense the grit that settles thick upon everything.

Yet at last out of it all, out of this primitive scene, emerges something so finished, so subtly perfect—

A razor, keen and brilliant, a very focus of light in the whole shop, with swift invisible edge running true from heel to point, and ringing so clear to the twang of the thumb-nail on it—

Emerges (his work done) a figure with dusty cap and light curls escaping from under it, large dove-grey eyes and Dutch-featured face of tears and laughter,

(So subtle, so rare, so finished a product,)

A man who understands and accepts all human life and character,

Keen and swift of brain, heart tender and true, and low voice ringing so clear,

And my dear comrade.

THE TRYSTING

FAR over the hills, ten miles, in the cloudless summer morning,

By grassy slopes and flowering wheatfields, and over the brooks, he strides—

A young man, slender, wistful-eyed—with a great bouquet of flowers in his hand.

Great roses, red and white (in the cottage-home garden gathered),

And sweet-scented ladslove and rich marigolds and mignonette and lilies,

All trembling in the glimmer of brimming eyes, and steeped in fragrant memories,

With full full heart he carries;

And calls in spirit, the while he goes, to her so loved—

More than all other women on earth beloved—

His mother who bore him.

Till at length by the town arriving,

On her grave in the cemetery ground he faithfully lays them.

And this the trysting.

This the trysting for which in the little garden, with tears, he gathered the flowers,

For which o'er the hills he hastened.—

And this, what means, what boots it?

There truly, below, with head fallen on one side, a shapeless indistinguishable mass, her body lies—

Three years already from this life departed—

Nor hears nor sees, nor understands at all,

The Trysting

Senseless as any clod.
Above, the flowers he has brought lie wilting in the sun;
Around, the common-place dingy scene extends—the dreary cemetery,
The stones, the walls, the houses.—
What boots it all?
These senseless things that neither see nor hear,
To senseless things what message can they bear?

Yet he, he hears and sees.
A natural child, untaught, reckless of custom and what they call religion,
He hears and sees things hidden from the learnéd;
He glimpses forms beyond the walls of Time.
Of bibles, creeds and churches he knows nothing,
And all that science has said about life and death and atom-dances and the immutable laws of matter,
And all the impassable lines and barriers that the professors and specialists have built up out of their own imaginations—
These simply exist not, for him.
He only knows she comes, the loved and worshiped—
Comes, takes the flowers,
Stands like a thin mist in the sun beside him,
Looks in his eyes, and touches him again.

And to its depth his heart shakes, breaking backward,
Tears rise once more, earth reels, the sun is splintered,
Stones, houses, and the solid sky dissolve,

And that far marvelous vibration of the soul,
Swifter than light, more powerful than sound,
Flies through the world, pierces the rocks and tombs,
And gains her Presence at the feet of God.

THE LOVER FAR ON THE HILLS

HERE on this high top far above the world—
    This mute and glorious scene, earth's panorama:
[The swelling mountains, all in green and gold,
Round-topped, or broken into savage crags;
The valleys scarcely shown, like narrow rifts;
The slate-dark shadows, and the tarns and lakes,
And vistas over them to sunny lands
Of tiny patchwork, with quaint fields and farms,
White sails on waters, and the sun-splashed sea:]
Here on this high top dreaming, to it all
I find but one fit likeness—
Namely the gracious form of her I love.
The limbs and hair, the lips, the eyes, I love—
Twin heavenlit lakes—
And undulant lines that run from hips to shoulder;
Fair world of hollow and rondure, hill and plain,—
So solid-fair like this, so dewy-fragrant,
And all inwrought with that dear life that holds me.

How calm this air! this silence here in heaven
Calm blue, and tender hanging clouds delaying
To kiss their shadows on the hills' deep breasts;

And far around this dream of human presence—
Nature, and my sweet Helpmate whom I worship,
With the dear god that dwells behind them both.

THE BABE

THE trio perfect: the man, the woman, and the babe:
And herein all Creation.

The two, with wonder in their eyes, from opposite worlds
Of sex, of ancestry, pursuits, traditions,
Each other suddenly, amazed, confronting—
A nameless glory each in each surmising.

A frenzy as of Gods—
Imperial rage, flinging the goods of the world aside as dross, to reach to a priceless treasure:
[He madly invasive,
She deeply wise, and drawing farther back
Even to the gates of Paradise as he approaches:]
Strange ecstasy of warfare!
Seisin and ravishment of souls and bodies,
Veils rent asunder,
Heaven opening measureless, overhead, in splendor,
And all life changed, transfigured!

And then a calm.
Weeks of humdrum and mortal commonplace,
And months perchance in monotone of toil,

But still behind it all some deep remembrance,
Some sure reliance,
And sweet and secret knowledge in each other.

And then the Babe:
A tiny perfect sea-shell on the shore
By the waves gently laid (the awful waves!)—
By trembling hands received—a folded message—
A babe yet slumbering, with a ripple on its face
Remindful of the ocean.

And two twined forms that overbend it, smiling,
And wonder to what land Love must have journeyed,
Who brought this back—this word of sweetest meaning:
Two lives made one, and visible as one.

And herein all Creation.

*O gracious Mother, in thy vast eternal sunlight
Heal us, thy foolish children, from our sins;
Who heed thee not, but careless of thy Presence
Turn our bent backs on thee, and scratch and scrabble
In ash-heaps for salvation.*

I Saw a Fair House

I SAW a fair house standing in a garden, but no one moved about it;

And I said to some who stood by, Who is the owner or dweller here?

And they said, We know not. Sometimes we see a form at a window, but it is for a moment only, and then it is gone.

Then I went up to the door of the house, and turned the handle very softly, and went in.

And the house was like a place deserted, yet was there a kind of order as if it might be used; and the tables were laid with victuals, and there was no lack of necessaries or of comforts;

And servants passed along the corridors; so I asked one of them, Where is the mistress of your house?

And he said, I know not.

Then I went on again, and passed softly through many rooms, and peeped into others;

And at last in a far chamber I came upon the figure of a woman, alone, and seated on a chair, with her head on her knees, and buried in her hands;

And I said, Are you the mistress of this house?

And when she lifted her face I saw it was very beautiful, and her eyes were glorious as the eyes of Love himself, but they were stained with weeping.

And she said, This is not my house, it is my prison.

And I said, Are not these servants here to minister to you?

She answered, Yes—but what is that if they are only here to minister to me?

But these rooms, I said, and well-set tables?

Yes—but what is that if they are only swept and garnished for me?

And this garden, and the fair outlook from it?

Yes—but since I may not even go my own errands beyond the gate?

And I said, How is that?

And she answered, Indeed I long to go down into the world, but I may not; no sooner do I show the face of Love than I am execrated as one forbidden and an outcast. For in this city so long as one remains within one's house one may do there what meanness and selfishness one will, provided one keeps fair the front of the house; but to go forth openly and share one's life and the gladness of life with others, that is not permitted.

And I said, It is a strange city.

And I went out and walked through the streets; but gloom and sadness reigned, and only in some houses the noise of feasting and debauchery, and in others a sound of weeping.

A Dream of Human Life

I DREAMED that I saw a wild and lonely promontory on which the sea beat; and the waves dashed against rocky cliffs and bastions, and flew in spray over the edges of them, and clouds drifted on overhead, mingling with the sea-mist below in one veil which wrapped and shadowed all, save where now and then a watery beam from the sun glanced through.

And in the midst among the rocks and crags was (it seemed to me) an ancient ancient fane, like some far forgotten Abbey Church built in an elder world—nor was it easy to say whether it was indeed built up of ordinary masonry, or whether by some rude art it had been shapen from the very crags themselves. But round about it and over the promontory on all sides the rocks and cliffs were carven in strange forms— sea-monsters half submerged beneath the waves, and serpents stretching along the bases of the cliffs, and evil shapes thrown up on land and grasping at the rocks with iron claws; and beside them forms heroic of men and women on ledges here and there and pinnacles, through the mist half-shown—as it might have been S. George against the dragon, or Andromeda to the rock-face chained, or Perseus with the Gorgon's head in hand.

But who they really were I could not well see. Only ever as the spray and wind wreathed by, the figures as in mortal combat seemed to move and menace each other, and serpents writhed and sea-beasts plunged through waves. And from the ancient fane came the sound of music continually—

now low and distant, now rising with the storm and mingling with the ocean-roar and wild cry of the wind: while overhead amid the breaking lights was a fluttering as of Wings.

And presently a change came over my dream; and looking again I saw that the storm had ceased, and the promontory was lying there in the sunshine, calm and peaceful; and the rocks were black no more, but full of color and glory; and the hero figures were in their places, at rest and beautiful to look on; and even the monsters that had seemed so terrible had a grace of their own, transformed in the peaceful light to harmless grotesque things. And the whole land seemed to thrill with a subterranean music, and on a high crag brooding over all was a figure with arms outstretched.

And once more my dream changed; and I looked, and the rocks had become like ordinary rocks and sea-cliffs, and grasses and wild flowers grew, and little habitations nestled, in the hollows of them; and the sea crawled about the boulders lying below them; and the promontory ran out into the ocean, and ships went past it to all parts of the world.

The Coast of Liguria

A THOUSAND years are nothing.
Once the Ligurian, sturdy and thickset, scaled these rocks,

And built his beehive huts of unhewn stone on the limestone terraces,

And gathered snails for food, and fought his tribal battles.

Now the Greek wanders along the shore, and oleander and rosemary

Shine in the moon for him, or Daphne hides

Among the laurel groves, or Heracles

Drives his red cattle home along the coast-line.

Later, the Roman makes great roads, and marches columns of soldiers through the dust,

Where overhead some temple of Castor and Pollux on the height

Gives omen of good fortune. The Christian follows,

Peacefully toiling in his olive-garden,

Hymning the gentle god,

And turns the Temple to a shrine of Michael—re-christens Mars, St. Martin.

But presently the Moor with fire and rapine sweeps the coast,

Or in his mountain-fastness, for a moment resting, watches the shining scimitar of the sea

Sheathed in the bay, its scabbard. Then, in their turn,

Bishops and Barons rule the land, and rage against each other. In the end the Modern

Buries it all in a big Hotel's foundations

Or the embankment of a Railroad.

Yet still beneath the surface all is alive.

Still the old peasant-woman—grin-faced, big-mouthed, with big-palmed hands, short fingers, and bandy climbing legs—among the rocks

Goes foraging for snails. The people still
Dimly athwart the mists of time remember,
Of Heracles the Savior,
How on this Plain, that Promontory, he rested
From his great labors in the West returning.
Still the little Church of St. Michael on the rock
Stands dearer to the folk for being pagan;
And still provençal songs and dances gladden the vintage;
And Moorish faces, and Greek, and old Phœnician,
Stir in the villages a stones-throw from the rail.

And still old names and festivals and customs
Linger along the coast and country side;
And still the hills stand, still the herbs diffuse
From the warm ground the old intoxication
Of aromatic sweetness. The waters still
Lap blue against the rocks. The snowy Alps
Look o'er the foot-hills and far out to sea,
To where and when perchance a worthier race
Than all that yet has been at length shall come
And gaze with grateful eyes upon their beauty,
And crown their slopes with gladness.

EASTER DAY ON MT. MOUNIER
(In the Alpes Maritimes)

SILENCE.—
    Here on a rock in blue mid-air nine thousand feet,
  The whole encircling sky flooded with light—the sun an unfaceable point in the dazzling zenith,

Warm, windless, basking—the snow at our feet a million bright points glittering;
And far around a multitudinous sea of peaks,
Frozen, of rock and ice, and fields of rounded whiteness,
And jutting shoulders, and slopes of shale, and walls,
Behind each other rising:
All drenched, dissolved, in light,
And waiting, silent, rapt, as if to break into song.

But not a sound.
Buried in invisible valleys—'mid pine and larch and torrent-beds below—
Villages ply their daily round of labor;
The peasant hacks deep the soil around his vine-roots, or with his long pole beats the boughs of olive;
Far by the sea, mid garden-terraces, hotels and villas, the great town keeps its carnival of Easter—
Unseen, unthought-of, here.

Here only rests the stillness of the Earth, waiting upon the glory of the Sun; or here and there in some calm lakelet imaged.
Ages fly by, and almost without change; dim lines of floating cloud just fringe the horizon; vistas of far lands, distant times, unfold;
And the silence of centuries holds the secret of history
Lost in the light of heaven.

At Mentone

WHY speak ye not, ye beautiful lands and seas,
    Hung like a magic curtain in the light?
What dumbness holds you, O divine vast Earth?

Ye stretches of smooth bare rock, dotted with cactus and aloe,
Rising so bold in the sun, from your deep dark gorges below;
Ye pine woods on the mountain flanks;
And ye, ye terraces of endless labor, planted with vine and lemon and the abounding olive,
With peasant cots and cabins here and there, and cisterns where the frogs croak night and day;
Why speak ye not, why speak ye not?
Why with that strange prophetic glance of yours
Hang ye in heaven there, magic lands and seas,
Nor say the word we wait for?

The Campanile and red roof of the village church show out seaward against the sky-line; and the cypresses stand sentinel in the cemetery on the hill above;
The borage-flowers beneath the lemon branches catch the hues of sea and sky; runnels of water sparkle through the grass by the pathside; the scent of orange-bloom is in the air;
Far back into the valleys stretch the gray shade and gloom of the olive-yards; and the narrow tumbled alleys of the mountain-villages are like huge rock-burrows of human beings;

The grizzled wrinkled old man on his little plot of ground, and the young man beside him, work doggedly on with their mattocks through the heat of the day;

The broad-bosomed placid-eyed girl tends her flock of goats on the higher ledges.

Ye leafing fig-trees, like silver candelabra of green flame!
And ye, pale-blossoming peaches, dainty bright!
And ye, ye immemorial aromatic herbs and bushes—arbutus, myrtle, lavender, rosemary, thyme—trampled to perfume by the feet of long-forgotten races;
And thou, blue bay, with myriad points of light, and sky above with subtle answering quiver,
And high far crests of gleaming purple crag, and snows beyond,
Flaming, all flaming in the light!
Why speak ye not?

Cave men and women and children, on your sides by the sea-shore,
Your long skulls resting still in the palms of your bony hands,
A score millenniums lying in the same position—
Why wake and speak ye not?
Why utter not the thoughts that were, for you, the world?
Ye dead that build the rocks, and are the Earth, and fill, without a void, the crystal air!
And Thou one dead (for each and all of us)—one dead for whom our life we'ld gladly give—

[Thou whose remembrance passes through all sights and sounds, transforming and transforming them]—

Why through the veil of this material texture showest thou not, dear soul of things, thy face?

What dumbness holds you?

O divine vast Earth,

Why utterest not the voice we long to hear?

Monte Carlo

ALL the long afternoon in a cloudless sky, slowly towards its setting the sinking sun

Looks on a scene of wonderful beauty.

Deep below over the rocks, through luscious tangles of geranium and rose and heliotrope in flower, the sea sparkles a rich turquoise blue;

Palms mingle with mimosa and myrtle amid the gardens;

The little cape of Monaco stands out, a stone's-throw across the harbour—the mountains of Mentone run down to the sea—and overhead in the clear air rise (two thousand feet) the great frowning rocks of Turbia, with their ancient Roman tower.

In front of the Casino, on a gravelled space, dazzling in light, a throng of all nationalities—Germans, Russians, French, Italians, English, Americans—goes to and fro,

Or sits at the Café tables, sipping coffee and cognac and maraschino :·

The puffy fussy Germans, the dull-eyed English, the feverish Russians and French.

The band, beneath its awning, plays; carriages drive up, and automatic cars with dusty occupants arrive; the new-comers alight and ascend the steps of the Casino; fashionable women are in evidence, some carrying long roulette-purses with chains;

Girls walk about singly or in pairs—pale, with carefully set profiles, lips, hair, and with immense hats and choice-colored costumes, orange-red or primrose or lavender or dead-white;

The knots, the groups, form and re-form; the waiters hurry to and fro; while in a corner with easel and palette an artist takes a sketch of the whole scene.

And still the sun nears its setting.

The air floats over, with the delicious scent of orange-blossom and mimosa from the gardens; the shadows form in blue folds on the distant mountains, the rocks overhead stand sturdier, more and more bastion-like, as though an earth-shock might tumble them on the crowd;

In the little harbour the wharf-men, with dusty sashes round their waists, are coaling a great white yacht, already half lost in shadow;

Along the shore in a green high-prowed boat some fishermen row and drop their seine net in the same old fashion of centuries;

The peasant climbs his terraces of olive, the goatherd looks down from his high perch among the rocks, and hears the faint strains of the band and catches the glance of the dresses.

And still the sun nears its setting.

And still, within, as all day since noon, the feverish crowd sits or stands round the tables;

Nigh twenty tables—well nigh a thousand people, for the most part bent on business—all but a few by the glitter dazed of the eyes of the great god Chance.

Hats doffed, a hush reigns; tiptoe they move about that huge saloon, as in some Temple.

And now the great shaded lamps are lighted, hanging close over the green cloth.

See! how beautiful is the face of this little old lady, with tiny shrunken body and trembling mittened hands—the deep eyes, and dark shades in the eye sockets, and pitiful tender mouth!

Each round she carefully places a gold piece on some compartment, and watches for the result—nor seems to doubt her occupation for a moment.

Next her a young girl of eighteen or nineteen, aristocratic-featured, sits intent, and hides her hot eyes and straight somewhat pinched mouth under the brim of a broad white hat.

Close by again, see, a woman in black, of clear frank simple-minded type, almost a rustic, standing behind a chair and trying one or two throws;

And here a man, faultlessly attired and with absurdly unconcerned manner, sitting close by a croupier, and every now and then changing a thousand-franc note for gold—which he dots about the board in the most casual way, and apparently with complete want of success;

And there, an old man with bald hot-veined forehead and

grey hair, deeply thinking, pencilling, computing, doubles his stakes with determination as he steadily loses.

Two demi-mondaines in waved and fretted hair, with long kid gloves covered with bracelets, push somewhat petulantly a little pile of gold across the board—then rake together their winnings and walk away.

There again, in the shade of many standing behind her, sits a strange Sibyll-like woman, with bat-wing trimmings in her hat. A half-formed smile dwells on her impassive face. She always wins, they say; and not a few furtively follow her lead in the chances.

Here is a young German student with old scars across his face; there, a Dundreary-whiskered yellow-haired Englishman of a type almost extinct at home; there, a business-like woman in mourning, with sharp nose and decided manner, evidently retrieving the fortunes of her family;

And there behind her an elderly respectable English matron, most anxious to speculate, but looking carefully round first to see if anyone recognises her;

And here again a big-chinned, flabby French youth with a suppressed boil on his neck.

Curious, the suppressed feverish sentiment of the whole scene, the quiet, the politeness; the occasional sharp glances, or hurried retirement from the table, the swift self-satisfactions, and the inward gnashings of teeth;

The many faces seamed with wrinkles spreading fan-shaped upwards from the bridge of the nose, or with twirled goat's-horn mustachios;

Monte Carlo

The little bald director on his high chair, white-skinned and white-haired, with big head, and quick beady eyes glancing through strong spectacles, watching closely the croupiers and the public;

The detectives among the throng;

The arrival at one of the tables of a roll of notes for a hundred thousand francs, to support the failing bank—the little stir of excitement among the gamblers, and the added stakes in consequence.

And now, outside, the sun has sunk.

Light-blue and white the calm sea lies beyond the palm-fronds, white sails speck the horizon, and the blue shadows on the silent hills are beautiful.

The fishermen have finished their haul, and stand chatting on the beach as they thumb from the meshes of the net and store in baskets the fish, which bring them a few pence for their day's labor, presently to be served up at fabulous prices in the restaurants.

The goatherds drive their goats homeward, with tinkling bells, and peering over the rocks look downward on the Eden which they may not enter.

The primitive peasant-woman, with great mouth and ears unlearned of aught so modern as French or Italian, returns to the arched streets of her hill-top village—Roccabruna or Eza or Turbia—and ere the glow of sunset dies from the sky is fast asleep.

But the lights of the Casino shine reflected in the water, and the strains of the band, through the scented air, vibrate, and from the gaming-tables the crowd drifts to its supper-tables —while late through the night the telegrams flash to Vienna or London or Paris.

India, the Wisdom-land

HERE also in India—wonderful, hidden—over thousands of miles,

Through thousands of miles of coco-nut groves, by the winding banks of immense rivers, over interminable areas of rice-fields,

On the great Ghauts and Himálayas, through vast jungles tenanted by wild beasts,

Under the cloudless glorious sky—the sun terrible in strength and beauty—the moon so keen and clear among the tree-tops,

In vast and populous cities, behind colors and creeds and sects and races and families,

Behind the interminable close-fitting layers of caste and custom,

Here also, hidden away, the secret, the divine knowledge.

Ages back, thousands of years lost in the dim past,

A race of seers over the northern mountains, with flocks and herds,

Into India, the Wisdom-land, descended;

The old men leading—not belated in the rear—

Eagle-eyed, gracious-eyed old men, with calm faces, resolute calm mouths,

India, the Wisdom-land.

Active, using their bodies with perfect command and power—retaining them to prolonged age, or laying them down in death at will.

These men, retiring rapt—also at will—in the vast open under the sun or stars,
Having circled and laid aside desire, having lifted and removed from themselves the clinging veils of thought and oblivion,
Saw, and became what they saw, the imperishable universe.
Within them, sun and moon and stars, within them past and future,
Interiors of objects and of thoughts revealed—one with all being—
Life past, death past—the calm and boundless sea
Of deep, of changeless incommunicable Joy.

And now to-day, under the close-fitting layers of caste and custom, hidden away,
The same seers, the same knowledge.
All these thousands of years the long tradition kept intact,
Handed down, the sacred lore, from one to another, carefully guarded;
Beneath the outer conventional shows, beneath all the bonds of creed and race, gliding like a stream which nothing can detain,
Dissolving in its own good time all bonds, all creeds,

The soul's true being—the cosmic vast emancipated life —Freedom, Equality—
The precious semen of Democracy.

Tanzbödeli

HIGH on a rock that juts above the Lauterbrunnen valley,
Seven thousand feet in air, a little floor of grass,
Even and smooth, with flowers—
The little dancing-ground, they call it (and have called, how many centuries?)—
And then across the gorge, and again some seven thousand feet higher,
In slopes of rock and ice, the Jungfrau towering over,
Proud and magnificent; and in her train seven mountains—
(Roth-thalhorn, Gletscherhorn, Ebne Fluh, Mittaghorn, Grosshorn, Breithorn and Tschingelhorn)—
Standing there like a wall and sending their glaciers to the valley.

[And far behind the wall, far miles and miles, but invisible from here,
Great rivers of ice between the glistening black and scarred crags
Flow, tossing and twisted, with sea-green escarpments and fissures, and scaly snaky moraines, and glittering snowfields above them, sharp on the dark blue sky,
All stretching, far as the eye may see, in endless silence,

Save for the fitful rattle of falling rocks, or muffled roar of an avalanche.]

But at the end of the train, and closing it and the valley,
Rises a huge bare cliff, the frowning G'spaltenhorn,
Diabolic and dark, an inferno of crags and pinnacles.

This on one side; on the other the landscape opens
To lower valleys and pastures—the huts of Gimmelwald and Mürren,
Lying serene in the sunlight, with herds of cows just visible,
And the blue-vista'd gorge of Lauterbrunnen running down to the distant hills of the twin lakes,
And tiny villages and towns, half seen and half imagined,
All folded in light and glory—as the peaks above are folded.

And there below us, in the huts of the upper pastures, the herdsmen gather and milk the cows, and in their great cauldrons warm the milk, and strain and press the cheeses;
Staying a few weeks in one spot till the feed is exhausted, and then leading the tinkling-belled herd by precipitous paths to other huts and pastures,
All summer long, till the autumnal return to the lowlands;
And in the little chalets the daily life goes on, with knitting and spinning and beating of flax, and storage of winter fuel and fodder;
And men with small short scythes mow the slopes of

grass almost too steep to stand on, or carry their heavy wooden brantes of milk, braced to their shoulders, down the mountain-bases;

And for a brief season the stream of visitors arrives, and the hotels wake from sleep, and distant music is heard;

And guides and climbers sally forth with lanterns in the dark, and are glad if they may remain for a few minutes at early morning in the thin icy wind of some silent summit;

And even tiny invisible trains attempt to ascend the unimaginable mountains.

But here on this little palm of grass, Earth's hand uplifted,
All is the same as though the centuries moved not;

And the peaks stand round and wreathe themselves in clouds, and take the colors and the lights of morning and evening;

And the moon sails, and an occasional eagle, overhead;

And the valleys plunge below in depths and darks invisible;

And the butterflies and flowers quiver and leap in the light and living air;

And we, in our turn, on the little dancing-ground of centuries,

Forming a circle, dance—till the mountains too wheel round us.

A Village Church

A STUMP of oak—a huge old ruin of a tree, shored up with props;
And close beside it a vast and splendid Yew—still flourishing though fully a thousand years of age—
With congregated stems upstanding, straight as a gothic pillar, and mighty outspread arms on every side—a home for birds for countless generations;
And almost underneath the branches of the yew, sunk somewhat in the ground,
A tiny little Church—squat roof and belfry—with Saxon walling and low dark Norman doorway.

And evening falls, and to us sitting in the lane
From the low door as from some cavern-mouth of the Earth
Come sounds of old old chants and murmur of ancient prayers, and the wailing of responses,
Wafted—and a faint faint odor of incense (for High Church is the service),
And dimly seen, as through the mists of time, the glint of candles on the altar-table.

Voices indeed of Time and the Earth, like some strange incantation,
Issuing from the gloom beneath the Yew-tree,
Coming adown forgotten centuries—

Voices and echoes of ages of Christianity, borne onward with the sound of Norman and Saxon chisels:

Phrases that Chrysostom wrote, or good St. Basil; or borrowed from primitive liturgies of the earliest Christians;

Scraps of antiphonies sung within the Catacombs; tags, litanies and Kyrie Eleisons, adapted from pagan rituals;

Fragments of Creeds and Glorias from the days of Athanasius and the Councils; or sanctioned by the use of Sarum;

Gregorian chants, and quaint melodic strains from far Greek sources:

These blent together,
And laden with hopes and fears of hearts long buried,
Come issuing from the doorway.

And all the while under the evening sky
The landscape stretches, so fair, so calm, so actual,
And in the air the delicious waft of hawthorn-blossom
Floats, and the red June sunset hangs in the West,
And high in the branches of the Yew, a peacock,
Preening its feathers, sits.

How strange!
To think of the old old life for a thousand years that has gathered round these stones, and since the yew was a seedling planted,

Of the generations of men and women to whom the Church has been the centre of their days—their first and latest home;

A Village Church

The old clock striking the hours and the quarters through years and decades,

The old bell tolling its way through the centuries, with pendulum-swing of life-times;

The infants and wide-eyed children brought in for baptism; and after eighty years brought in again—mere broken husks of aged folk—for burial;

And their children the same, and theirs again the same, and theirs, and theirs;

Till at length by the font where the monk once muttered his Latin blessing, a smug young curate stands and lisps the service;

The marriages, the festivals, the long tradition of the mass and the holy communion from that last supper in Jerusalem;

The glow of religious adoration, and the pain of broken hearts, age after age; the hopes of Heaven, the nightmare doubts of Hell;

And the trio of Gods aloft, looking on all the time,
The Father, the Son, and the Ghost,
And the dear Mother Mary, a little aside, apart,
And the crowd of Saints in the background—
The council-chamber of heaven.

And the terrestrial councils held in the Church,

The conferences of the local Barons with the clergy, the visitations of Bishops,

The stormy scenes in the vestry, while the congregation is waiting in the pews;

The Folk-motes called in the Churchyard, the preparations for defence in time of civil war;

The fierce fights on occasions all round the building and amongst the tomb-stones; and up the stone stairs of the Tower—the monks and priests laying about them with heavy candlesticks.

To think of it all:
Of the images that have stood in those niches and been cast down and broken to shards;

And of the tapestries and altar-cloths that have been woven and stitched with pious care, and that have long since faded away—

And the little church still standing!

And still the old vague-toned Gregorian phrases wandering down, and still the golden voice of Chrysostom sounding from afar over the hubbub of the ages,

Floating on the waft of incense, and mingling with the breath of the hawthorn, this June night, 1900.

How wonderful!

The romance, the poetry, the heart-yearnings—

As once perhaps they gathered round some Greek Temple:

[Where the young man, having washed his body and offered a sacrifice before the laurel-crowned priest, poured out his heart in prayer to Apollo, touching the knees of the god with a leafy olive-wand;

Or the expectant mother came to Juno Lucina with a branch of palm in her hands;

A Village Church

Or the old man at midnight, with a propitiatory offering, to the shrine of Proserpine:]
    So, all these centuries and round the village church,
    A like romance has gathered.

    And presently an alien folk will come, with alien thoughts and customs;
    And this little shrine half-buried in the ground, with its candles and incense and stuffy dingy interior,
    And its three Gods sitting up aloft, and its doubtful glances at Mary,
    Will seem as far back and strange as anything Greek or Egyptian.

    Thus as I dreamed, wandering away in thought through the long long past and future,
    The service ended, and in the last glow of sunset
    Out came a crowd of gaily-colored girls in silks and muslin, and village youths, and a top-hat squire or two—all modern as modern—
    And knowing or recking nothing of Chrysostom and Basil:
    Into the sweet evening air and dusk they came, with cheerful babble,
    Discussing the local fashions or last event in politics,
    When sudden a yell rang out in the sky, like the yell of a monstrous cat,
    And with a great rush of wings, and to a chorus of exclamations,

The peacock flew from its tree overhead to the East and into the Night.

Sheffield

WHERE a spur of the moors runs forward into the great town,
And above the squalid bare steep streets, over a deserted quarry, the naked rock lifts itself into the light,
There, lifted above the smoke, I stood,
And below lay Sheffield.

The great wind blew over the world,
The great soft Southwest, making a clear light along the far horizon;
The sky overhead was serenest blue, and here and there a solitary white cloud scudded swiftly below it.
The great soft wind! How it blew in gusts as it would unroot the very rocks, eddying and whistling round the angles!
The great autumnal wind! bearing from the valley below clouds of paper and rubbish instead of dead leaves.

Yet the smoke still lay over Sheffield.
Sullenly it crawled and spread;
Round the bases of the tall chimneys, over the roofs of the houses, in waves—and the city was like a city of chimneys and spires rising out of a troubled sea—
From the windward side where the roads were shining wet with recent rain,

Sheffield

    Right across the city, gathering, mounting, as it went,
    To the Eastward side where it stood high like a wall, blotting the land beyond,
    Sullenly it crawled and spread.

    Dead leaden sound of forge-hammers,
    Gaping mouths of chimneys,
    Lumbering and rattling of huge drays through the streets,
    Pallid faces moving to and fro in myriads,
    The sun, so brilliant here, to those below like a red ball just visible, hanging;
    The drunkard reeling past; the file-cutter humped over his bench, with ceaseless skill of chisel and hammer cutting his hundred thousand file-teeth per day—lead-poison and paralysis slowly creeping through his frame;
    The gaunt woman in the lens-grinding shop, preparing spectacle-glasses without end for the grindstone—in eager dumb mechanical haste, for her work is piecework;
    Barefoot skin-diseased children picking the ash-heaps over, sallow hollow-cheeked young men, prematurely aged ones,
    The attic, the miserable garret under the defective roof,
    The mattress on the floor, the few coals in the corner,
    White jets of steam, long ribbons of black smoke,
    Furnaces glaring through the night, beams of lurid light thrown obliquely up through the smoke,
    Nightworkers returning home wearied in the dismal dawn—
    Ah! how long? how long?

And as I lifted my eyes, lo! across the great wearied throbbing city the far unblemished hills,

Hills of thick moss and heather,

Coming near in the clear light, in the recent rain yet shining.

And over them along the horizon moving, the gorgeous procession of shining clouds,

And beyond them, lo! in fancy, the sea and the shores of other lands,

And the great globe itself curving with its land and its sea and its clouds in supreme beauty among the stars.

A LANCASHIRE MILL-HAND

SHE died at the age of sixty-three, mother of a family of four children, and having during that time worked for fifty-three years in a Lancashire cotton-mill!

You know the scene: the great oblong ugly factory, in five or six tiers, all windows, alive with lights on a dark winter's morning, and again with the same lights in the evening; and all day within, the thump and scream of the machinery, and the thick smell of hot oil and cotton fluff, and the crowds of drab-faced drab-dressed men and women and children—the mill-hands—going to and fro or serving the machines;

And, outside, the sad smoke-laden sky, and rows of dingy streets, and waste tracks where no grass grows, and tall chimneys belching dirt, and the same same outlook for miles.

Here she had grown up a bright-eyed strenuous girl, to blushing maidenhood, and had become a young woman, and in time married; and here she lived, and bore her family, and died.

In those days—it happens even now—whole families, father, mother and children, would go out (locking up the house behind them) to work in the Mills; thus to earn perhaps a decent combined wage.

And in this instance it was so. But the mother worked hardest of all: her one idea—her blind religion—being work: to bring up her children to work—never to give in.

During the last twenty-four years of her life she never missed a single work-morning being at the mill at 6 a.m.

Even before that, on each occasion of her confinement, she would only allow herself three weeks off. When she returned to the mill she would leave the new-born babe every morning at the house of a nursing woman on the way.

The youngest-born—and he it was who told it all—said he remembered very well as a child being picked out of bed in the early dawn, wrapped in a shawl, and carried through the streets, just as he was, to the house of an old woman.

Here his mother would just pop him down, and hurry on to *work*.

At the last, after her half-century of toil, she was terribly broken with bronchitis. Often, after going out at 5.30 a.m. into the cutting winds of winter, the gas-lamps would reveal her leaning for a while, wheezing and coughing, in the shelter of a doorway to get her breath and strength.

Nevertheless she never missed a single day, or even a quarter.

She never gave in till the very last.

Then one day at dinner-time she came home and went to bed.

But at 9 p.m. the youngest son going up found her dressed!—"O yes, the house wanted tidying, and she would attend to it, as she was going to work in the morning, and there was no one else to do so!"

But in the morning there *was* someone else, and the house was tidied without her;

For she lay in her chamber, dead.

A Trade

IN a little stinking shop, hardly seven feet square—

Just one room in a London back street, where nearly every room lodges a family—

With two or three little paraffin stoves in, and bowls and pots horribly steaming, for dyeing gloves—

A man, some forty years old, burly and well-brained but broken down and bloated with drink, plying a trade.

"Do you see?" he says, "I buy these white evening kids, what have been cast off, from the slop-dealers, at so much a score. Then I gets a woman to mend 'em and put buttons on, and then I dyes 'em black, in these 'ere pots.

[As good as new, d'yon see? See how they shine when they're got up—and the black'll never come orf.]

Then I goes out into the markets—Leather Lane and the street-markets I mean—and sells them at sixpence a pair.

[Yes, and I mean to get a stamp and stamp 'em inside; then they'll be *just* like new.]

O it aint so bad in mild weather, but when it's like this, cold and rainy, folk won't stop to buy nothing, they won't."

And there were the gloves, shriveled, black, and hanging in rows on stretched strings, like the corpses of weasels and moles strung by gamekeepers in the woods;

And there was the filthy suffocating odor of the den and the chemicals, and the intelligent eye of the man wavering in slavery to his protruding lower lip.

"Lor!" he said, "I often stay here at nights as well as days. I don't live with my wife now. She's a regular bad 'un!"

THE PLOUGHBOY

THE blackbirds sing so sweetly in the morning; They are building a nest yonder in the hedgerow, where I pass at sunrise: and I think their song is sweeter then than else at any time of day.

I take care not to disturb them: they work as hard as anybody for their living.

And I think they know me now, they are that bold. But they do not follow in the furrow, like the wagtails and robins; they seem to hang to the grass-lands.

It is pleasant then, in the morning: the air is so sweet.

And the smell of the earth—and I like the warm smell of the horses.

Jeannie goes in the furrow, and Rob on the fallow: they go very steady;

And when the ground is soft-like, it's good enough going, but when it's stiff it stretches your arms a bit:

Lord! it does make you sweat!

The Jackdaw

CHORK! chork!
The white sea-cliff, the crawling waves, the fringe of weed between,

Midway a cleft in the rock—from above, from below, unseen.

Chork! chork!
The sun alone looks in where my nest is; the moon shines in the blinking eyes of my children.

Sweet is the warm night nestling all together, sweet the dawn by the fresh air fanned,

Sweet to arise and soar into the blue weather—to see the brown fields and pastures inland!

To sail inland, a dozen together, to the feeding grounds, and unearth the fat white slugs, (chork! chork!)

To roam and range with the others—how sweet!—and yet not with them,

Forgetting never

My own particular cleft in the rock and the tuft of sea-poppies beside it—like yellow flames burning—

And the red wide throats of my chicks as they catch my black shadow upon them, returning.

By the Mersey

I WATCHED the sunlight on the river Mersey—all glorious with sailing clouds and shadows—and sailing craft and steamers on the tide—a stirring sight!

And heard the clang and clamor of Liverpool behind me;

And saw in front the crowded ferry-boats crossing, and gulls in clusters swooping down for garbage;

[Two steps on the green water with webbed feet—and up again, their full beaks raised in air!]

And the great Atlantic liner lay at the landing-stage, towering up, a mighty wall of iron, full thirty feet, over the little people who rushed to and fro below, completing the last shipments and farewells.

For even now the gong sounded in the ship's interior; and all was ready—every rope in place;

The shrouds and stays were taut on mast and spar;

Two slender wires, Marconi's, at the stern, ran sloping down from mizen-truck to wheel-house,

Ready to catch (far out at sea) a faint thrill from the home-land.

The little tug's towing-cable strained too at the monster; but still four mighty hawsers held her fast;

And still she delayed to move, and still the folk, on ship and shore, with jokes and quips beguiled the hour of parting.

Then sudden rang a bugle from the deck. Down came blue peter; and the foghorn sounded.
The hawsers fell, and she was free. A moment more, magnificent, she glided down the river.

And instantly from all the decks (from some of the portholes too) there burst a flutter of waving hands and scarves— a fringe of white, answered by such another fringe on shore;
And instantly I saw—what I had missed before—
[Stronger, it seemed, than even cable and hawser, more numerous and tense than shrouds and stays, finer and subtler than Marconi wires,]
A thousand invisible threads which bound the ship, and would not be cast off or loosed or snapt,
But tugged and strained at living human hearts—and strained and tugged and tore—
Till hearts were sore and broken:
Threads of some unseen world—that stretched and stretched, and floated like fair gossamers in the evening light—
So fine and strong, so stronger even than steel;
And followed lengthening as the great ship faded—lost in the glory of sunset—
Far out to the Atlantic.

In the British Museum Library

How lovely!
This vast vast dome—and the suspended sounds within it!

Sounds and echoes of the great city vibrating tirelessly night and day;

Voices and footfalls, of the little creatures that walk about its floor, half-lost in the huge concave;

Suspended whispers, from its walls, of far forgotten centuries.

How lovely!
All the myriad books—well-nigh two millions of volumes—the interminable iron galleries, the forty miles or so of closely-packed shelves;

The immense catalogue—itself a small library—of over a thousand volumes;

The thousands of editions of the Bible and parts of the Bible, with texts, commentaries, translations in every known tongue—these alone occupying sixteen volumes of catalogue;

The thousands of Shakespeare books, or of Aristotle, the hundreds of Homer, Virgil, Chaucer, Dante, Montaigne, Goethe, Voltaire, Byron;

The mountain-peaks of literature, and the myriads of lesser hills and shoulders and points—the mole-hills and grass-blades even;

The interminable discussions of the Schoolmen and Grammarians, the equally interminable discussions of modern

Science—the investigations into ghostly geometries of four or five dimensions, or into the values of c and g in the Lunar Theory, or into the alternation of generations in some obscure Annelids;

How bewildering! how impossible to sum up and estimate!

And then to think how slight it all is—
A little remnant of faded thought;
A little dust just crumbled through the fingers, hardly more;
The residue and deposit of ages;
The dead leaves, the skeleton foliage, which generations of trees have cast upon the earth—and which with infinite care we sort and catalogue!
And then to leave the mouldy stuffy vault, and go out, and breathe freely,
How lovely!
One living bud upon a little branch,
One face that looks and passes in the street,
And these contain it all.

How lovely!
To think there are all these books—and one need not read them;
To think of all the patient purblind accumulations, all the dry-as-dust, the fatuous drivel, the maundering vanity, the endless repetitions of vain things,
The endless care and industry and science used to sort out the pearls from the vast heap—

In the British Museum Library

[And we only know they are pearls because we already have the same within ourselves—]

And to think we need not stop to count them.

What is it, such a library?

It is the homage of industrious dulness to the human soul.

[Once there lived a man—he actually thought and felt—he wrote even a single sentence of sense—he uttered a word from his heart.

Then all the nations said, "O if we may but attain to save this divine spark from oblivion, let us erect even such a labyrinthine monument as this."]

Come, come away!

The single hair of Buddha encased in a dágoba-mountain of brick and mortar grows now, even such a hair, upon thy loved one's head.

Come, come away! leave books, traditions, all the dross of centuries,

Clean, clean thy wings, and fly through other worlds.

Heaven's stars shine all around thee;

Deep in thy Heart the ageless celestial Museum

Waits its explorer. All that they said—those wise ones—

They say and repeat it now, where the plough-boy drives his furrow:

Be still, O Soul, and know that thou art God.

EMPIRE

Blind, fooled, and staggering from her throne, I saw her fall,
Clutching at the gaud of Empire;
And wondering, round her, sons and daughter-nations stood—
What madness had possessed her;
But when they lifted her, the heart was dead,
Withered within the body, and all the veins
Were choked with yellow dirt.

O ENGLAND, fooled and blind,
 Come look, if but a moment, on yourself!
 See, through your streets—what should be living sap of your free blood—
 These brutish squalid joyless drink-sodden populations flowing;
 And in your mills and factories the weary faces, sad monotonous lives,
 Or miles of cottage tenements with weakly red-eyed children, worn-out mothers.
 See, from your offices and shops at closing hours, the morbid stream—as from unhealthy glands within the body—
 Crowds issuing of anæmic youths and girls, pale, prematurely sexual,
 With flabby minds and bodies (held together chiefly by their clothes) and perky pick-me-up manners;

See, on the land, where at least there should be courage and grit and sinew,
A thin-legged slouching apathetic population, ignorant even of agriculture,
And in the mines and coal-pits, instead of lusty power, poor rickety limbs and ill-built bodies;
And ask yourself the searching question straight,
How out of such roots shall a strong nation grow?

And then look upward, at the surface show and flaunt of society,
Those that are well-fed, and (out of the labor of the others) have plenty of chink in their pockets—
The club and drawing-room life—
Look well, look well, and see the feebleness and insincerity of it:
The scores and scores of thousands of titled and moneyed persons—a vast and ever-growing multitude—living the lives of idiots,
Faiblesse oblige their motto:
Of men scarce fit even to be good officers, much less good administrators; of women hardly worthy to be mothers;
A society wielding enormous wealth and privilege, skilled chiefly in the finesse of personal gain and advancement, and honeycombed by cynicism and unbelief:
And for the rest, the hundreds and hundreds of thousands swarming in commercial dens and exchanges,
The life of the successful business man, the company promoter, the lawyer; the manufacturer, traveller, factor,

dealer, merchant, speculator; the bank, the counting-house, the big store, the director's office; the advertising agent, and the vendor of patent medicines;

Think of all these, and of the ideals beneath and behind them—and ask again the question,

How out of such stuff can a strong nation grow?

Where (and the question must be faced),

Where, anywhere over the surface of England to-day, do the necessary conditions exist for the outcrop of a decent population—if only a body of a few hundreds at a time?

Where are the conditions for the growth of men and women,

Healthy and well-formed of limb, self-reliant, enterprising, alert, skilled in the use of tools, able to cope with Nature in her moods, and with the Earth for their sustenance, loving and trustful of each other, united and invincible in silent faith?

Where is the Statesman who makes it the main item of his programme to produce such a population? Where the Capitalist, where the Landlord?

Where indeed—in a country in which Politics are but a game of party bluff, where Labor is a modified slavery, and where Land (for such purposes as indicated) is simply not to be had?

And the answer comes: The conditions do not exist.

The conditions (says the doctor) of life and vitality are gone—already the process of decay has set in, which only a swift crisis can arrest:

The heart is dying down,
Withering within the body; and the veins
Are choked with yellow dirt.

And this Thing cries for Empire.

This Thing from all her smoky cities and slums, her idiot clubs and drawing-rooms, and her brokers' dens,
    Cries out to give her blessings to the world!
    And even while she cries
    Stand Ireland and India at her doors
    In rags and famine.

    These are her blessings of Empire!
    Ireland (dear Sister-isle, so near at hand, so fertile, once so prosperous),
    Rack-rented, drained, her wealth by absentees in London wasted, her people with deep curses emigrating;
    India the same—her life-blood sucked—but worse:
    Perhaps in twenty years five hundred millions sterling, from her famished myriads,
    Taken to feed the luxury of Britain,
    Taken, without return—
    While Britain wonders with a pious pretence of innocence
    Why famine follows the flag.

    Last, but not least, insult is added to injury.
    For, while she prates the blessings of her Empire, contempt and studied indifference are her methods of administering it:

An empty House to hear the burden of the sorrows of India,
And Irish questions treated with derision.

O England, thou old hypocrite, thou sham, thou bully of weak nations whom thou wert called to aid,
Thy day of ruin surely is near at hand,
Save for one thing—which scarcely may be hoped for—
Save that a heart of grace within thee rise
And stay the greed of gold—which else must slay thee.

For now I see thee like a great old tree,
A Mother of the forest,
Prone on the ground and hollow to the core, with branches spread and stretched about the world.
And truly these thy seedlings scattered round
May spring and prosper, and even here and there
One of thy great arms elbowed in the earth,
Or severed from the trunk, may live again;
But Thou—thy tale of ancient glory is told—
I fear thou canst but die.

And better so perhaps; for what is good shall live.
The brotherhood of nations and of men
Comes on apace. New dreams of youth bestir
The ancient heart of the earth—fair dreams of love
And equal freedom for all folk and races.
The day is past for idle talk of Empire;
And who would glory in dominating others—

The British

Be it man or nation—he already has writ
His condemnation clear in all men's hearts.
'Tis better he should die.

THE BRITISH, A.D. 1901

As the light descends to drown and redeem the world,
And the sea quivers answering to its depths,
And the rocks and trees stand up in the blue air like transparent creatures,
And the wheeling pigeons are a part of it all,
So is Love among the children of men—
Without which they have no being.

For I seemed to see in vision a people that knew not Love,
With cold-mutton faces and cod-fish eyes hurrying around,
Intent on endless quests, and gathering wealth in high and low places, and picking over the scrap-heaps of the world,
And building up carefully their own good names and reputations,
And following up clues of knowledge and philanthropy, and feeding piously and punctually the lusts of their bodies.
And it was like half-blind folk in a dark place hurrying up and down,
Hurting against one another in lost and aimless confusion,
Weary and senseless, stupefied and without originality,
Because indeed the one thing that might make life rational and vital was absent.

And it seemed to me that the most ignorant unbred girl or boy amongst them, who loved another and worshiped in mortal form a divine creature,

Knew more and possessed more even than them all.

PORTLAND

IN the grey North-East of winter the great granite rock, see, overhung with cloud!

And from the top no portion of the mainland visible—only a few war-ships below, and Chesil Bank, its far end rising into fog.

But behind, on the high plateau of the rock, among the quarries,

Where neither the sea nor the ships nor the mainland, but only the dreary piles of stone and drearier prison-walls, can at any time be descried, and the arméd sentinels,

There, behold! the convicts in gangs, ten or twelve to a gang—and to each gang one or two warders, with muskets—

The sullen heavy-faced convicts, and (in that place) every day more sullen growing—hauling at trollies, or quarrying or dressing the stone:

Damned,

Without interest in life.

And so onward, through more warders, some with and some without muskets,

And through huge stone gateways and bastions, and

through heavy clamped doors, with endless turning of keys;

   Till at last amid all this absurd and lumbering display of brute force, as if for wild beasts—behind bars thick enough to confine an elephant—

   Lo! a well-known face!

   A gentle unharmful face, making the whole apparatus look foolish and ashamed of itself—

   The face of your friend whom you came to see—
   So tender and hesitating, thoughtful, and lover of children:
   His face, also alas! grown monotone,
   And like a caged wild animal's indeed,
   With dull and quavering eyes, that fill with tears,
   And lips whose tremulous smile belies the words
   They speak so bravely.

   And so more clanging of doors and turning of keys, and this one left behind again, clamped down,
   And buried in stone and iron.

   Damned,
   Without interest in life:
   Neither to speak nor to hear, to speed nor to welcome, a word of fellowship, a single act of kindness;
   [Even a warder for tucking the scanty blanket round an ailing prisoner was fined;]
   Never to use nor exercise the sense of helpfulness—the source of all human virtue;
   Never to feed but only starve the soul;
   Is this the Doom?

To hear no news from the outer world, save at unimaginable intervals a letter;

To read no book—save some goody-goody inhuman rubbish recommended by the Chaplain;

To nauseate, and yet to hunger ravenously for the same scant ever-same food;

To sicken at and hate the same insults and loud imperatives of the jailer, unendingly continued, unendingly borne—the same idiotic vacancy of the cell—

The three-legged stool, the can, the barred little window;

The same long hours of the night with pain at the heart, the sound of silly fingers every hour at the slide of the spyhole, and the flashing of the night-officer's lantern in one's face;

The recurring effort of the irritated mind and starved body to compose themselves to sleep;

In vain: the same same thoughts thought over and over and over and over again;

The same little stock of memories and fancies brought with one into this whited sepulchre—getting smaller and slighter daily—now like a wheel with ever rapider motion going round and round,

Till the brain itself is reeling.

[And now a Fear, perhaps for the safety of some loved one outside, leaps into the grinning circle and courses with it; and now another, perhaps for one's own fate in the years still in front; and now—worst of all phantoms—the Dread that one's mind is giving way: till, in fact, out of momentary sleep awaking to the same awful nightmare, a chill runs down the back, the body breaks in sweat, forms gibber and voices jabber—and presently the doctor is called.]

Mind starved and body starved, and heart, too, starved—
Is this the Doom of Man to his outcast fellow?

Only for those whose minds and hearts are already stunted—for the merely brutish by nature—the fate reserved is easier.

For them, two thoughts alone dominate—Hunger, the ever-present craving for food, the counting and computing of meals in prospect, sufficiently degrading;

And Sex, the everlasting curiosity and imagination (and act if possible);

But no word, no possibility presented to them, of **Manhood**; no word, no possibility, of Love.

And so for those who care not that such possibilities should be presented,

Is the easier fate reserved!

CHINA, A.D. 1900

FAR in the interior of China,
Along low-lying plains and great river-valleys, and by lake-sides, and far away up into hilly and even mountainous regions,

Behold! an immense population, rooted in the land, rooted in the clan and the family,

The most productive and stable on the whole Earth.

A garden one might say—a land of rich and *recherché* crops, of rice and tea and silk and sugar and cotton and oranges;

Do you see it?—stretching away endlessly over river-lines and lakes, and the gentle undulations of the lowlands, and up the escarpments of the higher hills;

The innumerable patchwork of cultivation—the poignant verdure of the young rice; the sombre green of orange groves; the lines of tea-shrubs, well-hoed, and showing the bare earth beneath; the pollard mulberries; the plots of cotton and maize and wheat and yam and clover;

The little brown and green-tiled cottages with spreading re-curved eaves, the clumps of feathery bamboo, or of sugar-canes;

The endless silver threads of irrigation-canals and ditches, skirting the hills for scores and hundreds of miles, tier above tier, and serpentining down to the lower slopes and plains—

The accumulated result, these, of centuries of ingenious industry, and of innumerable public and private benefactions, continued from age to age;

The grand canal of the Delta-plain extending, a thronged waterway, for six hundred miles, with sails of junks and bank-side villages innumerable;

The chain-pumps, worked by buffaloes or men, for throwing the water up slopes and hillsides, from tier to tier, from channel to channel;

The endless rills and cascades flowing down again, into pockets and hollows of verdure, and on fields of steep and plain;

The bits of rock and wild wood left here and there, with the angles of Buddhist temples projecting from among the trees;

The azalea and rhododendron bushes, and the wild deer and pheasants unharmed;

The sounds of music and the gong—the Sin-fa sung at eventide—and the air of contentment and peace pervading;

A garden you might call the land, for its wealth of crops and flowers,

A town almost for its population.

A population denser, on a large scale, than anywhere else on the earth—

Five or six acre holdings, elbowing each other, with lesser and larger, continuously over immense tracts, and running to plentiful market-centres;

A country of few roads, but of innumerable footpaths and waterways.

Here, rooted in the land, rooted in the family,

Each family clinging to its portion of ancestral earth, each offshoot of the family desiring nothing so much as to secure its own patrimonial field,

Each member of the family answerable primarily to the family-assembly for his misdeeds or defalcations,

All bound together in the common worship of ancestors, and in reverence for the past and its sanctioned beliefs and accumulated prejudices and superstitions;

With many ancient wise simple customs and ordinances,

coming down from remote centuries, and the time of Confucius,

This vast population abides—the most stable and the most productive in the world.

And Government touches it but lightly—can touch it but lightly.

With its few officials, its scanty taxation (about half-a-crown per head), and with the extensive administration of justice and affairs by the clan and the family—little scope is left for Government.

The great equalized mass-population pursues its even and accustomed way, nor pays attention to edicts and foreign treaties, unless these commend themselves independently;

Pays readier respect, in such matters, to the edicts and utterances of its literary men, and the deliberations of the Academy.

And religious theorizing touches it but lightly—can touch it but lightly.

Established on the bedrock of actual life, and on the living unity and community of present, past, and future generations,

Each man stands bound already, and by the most powerful ties, to the social body—nor needs the dreams and promises of heaven to reassure him.

And all are bound to the Earth.

Rendering back to it as a sacred duty every atom that the Earth supplies to them (not insensately sending it in sewers to the sea),

By the way of abject common sense they have sought the gates of Paradise—and to found on human soil their City Celestial!

And this is an outline of the nation which the Western nations would fain remodel on their own lines—

The pyramids standing on their own apexes wanting to overturn the pyramid which rests foursquare on its base!

But China remembers too well the time when it too endured the absurdities of monopolized Land and Capital, of private property in water and other necessaries, of glaring wealth and poverty, and the practical enslavement of one man by another;

It remembers even yet the discomfort of standing on its own apex,

And oddly enough has no intention of returning to those times.

Standing beyond Time,
As the Earth to the bodies of all men gives footing and free passage, yet draws them to itself with final overmastering force, and is their bodies—
So I their souls.

I am the ground of thy soul;
And I am that which draws thee unbeknown—veiled Eros,
Visitor of thy long night-time;
And I that give thee form from ancient ages,
Thine own—yet in due time to return to Me
Standing beyond Time.

Who but the Lover should Know

AH! who but the lover at last should know Death is?

To give one's body to the earth;
To rise through the roots of the trees and to feel once more the sunshine—floating as a leaf in air;
To star out months together with mosses and bog-plants on the lonely mountain-sides, to lurk under the speckled fungi in the woods, looking up at the traveller as he passes;
To be sucked in, in the mad rush of the sap through the veins of the chestnut in spring, and to burst in its great shining buds;
To catch at, dimly as in dreams, the wonderful thoughts that sweep through—the great rushing prophetic dreams of the life-laden earth;
To feel the call of existence in new and strange fashion:

To arise and ascend;
To mix with the animals roaming over the Earth;
To be and to include them—to put on purposely the mask which they put innocently on;
To be one of two swallows clinging to the southern wall, twittering, discussing sites for a nest; to be a snake basking coiled on a rock in the sun;
To rejoice in my swiftness and strength, my inevitable action and instinct;

To pass into the bodies of men and women, to be arrayed in their hair, and to look forth out of their eyes;

To be the long lines of habit in them, the food that is sweet in their mouths, the poison that is bitter;

To be the thoughts that they think, and the dreams that they dream; to circle very close;

To circle closer than all thought; to touch and startle— like the sound of distant music heard through the rushing of a storm;

To be the presentation of new unsuspected ideals:

To be buried in the ground;
To be buried deep in the ground of all existence;
To lie in the soil whence all human life springs, and whither it returns again;

Listening as in a dream of joy to the sound of innumerable voices,

And to the sound of innumerable footsteps coming nearer through all the ages;

To see and to be unseen; to hear and to be that which no ear hath heard;

To turn an open impartial eye without blame on every creature; to hold up a mirror,

So tallying nature that to it all men and things run to look upon themselves and learn their parts;

To give products and receive materials;

To have the adit, to be the hidden link, the life which does not appear;

To love without sorrow; and to send love forth to bathe the world, healing it from its wounds:

Ah! who at last but the lover should know what Death is?

The Everlasting Now

WHEN all life has been rich in experience shall not Death be rich in experience also?

Hold fast to the actual, and do not go outside good sense;
Do not let your mind stray into a world of negations and impossibilities, or try to image some future time when it will be unable to image anything—for there is no sense in that.
Do not wander too far into time at all, lest with the everlasting Now—the centre of all life and experience, and your own true lover—
You fail to keep your first appointment.

Now is the Accepted Time

AMID all the turmoil and the care—the worry, the fever, the anxiety,
The gloomy outlook, fears, forebodings,
The effort to keep up with the rush of supposed necessities, supposed duties,
The effort to catch the flying point of light, to reach the haven of Peace—always in the future—

Amid all, glides in the little word Now.

As when the winds of March with their long brooms sweep the dead leaves from the surface of the ground, and the Earth in virgin beauty with the growing grass once more appears;

So when all this debris of thought from the Past, of anxiety about the Morrow, is at last swept away,

Does the vast ever-Present beneath reveal its perfect rondure.

A Summer Day

SEEING once again the ethereal blue of the sky—the limpid air—the all-enfolding sunlight,

Here in the great tumultuous abounding city, or again in the far woods among the fallen oak-boles and the fox-gloves,

The far floating ever haunting shimmer of uncaught beauty:

I recognise that in all and everywhere it is the same:

Somehow to hold and have this in oneself—

This light and everlasting space,

This real eternal, whence the sensible light and space are born—

Somehow to hold from all things still a little aloof for this;

No rock that stands above the river's edge—but that which illumines the rock;

No brown sail in the bay—but the sweet undirected air that wafts it;

No pleasure, but the greater which lets the pleasure go or come;

Not anything, but that which brings to all things grace and light.

Still the far clouds just rim the Western sky—domed masses clear above, below lost in the summer haze:

So vast the orb of heaven enfolds the earth—the rocks and seas and rivers—and the dream-walking millions of the earth;

So vast the soul of every man enfolds his mortal deeds and thoughts,

Deeds, thoughts, desires, confused and contrary, vexing each other and vexed, in myriads, every shade and color, form and tongue, strange wanderers,

Dream-walking, till at length the real day may dawn.

The Central Calm

DRAWING back for a moment from Time, and its superficial claims and conclusions,

Realising for a moment the artistic nature of the utterance of the Universe:

That all is for expression, and that for this end commencement and finale, first evolved and latest evolved, are equally important;

That Progress is a word which may be applied to any world-movement or individual career in the same sense as it may be applied to the performance of a musical work,

Which progresses indeed to its final chord, yet the conclusion of the whole is not in the final chord, but in that which runs beneath and inspires the entire web—in that which from first to last the whole complex succession of chords and phrases indicates:

Realising this,

Realising—thus for a moment withdrawn—that there is no need to hurry, no need to dash against the bars;

But that Time itself rushing on with amazing swiftness in its vast and endless round, with suns and systems, ages and geologic epochs, races and tribes of beings, mineral, vegetable, animal, and ethereal, circle beyond circle, infallibly fulfils and gives utterance to the glorious whole:

Like one in the calm that is the centre of a cyclone—guarded by the very tornado around—

Undisturbed, yet having access equally to every side,
I drink of the deep well of rest and joy,
And sit with all the gods in Paradise.

WIDENING CIRCLES

THERE is no gap nor any flaw.

I establish my base of operations here, you establish yours in distant grounds, a million years back or a million years forward:

It makes no difference,

Our widening circles inevitably meet and interfuse some time.

When I Look upon Your Faces

CHILDREN, dear children, when I look upon your faces,
Lo! all the hidden griefs, the sorrows and the vain imaginings,
The longings, and the desperate struggles and hatreds,
The jealousies, angers—and the sudden joys, breaking the heart's doors open—
Pass in dumb show before me.
Like figures in a dream I see them there gesticulating—behind a veil, in silence.

And still you move to your daily ways and works, seeming so unconcerned—as I to mine—
And still the waves of Time wash down between us,
And soon shall wash even you and all your dreams
Into the void—and mine.

But even so, dear children, I forebode
Deliverance;
Some better thing than all our dreams and longings:
One Life — and all these images in their strange procession,
Its mystic intimation.

Life Behind Life

WHAT joys, what strange joys, lurk behind the actual!
See how great the pleasures of the body, of eating,

drinking, resting; or of the mind, of knowledge, ambition, power;

And yet behind these what strange pleasures:

Pleasures of fierce pain endured, pleasures of the body exposed to bullet-wounds, scourges, fire—shattered and cast away;

Pleasures of pleasure refused, of simple withdrawnness and indifference, or of mastery and ascendancy.

Ever breaking out behind the actual some unknown force or being,

Throwing the whilom body off like a husk, with its former capacities and needs,

Creating new joys, fiercer wilder than those of old.

The Stupid old Body

Do not pay too much attention to the stupid old Body.

When you have trained it, made it healthy, beautiful, and your willing servant,

Why, do not then reverse the order and become its slave and attendant.

[The dog must follow its master—not the master the dog.]

Remember that if you walk away from it and leave it behind, it will have to follow you—it will grow by following, by continually reaching up to you.

Incredibly beautiful it will become, and suffused by a kind of intelligence.

But if you turn and wait upon it—and its mouth and its belly and its sex-wants and all its little ape-tricks—preparing and dishing up pleasures and satisfactions for these,

Why, then instead of the body becoming like you, you will become like the body,

Incredibly stupid and unformed—going back in the path of evolution—you too with fish-mouth and toad-belly, and imprisoned in your own members, as it were an Ariel in a blundering Caliban.

Therefore quite lightly and decisively at each turning point in the path leave your body a little behind—

With its hungers and sleeps, and funny little needs and vanities—paying no attention to them;

Slipping out at least a few steps in advance, till it catch you up again,

Absolutely determined not to be finally bound or weighted down by it,

Or fossilized into one set form—

Which alone after all is Death.

THE WANDERING LUNATIC MIND

Do not pay too much attention to the wandering lunatic Mind.

When you have trained it, informed it, made it clear, decisive, and your flexible instrument and tool,

Why, do not then reverse the order and become the mere

fatuous attendant and exhibitor of its acrobatic feats (like a keeper who shows off a monkey).

Remember that if you walk away from it, leaving it as dead, paying it no attention whatever—it will have to follow you—it will grow by following, by reaching up to you, from the known to the unknown, continually;

It will become at last the rainbow-tinted garment and shining interpreter of Yourself, and incredibly beautiful.

But if you turn and wait always upon it, and its idiotic cares and anxieties, and endless dream-chains of argument and imagination—

Feeding them and the microbe-swarms of thought continually, wasting upon them your life-force;

Why, then, instead of your Mind becoming your true companion and interpreter, it will develop antics and a St. Vitus' dance of its own, and the form of a wandering lunatic,

Incredibly tangle-haired and diseased and unclean,

In whose features you, in sadness and in vain, will search for your own image—terrified lest you find it not, and terrified too lest you find it.

Therefore quite decisively, day by day and at every juncture, leave your Mind for a time in silence and abeyance;

With its tyrannous thoughts and demands, and funny little fears and fancies—the long legacy of ages of animal evolution;

Slipping out and going your own way into the Unseen—feeling with your feet if necessary through the darkness—till some day it may follow you;

Absolutely determined not to be bound by any of its conclusions; or fossilized in any pattern that it may invent;

For this were to give up your kingdom, and bow down your neck to Death.

As a Mould for some Fair Form

AS a mould for some fair form is made of plaster, and then when it is made and the form is cast therein, the plaster is broken and flung aside—

So, and for a form fairer than aught thou canst imagine, thy body, thy intellect, thy pursuits and accomplishments, and all that thou dost now call thyself,

Are the mould which in time will have to be broken and flung aside.

Their outlines are the inverse of thy true form: looking on them thou beholdest—what thou art not.

Nothing Less than All

ALL, all—and nothing less than all.

Ever men say: Here lies the truth, There lies the truth —Take this, cast that aside—Throw in thy lot with us—We are the wise, the rest are fools.

But I am as one dumb—I try to speak, to say what is in my mind, but words fail me.

I go with these wise folk a little way, and then I draw back again; I throw in my lot with them, and then alas! I throw in with the fools.

I stultify myself, and am like a thing of no shape.

The fault is mine, that I cannot say what I want to say —I cannot for the life of me answer the questions that are continually being asked.

Is it for pleasure and the world and the present, or for death and translation and spirituality, that we must live? Is it for asceticism and control, or for ingenuity and sweet enjoyment?

Does the truth lie with the East or with the West—with Buddhists and the followers of Lao Tsze, or with those who span seas and rivers by bridges and wing aerial flights by machinery?

Is it best to be an idler or a worker, an accepted person or a criminal?

Shall the town be my home, with its rush of interests and sympathies, its fascinations and magnetisms of the crowded pavements?

Or the country, with its gracious solitude and the pure breath and beauty of the air and the fields?

Shall. I give my life (how gladly!) to my one, my only lover—absorbed, we two, our days, in single devotion to each other—

Or shall I pour it out upon a hundred and a thousand beautiful forms (so beautiful) to spread from them as in an ever-widening ring to others?

Which is the most desirable or useful trade—to be a musician, or a geologist, or a navvy? to work laughing and joking with one's mates in a big workshop, or to walk at the plough-tail all day in the quiet landscape under the slow changes of the weather and the clouds?

To be a mathematician tracking in one's study the hidden properties of curves and closed figures, or an astronomer noting the star-transits on which a nation's time-reckoning depends?

To be a file-forger with hooved palm sweating before one's fire in summer, or a cobbler cursing the brittleness of his wax in winter?

Or a potter or a moulder or a parson or a prostitute or a town-councillor?

Is it better to be surly and rude, or sympathetic and suave, to be quick-tempered or patient, hot-blooded or cold-blooded, 'cute or simple, moral or immoral?

To join the society for the suppression of Vice, or to be one of the persons to be supprest? to be partial to drink, or to be a teetotaler?

For the life of me I cannot answer all these questions—I acknowledge that I am a fool.

Sometimes with this inability to take sides comes a strange terror of losing all outline, of losing my identity, my proper consciousness, everything;

Till I think of the Present and the work I have actually to do—and then comes relief;

Then instantly everything is decided—one's place, and the part one has to play—nor is there any doubt whatever about the next move.

For the moment I am pledged to this or that;
Yet I feel that in the end I must accept all,
And shall be content with nothing less than all.

Believe Yourself a Whole

BELIEVE yourself a Whole.
These needs, these desires, these faculties—

This of eating and drinking, the great pleasure of food, the need of sex-converse and of renewal in and from the bodies of others;

The faculty of sight, the wonderful panorama of the visible, and of hearing;

The inquisitive roaming brain, the love of society and good fellowship;

The joy of contest, the yearnings of Religion, the mystic impulses of night, of Nature, of solitude;

All these and a thousand other impulses, capacities, determinations, are indeed Yourself—the output and evidence and delineation of Yourself.

They cannot (in any permanent sense) be peeled off and thrown away;

They spring inevitably deep down out of yourself—and will recur again wherever you are.

There is no creature in the whole range of Being from the highest to the lowest which does not exhibit these and similar capacities, or the germs of them, in itself.

You are that Whole which Nature also is—and yet you are that Whole in your own peculiar way.

Were your eyes destroyed, still the faculty of sight were not destroyed:

Out of the same roots again as before would the optic apparatus spring.

Should you die of starvation you would only begin immediately after death to take food in another way; and the impulse of union which is at the base of sex lies so deep down that the first reawakening of consciousness would restore it.

Believe yourself a Whole, indivisible, indefeasible,
Reawakening ever under these, under those, conditions,
Expanding thus far, expanding less far, expanding farther;
Expanding this side, expanding that side, expanding all sides;
Ever diverse yet the same, the same yet diverse—inexhaustibly continuous with the rest;
And made for love—to embrace all, to be united ultimately with all.

THE BODY WITHIN THE BODY

WHEN life like a ghastly panorama stretches before the eye of the spirit—

A festal procession, as it were, continually gulfing itself in a quicksand;

When—waking as in a nightmare at dead of night—

One thinks of all the disease, the weariness, the suffering of the world as it is:

Of the cancer eating slowly onward with its roots entwined in the vitals—the vista of agony and defeat by the curséd thing;

Of the incurable filth, the venom in the lungs, breeding slime and death within one through the interminable months;

And these but samples of what waits, more or less, for almost all;

When one thinks of the sudden senseless accidents which are for ever occurring—the ship returning home, full, with brimming hearts, from the Antipodes, ripped on a rock and gone in a moment to the bottom;

A lurch, somewhere, of the shrinking earth-strata, and a whole city tumbled in shrieks and ruin;

The 'weight' coming on in the coal-pit, the ominous fall of small stones from the roof, the awful cracking of the great oak-props, the hurried rush of the miners and their swifter still entombment;

The breaking of a cable, or of a driving band in machinery, a flaw in a wheel, a random step on a stairway— and husband torn from wife, and mother from child, or child from mother;

Death and destruction and the messengers of death and destruction in myriad forms still waiting to fulfil the inevitable doom;

When, I say, the necessity arises to face all this—and face it out

Then somehow, underneath it all,
I seem to see that the strands of affection and love,

The Body Within the Body

auroral, shooting from one to another—so tender, so true, and life-long,

And longer than life—holding together the present and past generations;

The currents of love and thought streaming in the watches of the night from far and near, from one to another,

(Streaming all the more powerfully for the very hindrances and disasters which arrive or threaten,)

And building in the bustle of the day such likeness of their dreams as may be—

That these inner are after all more real in some sense than the outer things—that they surpass in actual vitality and significance even all this artillery of horrors.

I dream that these are the fibres and nerves of a body that lies within the outer body of society,

A network, an innumerable vast interlocked ramification, slowly being built up—all dear lovers and friends, all families, groups, all peoples, nations, all times, all worlds perhaps—

Of which the outer similitudes and shells, like the minute cells of an organism, are shed and die in endless multitudes with continual decay and corruption;

But the real individuals persist and are members of a Body, archetypal, eterne,

Glorious, the centre and perfection of life and organisation,

And the source of all the Light in the universe.

In an Old Quarry

ONCE in an old quarry,
   In a heathery nook among the rocks, unclothed as I reclined in the sun, facing only the great hills and the sky;
   Millions of years floating softly down through the aerial blue,
   Thy words—millions millions of human forms—
   I saw descending.

   Tiny, into the tissue of grass and tree and herb passing—into the mouths and bodies of men and animals—and here and there a fitting home in the sex-cells finding,
   At length, clothed mortal men and women,
   Out on the actual world I saw them step:
   Thy words—thy wandering words—each one alone, so lost, so meaningless,
   Each seeking his true mates, if so to spell
   One sentence of thy great world-wisdom out.

The Soul to the Body

NOW at last after thousands of years, dear Body, from thy prison emerging,
   Thy agelong tomb and sepulchre,
   [Where, with what swathing-bands, like Lazarus, what mummy-cloths, what cerements of fashion custom ignorance, thou wast bound,]
   Strange chrysalis, thy dead sheath bursting!

The Soul to the Body

Strange glorious Lover!
To feel again thy arms enfolding, to breathe the fragrance of thy sun-kist skin, how sweet!

What long estrangement, dear, what nightmare has it been, divided us?
From far away what long slow exodus?
Why to the tomb in ages past didst thou descend—of Death and dread Corruption?—
While I, poor ghost, went wandering belated, and homeless and forlorn about the world?
For, as the delicate vein-winged gnat from its watery case, as Eve from Adam's side, as Psyche from the dark embrace of Eros,
So from thee gliding, far-back, long ago—dimly I mind me now—
Slow-differenced, this wondering wandering Self was I.

[Dimly I mind the agelong alienation:
Thou body, of thy mate bereft, and falling unclean, diseased, by devils possest, in mire and filth—
Blind Maenad by thy own senses led astray!
While I, poor soul, half formed and maimed of half,
Abstract, absurd, amazed, and crucified,
To arid and unending toils was doomed, and loneliness.]

After it all to thee, dear, to return,
To feel again thy close-enfolding arms—how sweet!
To know Thee now at last—(long veiled and hidden)—

Through Nature moving, as the Sun and Moon
Move through the crystal heaven, self-sent, divine,
Transparent, tameless, more than spirit or matter;
Dear body, brushing with thy feet the grasses, or resting outlined by the rocks and sea—
To rest with thee, content, in perfect union,
O in such deep and fathomless joy to rest beside thee,
Thy mate and friend, stricken with doubts no more.

Now once more in thy lungs the winds of heaven—as out there in the forest-branches—nestle;
The waters flowing in the brooks flow on in crimson tide through artery and vein; and lift the little valve-doors and pass by with whispered secrets from the clouds and hills.
Sweet now the food-fruits pass without corruption inward and outward of the body's frame;
Clean is the ark and holy chamber of the woman, the seed-vessel of the man;
And clean the body all suffused with passion
Till the right mate arrives.

O Love, with fragrance of whose wine the world is vanquished!
Great Ocean swaying far from atom to atom! sweet aromatic transpiration of the clods!
Diffused vast Life, now here, now there, in definite lightning-flash thy visible work fulfilling!
For this, even for thy habitation, hast thou prepared these bodies.

And thou, little one, so soon to dissolve into earth and air and sea,

Thy form, my love, I accept—and am no more divided from thee.

To Become a Creator

I HEARD a Voice saying:
See now in the end you shall stand Lord of the World.

When those desires which are injurious to others have departed from you—when all desires born of hate;

When you have become strong to conquer the world, strong to endure and conquer so the hatred and the injuriousness of others;

When what you will, you will with the whole force of your nature, undivided,

Undivided by fear, conscience, conventions, and the distinctions of self and not-self;

Then, lo! all that you wish—all that your heart forms for an image of its longings—shall take shape before you;

You shall create the things which are the fulfilment of your needs;

There is nothing that shall not be yours.

For this world you see around—these trees, mountains, these high city streets and the myriad faces that pass among them—are not all these but images?

Images, to the Heart of which with restless longing you have indeed so often sought to penetrate.

Say then, if you attain to be ruler of your own thoughts, and of the images which spring from your heart, is it so much that you should be arbiter also of these others, and touch to the Heart they spring from?

For deep down there is, may-be, no difference—
And when the desires that are born of Hate and Fear and Distrust are gone, there is no difference.

And I said: Am I not my own thoughts, and when these die, shall I not also die?
And the Voice said: Look again—
These thoughts, these images, that pass before you—they pass before You.
Then how can they be Yourself?
Nevertheless it is true that they proceed from you.
They proceed from the Heart, and the mind perceives them.
And so it shall be eternally.

And all This, and all that you see, and all that you think, and all that you experience, is the evidence of Yourself,
Yourself coming to you over the ages.
Therefore go forth—and be in truth thine own Creator—
No longer in fear and trembling but in kingship and power meeting the mystery of the world;
By the pure and beautiful desires which spring within

thee, like fountain-waters from a hillside welling (which flow and grow into an endless stream running ever towards the centre of the Earth)—by these guided,

Take with unerring choice, and make and mould, and carve and cut and force thy way,

To the centre of all creation—to the Heart indeed of all lovers.

After Fifty Years

Looking back now, after fifty years and more, when the main work of life is done,

When its acquisitions, its results, its alliances, are before me, and but few new elements remain to be added,

I ask myself: What is the gist, what the end, what the gain of it all?

What shall I take with me now when Death comes—as one coming homeward takes a flower in his hand for a token that he has strayed in gracious fields?

Is it applause and fame? But this, if it came to me, were only as a little stir of wind might be, to one seeking his lover in the night: a pleasant breeze—that yet might blow his lamp out!

Is it all the pleasure of life that I have had—in the beautiful woods and on the mountains, in the sun and in the waters, in social life and jollity, in my actual work?

Yea, these things were beautiful, but I have passed and left them and can return no more. The fields remain, but the flowers I plucked there are fading already on my bosom.

Is it all my acquisitions—of goods, of skill, of knowledge, of character—but what are they for myself but weariness, save I can yield them to the hands of one I love?

O little heart, where my friends my dear ones live, thou alone remainest!
While I live thou livest, and while thou livest they live, whose home is within thy walls.
Methinks that when I die I still shall hold Thee;
Methinks that when the world fades my little heart shall grow,
And grow and grow into another World,
And be my Paradise where I shall find
My lovers, and they me, for evermore.

Out of the House of Childhood

To take by leaving, to hold by letting go.

Now, when out of the house of your childhood you are departing,
Where you suffered, where you joyed, in the old confused childish way, not certainly distinguishing things,
Now suddenly, as you leave, how it all becomes clear, as in a kind of new and incomparable light!
This is the corner where your little bed stood against the wall, this the window where the moon peeped, and the white and ghostly dawn came;
These are the closed rooms and chests into which you

were so seldom permitted to look; this was the daily routine of life which for some inscrutable reason was so rigidly adhered to;

These are the stairs where up and down moved such queer processions—funerals and weddings, and bustling visitors and elderly aunts and uncles, and the parson and the doctor in their turn;

And you were bade stand aside since you could not understand—

But now you understand it all.

Now, leaving it all,

The window truly for you will never stand open again, nor the sweet night-air through it blow—never again for you on the little coverlet of your bed will the moonlight fall;

And yet mayhap for the first time will the wind really blow and the moonlight fall,

For the first time shall you really see the face of your father whom you used to meet so often on the stairs.

All the spaces and corners of the house, and the swinging of the doors, and the tones and voices of those behind them, shall be full of meanings which were hidden from you while you dwelt among them.

Nor shall they ever leave you.

Never so long as yourself lasts shall you forget your mother smoothing out the pillow under your head, last thing at night, and kissing you as you slept;

Nay, every year so long as you live shall you understand

that act better—shall you come closer in reality to **her** whom as a child you saw but through a glass darkly.

    Leaving and again leaving, and ever leaving **go** of the surfaces of objects,
    So taking the heart of them with **us,**
    This is the law.

    The beauty of a certain scene in Nature,
    The beauty, the incomparable beauty of the face and presence of the loved **one;**
    The sweetness of pleasure—of food, of music, of exercise, or of rest and sleep;
    All these are good to obtain and to hold;
    Yet (when the need arises) to be able to dispense with them—that is indeed to hold and to realise them even more deeply.

    When at last Death comes, then all of Life shall be to us as the house of our childhood—
    For the first time we shall really possess it.
    But who is ready to die to life now, he even now possesses it.

LITTLE BROOK WITHOUT A NAME

LITTLE brook without a name, that hast been my companion so many years;
    Hardly more than a yard wide, yet **scampering** down

through the fields, so bright so pure, from the moorland a mile away;—

The willows hang over thee, and the alders and hazels; and the oak and the ash dip their feet in thy waves;

And on thy sunny banks in Spring the first primroses peep, and celandines, and the wild hyacinths lavish fragrance on the breeze—

Little brook, so simple so unassuming—and yet how many things love thee!

Here where I have my nest,
[And the white-throat through the day and through the long night sits patient on her brood among the grasses,]
Lo! Sun and Moon look down and glass themselves in thy waters,
[In the faithful watchful eyes of the bird they lovingly glass themselves;]
And the wren creeps like a mouse from twig to twig, and utters her thin sweet note; and the willow-warbler chimes his endless cadence of gratitude; and the night-jar sweeps silently by in the dusk, and the pheasant at midday comes down from the wood to drink;

And the trout balances itself hour-long against the stream, watching for its prey; or retires under a stone to rest;

And the water-rats nibble off the willow leaves and carry them below the wave to their nests—or sit on a dry stone to trim their whiskers;

And the little mouse, the water-shrew, walks (even like

Jesus Christ) upon the flood, paddling quickly over the surface with its half-webbed feet;

And the may-fly practises for the millionth time the miracle of the resurrection, floating up an ungainly grub from the mud below, and in an instant, in the twinkling of an eye (even from the jaws of the baffled trout) emerging, an aerial fairy with pearl-green wings;

And the caddis-fly from its quaint disguise likewise emerges;

And the bee, as ever, hums, and the butterfly floats, and the little winged beauty with shining mail of crimson and blue —the ruby-tail—searches in and out of every crevice and chink for a suitable place for her eggs;

And the early daffodil and narcissus from the garden stray forward to peer into thy mirror; and the wild garlic in the shade, and in the sun the king-cups, fringe thy margin;

And the prick-eared earth-people, the rabbits, in the stillness of early morning play beside thee undisturbed, while the level sunbeams yet grope through the dewy grass;

And the land-rail cranes its neck, to peer and peep from its cover;

And the weasel canters by on its quest, and the loose-jointed fox returning from a foray;

And the squirrel on a tree-root—its tail stretched far behind—leans forward to kiss thee,

Little brook,

For so many things love thee.

Little Brook without a Name

Say, what indeed art Thou—that hast been my companion now these twenty years?

Thou, with thy gracious retinue of summer, and thy fringes and lace-work of frost in winter, and icy tassels bobbing in the stream;

And sound of human voices from thy bosom all the day, and mystic song at night beneath the stars—

What art Thou, say!

While I have sat here, lo! thou hast scampered away, little brook, with all thy lace-work and tassels,

Three hundred and fifty thousand miles;

So quiet, so soft—and no one knew what a traveller thou wert;

Three hundred and fifty thousand miles in these few years, and so thou hast flowed for centuries;

And all the birds and fish and little quadrupeds have gone with thee, and herbs and flowers;

Yet I sit here and prate as though I knew all about thee;

And the country-folk too, who reckon thou camest to turn the Mill—they think they know all about thee.

But now I see how, soft-footed, thou passest by on a secret quest,

Cantering quietly down through the grasses,

And gatherest even from all wide earth and heaven thy waters together—to lave these turfy banks and the roots of the primroses;

I see how thou sheddest refreshment and life on thousands of creatures—who ask no questions;

Nor disdainest even to give the old millwheel a turn as thou goest, or bring me a tiny thought or two from thy store in cloudland,

Little brook, so strange, so mystical,

That all things love—though they know not what thy Name is.

I see where thou passest graciously by, and hastenest seaward,

Scattering once more thy waters to earth and heaven;

And I pray thee take again these thoughts thou hast brought me,

And bear away on thy bosom, and scatter them likewise.

Lo! what a World I Create

Lo! what a world I create for my own, my lovers.

As the moonbeams in winter gliding along the forest-glades reveal the beauty of the trees—the hushed soft masses of light and darkness, the mysterious depths, the thousand fairy outlines—all merged and blent in one serene Presence;

As a figure dimly seen, from glade to glade, from perspective to perspective, through the wilderness wanders content—his soul with the forest-soul mated;

So dear friends, dear lovers, through this world of mine that I weave for you here, methinks sometimes I see you moving.

And I wait of you that in time you also spread worlds equally beautiful, more beautiful, for me,

Lo! what a World I Create

[Not in written words only, but in spoken words, or the mere sound of the voice or look of the face, and in beauties of body and limb and brain and heart, and in beauty of deed and action, and in a thousand ways,]

Forest-glades and glooms where I in turn (as indeed already) may dwell and dream and be content, mated to the soul thereof.

Thus, dear ones, building up these spheres of ourselves continually for the joyance of each other, it shall come about that at length

We shall need no other world, no other worlds.

THE END

A NOTE ON
"TOWARDS DEMOCRACY"

A Note on "Towards Democracy"

(*Reprinted from* THE LABOUR PROPHET, *May*, 1894)

HAVING sometimes been asked questions about "Towards Democracy" which I found it difficult to answer, I will try and shape a few thoughts about it here.

Quite a long time ago (say when I was about 25, and living at Cambridge) I wanted to write some sort of a book which should address itself very personally and closely to any one who cared to read it—establish so to speak an intimate personal relation between myself and the reader; and during succeeding years I made several attempts to realise this idea—of which beginnings one or two in verse may be found in a little volume entitled "Narcissus and other Poems," now well out of print, which I published in 1873. None of these attempts satisfied me however, and after a time I began to think the quest was an unreasonable one—unreasonable because while it might not be difficult for any one with a pliant and sympathetic disposition to touch certain chords in any given individual that he might meet, it seemed impossible to hope that a *book*—which cannot in any way adapt itself to the idiosyncrasies of its reader—could find the key of the personalities into whose hands it should happen to come. For this it would be necessary to suppose, and to find, an absolutely common ground to all individuals (all at any rate who might have reached a certain stage of thought and experience)—and to write the book on and from that common ground: but this seemed at that time quite impracticable.

Years followed, more or less eventful, with flight from Cambridge, and university lectures carried on in the Provincial Towns, and so forth; but of much dumbness as regards writing; and inwardly full of tension, and suffering. At last early in 1881, no doubt as the culmination and result of struggles and experiences that had been going on, I became conscious that a mass of material was forming within me, imperatively demanding expression—though what exactly its expression would be I could not then have told. I became for the time overwhelmingly conscious of the disclosure within of a region transcending in some sense the ordinary bounds of personality, in the light of which region my own idiosyncrasies of character—defects, accomplishments, limitations, or what not—appeared of no importance whatever—an absolute Freedom from mortality, accompanied by an indescribable calm and joy.

I also immediately saw, or rather *felt*, that this region of Self existing in me existed equally (though not always equally *consciously*) in others. In regard to it the mere diversities of temperament which ordinarily distinguish and divide people dropped away and became indifferent, and a field was opened in which all might meet, in which all were truly Equal. Thus I found the common ground which I wanted; and the two words, Freedom and Equality came for the time being to control all my thought and expression.

The necessity for space and time to work this out grew so strong that in April of that year I threw up my lecturing employment. Moreover another necessity had come upon me which demanded the latter step—the necessity namely for an open air life and manual work. I could not finally argue with this any more than with the other, I had to give in and obey. As it happened at the time I mention I was already living in a little cottage on a farm (at Bradway, near Sheffield) with a friend and his family, and doing farm-work in the intervals of my lectures. When I threw up the lecturing I had everything clear before me. I knocked together a sort of wooden sentinel-box, in the garden, and there, or in the fields and the woods, all that spring and summer, and on through the winter, by day and sometimes by night, in sunlight or in rain, by frost and snow and all sorts of grey and dull weather, I wrote "Towards Democracy"—or at any rate the first and longer poem that goes by that name.

By the end of 1881 this was finished—though it was worked over and patched a little in the early part of 1882; and I remember feeling then that, defective and halting and incoherent in expression as it was, still if it succeeded in rendering even a half the splendour which inspired it, it would be good, and *I need not trouble to write anything more* (which, with due allowance for the said "if," I even now feel was a true and friendly intimation)!

The writing of this and its publication (in 1883) got a load off my mind which had been weighing on it for years—a sense of oppression and anxiety which I had constantly suffered from before—and which I believe, in its different forms, is a common experience in the early part of life.

In this first poem were embodied with considerable alterations and adaptations a good number of casual pieces, which I had written (merely under stress of feeling and without any particular sense of proportion) during several preceding years. They now found their interpretation under the steady and clear light of a new mood or state of feeling which previously had only visited me fitfully and with clouded beams. The whole of "Towards Democracy"—I may say, speaking broadly and including the later pieces—has been written under the domination of this mood. I have tested and measured everything by it; it has been the sun to which all the images and conceptions and thoughts used have been as material objects reflecting its light. And perhaps this connects itself with the fact that it has been so necessary to write in the open air. The more universal feeling which I sought to convey refused itself from me within doors; nor could I at any time or by any means persuade the rhythm or style of expression to render itself up within a room—tending there always to break back into distinct metrical forms; which, however much I admire them in certain authors, and think them myself suitable for certain kinds of work, were not what I wanted, and did *not* express for me the feeling which I sought to express. This fact (of the necessity of the open air) is very curious, and I cannot really explain it. I only know that it is so, quite indubitable and insurmountable. I can feel it at once, the difference, in merely passing through a doorway—but I cannot explain it. Always especially the *sky* seemed to contain for me the key, the inspiration; the sight of it more than anything gave what I wanted (sometimes like a veritable lightning-flash coming down from it onto my paper—I a mere witness, but agitated with strange transports).

But if I should be asked—as I have sometimes been asked—What is the exact nature of this mood, of this illuminant splendour, of which you speak? I should have to reply that I can give no very concise and clearcut answer. The whole of "Towards Democracy" is an endeavour to give it utterance; any mere single sentence, or direct definition, would be of no use—rather indeed would tend to obscure by limiting. All I can say is that there seems to be a vision possible to man, as from some more universal stand-point, free from the obscurity and localism which especially connect themselves with the passing clouds of desire, fear, and all ordinary thought and emotion; in that sense another and separate faculty; and as vision always means a sense of light, so here is a sense of inward light, unconnected of course with the mortal eye, but bringing to the eye of the mind the impression that it *sees*, and by means of a medium which washes as it were the *interior* surfaces of all objects and things and persons—how can I express it?—and yet this is most defective, for the sense is a sense that one *is* those objects and things and persons that one perceives, (and even that one is the whole universe,)—a sense in which sight and touch and hearing are all fused in identity. Nor can the matter be understood without realising that the whole faculty is deeply and intimately rooted on the far side of the moral and emotional nature, and beyond the thought-region of the brain.[1]

And now with regard to the "I" which occurs so freely in this book. In this and in other such cases the author is naturally liable to a charge of egotism—and I personally do not feel disposed to combat any such charge that may be made. That there are mere egotisms and vanities embodied in these pages I do not for a moment doubt; and that so far as they exist they mar the expression and purpose of the book I also do not doubt. But the existence of these things does not affect the real question: What or Who in the main is the "I" spoken of?

---

[1] I do not know any description in its way better that one attributed to Tennyson:—"All at once, as it were, out of the intensity of the consciousness of individuality, the individuality itself seemed to dissolve and fade away into boundless being, and this not a confused state, but the clearest of the clearest, the surest of the surest, utterly beyond words, where death was an almost laughable impossibility, the loss of personality —if so it were—seeming no extinction but the only true life. I am ashamed of my feeble description. Have I not said the state is utterly beyond words?" Compare also his poem, "The Ancient Sage."

To this question I must also frankly own that I can give no answer. I do not know. That the word is not used in the dramatic sense is all I can say. The "I" is myself—as well as I could find words to express myself: but what that Self is, and what its limits may be; and therefore what the self of any other person is and what *its* limits may be—I cannot tell. I have sometimes thought that perhaps the best work one could do—if one felt at any time enlargements and extensions of one's *ego*—was to simply record these, as faithfully as might be; leaving others, the science-man and the philosopher, to explain—and feeling confident that what really existed in oneself would be found to exist either consciously or in a latent form in other people. And I will say that I have in these records above all endeavored to be genuine. If I have said "I, Nature" it was because at the time, at any rate, I felt "I, Nature"; if I have said "I am equal with the lowest," it was because I could not express what I felt more directly than by those words. The value of such statements can only appear by time; if they are corroborated by others then they help to form a body of record which may well be worth investigation, analysis and explanation. If they are not so corroborated, then they naturally and properly fall away as mere vagaries of self-deception. I have not the least doubt that anything which is really genuine will be corroborated.

It seems to me more and more clear that the word "I" has a practically infinite range of meaning—that the *ego* covers far more ground than we usually suppose. At some points we are intensely individual, at others intensely sympathetic; some of our impressions (as the tickling of a hair) are of the most local and momentary character, others (as the sense of identity) involve long periods of time. Sometimes we are aware of

A Note 517

almost a fusion between our own identity and that of another person. What does all this mean? Are we really separate individuals, or is individuality an illusion, or again is it only a part of the *ego* or soul that is individual, and not the whole? Is the *ego* absolutely one with the body, or is it only a small part of the body, or again is the body but a part of the self—one of its organs so to speak, and not the whole man? Or lastly is it perhaps not possible to express the truth by any direct use of these or other terms of ordinary language? Anyhow, what am I?

These are questions which come all down Time, demanding solution—which humanity is constantly endeavoring to find an answer to. I **do** not pretend to answer them. On the contrary I am sure that *not one* of the pieces in "Towards Democracy" has been written with the deliberate view of providing an answer. They have simply been written to express feelings which insisted on being expressed. Nevertheless it is possible that some of them—by giving the experiences and affirmations even of one person—may contribute material towards that answer to these and the like questions which in some region must assuredly be given.

That there **is** a region of consciousness removed beyond what we usually call mortality, into which we humans can yet pass, I practically do not doubt; but granting that this is a fact, its explanation still remains for investigation.

I have said in this brief note on "Towards Democracy" nothing about the influence of Whitman—for the same reason that I have said nothing about the influence of the sun or the winds. These influences lie too far back and ramify too complexly to be traced. I met with William Rossetti's little selection from "Leaves of Grass" in 1868 or 1869, and read that and the original editions continuously for **ten** years.

I never met with any other book (with the exception perhaps of Beethoven's sonatas) which I could read and re-read as I could this one. I find it difficult to imagine what my life would have been without it. "Leaves of Grass" "filtered and fibred" my blood: but I do not think I ever tried to imitate it or its style. Against the inevitable drift out of the more classic forms of verse into a looser and freer rhythm I fairly fought, contesting the ground ("kicking against the pricks") inch by inch during a period of seven years in numerous abortive and mongrel creations—till in 1881 I was finally compelled into the form (if such it can be called) of "Towards Democracy." I did not adopt it *because* it was an approximation to the form of "Leaves of Grass." Whatever resemblance there may be between the rhythm, style, thoughts, constructions, etc., of the two books, must I think be set down to a deeper similarity of emotional atmosphere and intension in the two authors—even though that similarity may have sprung and no doubt largely did spring out of the personal influence of one upon the other. Anyhow our temperaments, standpoints, antecedents, etc., are so entirely diverse and opposite that, except for a few points, I can hardly imagine that there is much real resemblance to be traced. Whitman's full-blooded, copious, rank, masculine style must always make him one of the world's great originals—a perennial fountain of health and strength, moral as well as physical. He has the amplitude of the Earth itself, and can no more be *thought away* than a mountain can. He often indeed reminds one of a great quarry on a mountain side—the great shafts of sunlight and the shadows, the primitive face of the rock itself, the power and the daring of the men at work upon it, the tumbled blocks and masses, materials for endless buildings, and the beautiful tufts of weed or flower on inaccessible ledges—a picture most artistic in its very incoherence and formlessness.

"Towards Democracy" has a milder radiance, as of the moon compared with the sun—allowing you to glimpse the stars behind. Tender and meditative, less resolute and altogether less massive, it has the quality of the fluid and yielding air rather than of the solid and uncompromising earth.

Printed by S. CLARKE LIMITED
41, Granby Row, Manchester.

Works by Edward Carpenter:

(Published by GEORGE ALLEN & COMPANY LTD. Those marked * published also by S. CLARKE LIMITED, Manchester.)

*TOWARDS DEMOCRACY: Complete poems in four parts. Library Edition, with two portraits, one vol., large crown 8vo, pp. 520, cloth gilt. 4/6 net.

*The same. Pocket Edition, without portraits, one vol., India paper, limp binding, gilt edge. 3/6 net.

ENGLAND'S IDEAL, and other Papers on Social Subjects. Eleventh Thousand, pp. 176. Cloth, 2/6; paper, 1/-

CIVILISATION: ITS CAUSE AND CURE. Essays on Modern Science, etc. Eleventh Thousand, pp. 176. Cloth, 2/6; paper, 1/-

*LOVE'S COMING-OF-AGE: a Series of Papers on the Relations of the Sexes. Eighth Thousand, pp. 190. Cloth gilt, 3/6 net.

*THE INTERMEDIATE SEX: a Study of some Transitional Types of Men and Women. Third Edition. Cloth gilt, pp. 176. 3/6 net.

ANGELS' WINGS: Essays on Art and Life, with nine full-page plates. Third Edition. Cloth gilt, pp. 248. 4/6 net.

ADAM'S PEAK TO ELEPHANTA: Sketches in Ceylon and India. Copiously illustrated, and containing four chapters on "A visit to a Gñani." Third Edition. Cloth gilt, 4/6.

A VISIT TO A GÑANI, or Wise Man of the East: extracted from the above work, with portraits. 1/6 net.

*IOLÄUS: An Anthology of Friendship. Printed in Old Face Caslon type, with ornamental initials and side notes. New and Enlarged Edition. Cloth gilt, 2/6 net.

Works by Edward Carpenter (continued):

(Published by GEORGE ALLEN & COMPANY LTD.)

CHANTS OF LABOUR: a Song-book for the People, edited by EDWARD CARPENTER. With frontispiece and cover by WALTER CRANE. Paper, 1/- Seventh Thousand.

THE ART OF CREATION: Essays on the Self and its Powers. Second Edition, enlarged. Crown 8vo, cloth gilt, pp. 266, 3/6 net.

DAYS WITH WALT WHITMAN, with some Notes on his Life and Work, and three portraits. Crown 8vo, cloth gilt. 3/6 net.

SKETCHES FROM LIFE IN TOWN AND COUNTRY, with some verses and a portrait of the author. Cloth gilt, pp. 270, 3/6 net.

(Published, March, 1912.)
THE DRAMA OF LOVE AND DEATH: a Study of Human Evolution and Transfiguration. Cloth gilt, pp. 300. 5/- net.

(Published by A. C. FIFIELD, 13, Clifford's Inn, E.C.)

PRISONS, POLICE AND PUNISHMENT: An Inquiry into the Causes and Treatment of Crime and Criminals. Crown 8vo, cloth. 2/- net. Paper, 1/- net.

BRITISH ARISTOCRACY AND THE HOUSE OF LORDS. Pamphlet. Price, 6d. net.

EDWARD CARPENTER; THE MAN AND HIS MESSAGE. Pamphlet by TOM SWAN, with two portraits and copious extracts from the above works. Price 6d. net.

PHOTOGRAVURE PORTRAIT OF E. C., by MATTISON, 1905. Size 8 × 5½, on Mount 12 × 10. Price 2/- net, by post, 2/3.